World Cultures
AND
GEOGRAPHY

Reading Study Guide

McDougal Littell

Evanston, Illinois • Boston • Dallas

Acknowledgments

Unless otherwise noted, all artwork created by Publicom, Inc.

This product contains proprietary property of **MAPQUEST**.
Unauthorized use, including copying, of this product, is expressly prohibited.

Contents

UNIT 7 **Southern Asia**

UNIT 8 East Asia, Australia, Oceania, and Antarctica

Being a Strategic Reader

HOW TO USE THIS READING STUDY GUIDE

The purpose of this *Reading Study Guide* is to help you read and understand your social studies textbook, World Cultures and Geography. You can use this *Reading Study Guide* in two ways.

1. Use the *Reading Study Guide* side-by-side with your social studies book.
- Turn to the section that you are going to read in the textbook. Then, next to the book, put the pages from the *Reading Study Guide* that accompany that section. All of the heads in the *Reading Study Guide* match the heads in the textbook.
- Use the *Reading Study Guide* to help you read and organize the information in the textbook.

2. Use the *Reading Study Guide* to study for tests on the textbook.
- Reread the summary of every chapter.
- Review the definitions of the Terms and Names in the *Reading Study Guide*.
- Review the information that you filled out as you read the summaries.
- Review your answers to questions.

Name _____ Date _____

CHAPTER 1

Section 1 (pages 17–21)

Reading Study Guide

The World at Your Fingertips

BEFORE YOU READ
In this section, you will learn about the five fields of learning that make up social studies.

AS YOU READ
Use this chart to organize definitions of terms.

Term	Definition
history	
geography	
government	
economics	
culture	

TERMS & NAMES
history a record of the past
geography the study of people, places, and the environment
government people in a society who make laws, enforce them, and settle disagreements about them
citizen a legal member of a country
economics how people manage their resources by producing, exchanging, and using goods and services
scarcity the conflict between unlimited desires and limited resources
culture the beliefs, customs, laws, art, and ways of living that a group of people share
culture traits specific foods, clothing, beliefs, languages, or tools shared by a culture

The Peoples of the World (page 17)
Why is it important to learn about other peoples' ways of life?
Advances in communication, transportation, trade, and immigration have brought peoples of the world closer together.

1. What are some examples of ways people have been brought together?

_____

_____

_____

Learning About the World (page 18)
How can social studies help you learn about the world?
Social studies draws on five fields of learning: geography, history, economics, government, and culture. Suppose you were at a new school.

Figuring out how to get around is learning your school's geography. Asking other students about themselves is learning their history. Making choices about buying school supplies is economics. Learning the school's rules is learning about its government. Clubs, clothing styles, holidays, and even ways of saying things are part of the school's culture.

2. What are the five fields of learning that make up social studies?

_____

_____

_____

History and Geography (pages 18–19)
What can you learn about a place from studying its history and geography?
History is a record of the past. Historians use *primary sources* such as newspapers and journals to find out about the past. Archaeologists study

Copyright © McDougal Littell Inc.

④ UNIT 1 CHAPTER 1

Strategy: Read the Terms & Names and the definition of each. The Terms and Names are in dark type in the section.

Try This: What are the definitions of "history" and "culture"?

Strategy: Fill in the chart as you read. The chart will help you organize information in the section.

Try This: What is the purpose of this chart?

Strategy: Read the summary. It contains the main ideas and the key information under the head.

Try This: What do you think this section will be about?

artifacts such as tools and artwork to learn about people's culture and history.

Geography is the study of people, places, and the environment. Geography focuses on five themes: location, region, place, movement, and human-environment interaction.

3. What are three ways to learn about the history and geography of a place?

_____

_____

Government (pages 19–20)

What is the purpose of government?

Government is the people in a society who have the power to make laws, to see that they are carried out, and to settle disagreements about them. In a *limited government*, everyone, including those in charge, must obey the laws. Democracy is a form of limited government.

Rulers in an *unlimited government* have total control and can disregard the law.

A **citizen** is a legal member of a country. Citizens in a democracy have rights and responsibilities. A citizen may be native-born or naturalized.

4. What is the difference between a democracy and a totalitarian government?

_____

_____

Economics (page 20)

What can you learn about a country by studying its economics?

Economics is the study of how people manage their resources by producing, exchanging, and using goods and services.

Resources to satisfy people's desires are limited. The conflict between the unlimited desires and limited resources is called **scarcity**.

Natural resources are gifts of nature, such as forests, fertile soil, and water. *Human resources* are skills people have. *Capital resources* are tools people make.

5. Give examples of the three types of resources that affect a country's economy.

_____

_____

Kinds of Economies (pages 20–21)

What is the difference between a command economy and a market economy?

In a *command economy,* the government decides whether a product should be manufactured, in what quantity, and at what price. In a *market economy*, individual businesses make those decisions based on what consumers want. In a highly developed country, most people are well educated and healthy. Services are plentiful, technology is advanced, and businesses flourish.

A country with a low level of development is marked by few jobs in industry, poor services, and low literacy rates. *Life expectancy* is low.

6. What are some of the characteristics of a country with a high level of development?

_____

_____

Culture (page 21)

What can you learn about a group of people when you study their culture?

Culture consists of the beliefs, customs, laws, art, and ways of living that a group of people share. Religion is part of most cultures; so is a shared language. Music, dance, literature, and the visual arts are important parts of every culture. So are the technology and tools people use to accomplish various tasks. Each kind of food, clothing, or technology, and each belief, language, or tool shared by a culture is called a **culture trait**. The culture traits of a people shape their way of life.

7. What are some examples of culture traits?

_____

_____

Strategy: Underline main ideas and key information as you read.

Try This: Read the summary under the head "Kinds of Economics." Underline information that you think is important.

Strategy: Answer the question at the end of each part.

Try This: Write an answer to Question 4.

Strategy: When you see a word in italic type, read the definition in the on the chapter review page.

Try This: What does limited government mean? Look at the Glossary on the chapter review page to find the definition.

Being a Strategic Reader

HOW TO USE THIS READING STUDY GUIDE

At the end of every chapter in the *Reading Study Guide*, you will find a Glossary and a section called After You Read. The Glossary gives definitions of all the words in italic type in the chapter summaries. After You Read is a two-page chapter review. Use After You Read to identify those parts of the chapter that you need to study more for the test on the chapter.

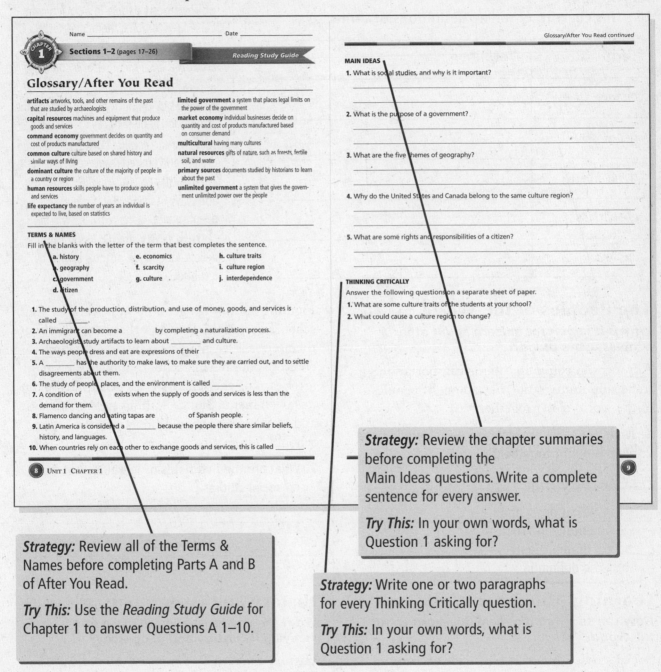

Name _____ Date _____

Glossary/After You Read continued

Glossary/After You Read

artifacts artworks, tools, and other remains of the past that are studied by archaeologists

capital resources machines and equipment that produce goods and services

command economy government decides on quantity and cost of products manufactured

common culture culture based on shared history and similar ways of living

dominant culture the culture of the majority of people in a country or region

human resources skills people have to produce goods and services

life expectancy the number of years an individual is expected to live, based on statistics

limited government a system that places legal limits on the power of the government

market economy individual businesses decide on quantity and cost of products manufactured based on consumer demand

multicultural having many cultures

natural resources gifts of nature, such as forests, fertile soil, and water

primary sources documents studied by historians to learn about the past

unlimited government a system that gives the government unlimited power over the people

TERMS & NAMES

Fill in the blanks with the letter of the term that best completes the sentence.

a. history	**e.** economics	**h.** culture traits
b. geography	**f.** scarcity	**i.** culture region
c. government	**g.** culture	**j.** interdependence
d. citizen		

1. The study of the production, distribution, and use of money, goods, and services is called _____.
2. An immigrant can become a _____ by completing a naturalization process.
3. Archaeologists study artifacts to learn about _____ and culture.
4. The ways people dress and eat are expressions of their _____
5. A _____ has the authority to make laws, to make sure they are carried out, and to settle disagreements about them.
6. The study of people, places, and the environment is called _____.
7. A condition of _____ exists when the supply of goods and services is less than the demand for them.
8. Flamenco dancing and eating tapas are _____ of Spanish people.
9. Latin America is considered a _____ because the people there share similar beliefs, history, and languages.
10. When countries rely on each other to exchange goods and services, this is called _____.

8   UNIT 1 CHAPTER 1

MAIN IDEAS

1. What is social studies, and why is it important?
_____
_____

2. What is the purpose of a government?
_____
_____

3. What are the five themes of geography?
_____
_____

4. Why do the United States and Canada belong to the same culture region?
_____
_____

5. What are some rights and responsibilities of a citizen?
_____
_____

THINKING CRITICALLY

Answer the following questions on a separate sheet of paper.
1. What are some culture traits of the students at your school?
2. What could cause a culture region to change?

9

Strategy: Review all of the Terms & Names before completing Parts A and B of After You Read.

Try This: Use the *Reading Study Guide* for Chapter 1 to answer Questions A 1–10.

Strategy: Review the chapter summaries before completing the Main Ideas questions. Write a complete sentence for every answer.

Try This: In your own words, what is Question 1 asking for?

Strategy: Write one or two paragraphs for every Thinking Critically question.

Try This: In your own words, what is Question 1 asking for?

Name _____ Date _____

The World at Your Fingertips

BEFORE YOU READ

In this section, you will learn about the five fields of learning that make up social studies.

AS YOU READ

Use this chart to organize definitions of terms.

Term	Definition
history	
geography	
government	
economics	
culture	

TERMS & NAMES

history a record of the past

geography the study of people, places, and the environment

government people in a society who make laws, enforce them, and settle disagreements about them

citizen a legal member of a country

economics how people manage their resources by producing, exchanging, and using goods and services

scarcity the conflict between unlimited desires and limited resources

culture the beliefs, customs, laws, art, and ways of living that a group of people share

culture traits specific foods, clothing, beliefs, languages, or tools shared by a culture

The Peoples of the World (page 17)

Why is it important to learn about other peoples' ways of life?

Advances in communication, transportation, trade, and immigration have brought peoples of the world closer together.

1. What are some examples of ways people have been brought together?

_____

_____

_____

Learning About the World (page 18)

How can social studies help you learn about the world?

Social studies draws on five fields of learning: geography, history, economics, government, and culture. Suppose you were at a new school.

Figuring out how to get around is learning your school's geography. Asking other students about themselves is learning their history. Making choices about buying school supplies is economics. Learning the school's rules is learning about its government. Clubs, clothing styles, holidays, and even ways of saying things are part of the school's culture.

2. What are the five fields of learning that make up social studies?

_____

_____

_____

History and Geography (pages 18–19)

What can you learn about a place from studying its history and geography?

History is a record of the past. Historians use *primary sources* such as newspapers and journals to find out about the past. Archaeologists study *artifacts* such as tools and artwork to learn about people's culture and history.

Geography is the study of people, places, and the environment. Geography focuses on five themes: location, region, place, movement, and human-environment interaction.

3. What are three ways to learn about the history and geography of a place?

_____

_____

Government (pages 19–20)

What is the purpose of government?

Government is the people in a society who have the power to make laws, to see that they are carried out, and to settle disagreements about them. In a *limited government*, everyone, including those in charge, must obey the laws. Democracy is a form of limited government.

Rulers in an *unlimited government* have total control and can disregard the law.

A **citizen** is a legal member of a country. Citizens in a democracy have rights and responsibilities. A citizen may be native-born or naturalized.

4. What is the difference between a democracy and a totalitarian government?

_____

_____

Economics (page 20)

What can you learn about a country by studying its economics?

Economics is the study of how people manage their resources by producing, exchanging, and using goods and services.

Resources to satisfy people's desires are limited. The conflict between the unlimited desires and limited resources is called **scarcity**.

Natural resources are gifts of nature, such as forests, fertile soil, and water. *Human resources* are skills people have. *Capital resources* are tools people make.

5. Give examples of the three types of resources that affect a country's economy.

_____

_____

Kinds of Economies (pages 20–21)

What is the difference between a command economy and a market economy?

In a *command economy*, the government decides whether a product should be manufactured, in what quantity, and at what price. In a *market economy*, individual businesses make those decisions based on what consumers want. In a highly developed country, most people are well educated and healthy. Services are plentiful, technology is advanced, and businesses flourish.

A country with a low level of development is marked by few jobs in industry, poor services, and low literacy rates. *Life expectancy* is low.

6. What are some of the characteristics of a country with a high level of development?

_____

_____

Culture (page 21)

What can you learn about a group of people when you study their culture?

Culture consists of the beliefs, customs, laws, art, and ways of living that a group of people share. Religion is part of most cultures; so is a shared language. Music, dance, literature, and the visual arts are important parts of every culture. So are the technology and tools people use to accomplish various tasks. Each kind of food, clothing, or technology, and each belief, language, or tool shared by a culture is called a **culture trait**. The culture traits of a people shape their way of life.

7. What are some examples of culture traits?

_____

_____

Many Regions, Many Cultures

BEFORE YOU READ

In the last section, you read about the five fields of learning that are part of social studies.

In this section, you will read about how the world can be divided into regions according to culture.

AS YOU READ

Use this diagram to identify and take notes about the world's seven major culture regions.

TERMS & NAMES

culture region an area of the world in which many people share similar beliefs, history, and languages

interdependence the economic, political, and social dependence that culture regions have on each other

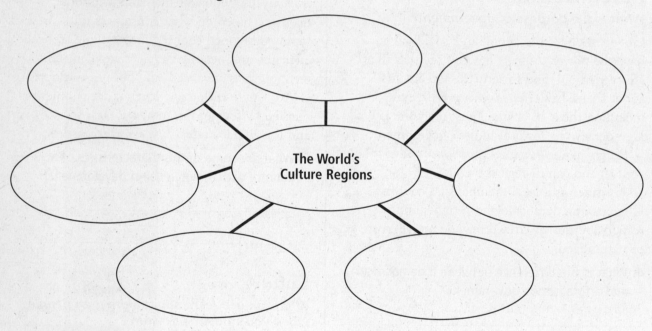

The World's Culture Regions

Different Places, Different Cultures (page 24)

What is a culture region?

A **culture region** is an area of the world in which many people share similar beliefs, history, and languages. They may have religion, technology, and ways of earning a living in common as well. They may grow and eat similar foods, wear similar clothing, and build similar houses.

1. What are a few things that people in a culture region have in common?

_____

_____

The World's Culture Regions
(page 25)

What is a common culture?

The map on the next page shows the major culture regions of the world. Latin America is one culture region. A common history and common languages help to tie its people together. In the Southwest Asia and Northern Africa culture region, most countries share a desert climate. People have adapted to the desert in similar ways, thus creating a *common culture*. Islam, which is the major religion in this region, also helps shape a common culture.

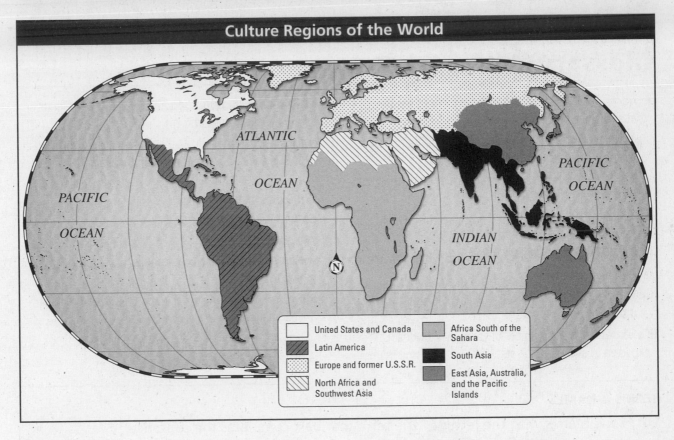

Culture Regions of the World

Legend:
- United States and Canada
- Latin America
- Europe and former U.S.S.R.
- North Africa and Southwest Asia
- Africa South of the Sahara
- South Asia
- East Asia, Australia, and the Pacific Islands

Usually, not every person in a region belongs to the *dominant culture*. Some regions are *multicultural*. For example, the United States and Canada contain other cultures besides the dominant one. Although most people in this region speak English, many people in Canada speak French, and many in the United States speak Spanish. In both countries, several religions flourish.

2. Why are the United States and Canada considered multicultural?

_____

_____

Culture Regions Change (page 26)
What is interdependence?

Cultural regions have changed and evolved as they have borrowed culture traits from one another. They have also come to depend upon each other economically. Advances in transportation and communication have increased this **interdependence**. When oil-producing nations in the Middle East raise the price of oil, for example, the price of gasoline at your local gas station is likely to rise. More and more, people of different countries are becoming part of one world.

3. How are the United States and nations of the Middle East interdependent?

_____

_____

Glossary/After You Read

artifacts artworks, tools, and other remains of the past that are studied by archaeologists

capital resources machines and equipment that produce goods and services

command economy government decides on quantity and cost of products manufactured

common culture culture based on shared history and similar ways of living

dominant culture the culture of the majority of people in a country or region

human resources skills people have to produce goods and services

life expectancy the number of years an individual is expected to live, based on statistics

limited government a system that places legal limits on the power of the government

market economy individual businesses decide on quantity and cost of products manufactured based on consumer demand

multicultural having many cultures

natural resources gifts of nature, such as forests, fertile soil, and water

primary sources documents studied by historians to learn about the past

unlimited government a system that gives the government unlimited power over the people

TERMS & NAMES

Fill in the blanks with the letter of the term that best completes the sentence.

a. history	**e.** economics	**h.** culture traits
b. geography	**f.** scarcity	**i.** culture region
c. government	**g.** culture	**j.** interdependence
d. citizen		

1. The study of the production, distribution, and use of money, goods, and services is called _____.

2. An immigrant can become a _____ by completing a naturalization process.

3. Archaeologists study artifacts to learn about _____ and culture.

4. The ways people dress and eat are expressions of their _____.

5. A _____ has the authority to make laws, to make sure they are carried out, and to settle disagreements about them.

6. The study of people, places, and the environment is called _____.

7. A condition of _____ exists when the supply of goods and services is less than the demand for them.

8. Flamenco dancing and eating tapas are _____ of Spanish people.

9. Latin America is considered a _____ because the people there share similar beliefs, history, and languages.

10. When countries rely on each other to exchange goods and services, this is called _____.

MAIN IDEAS

1. What is social studies, and why is it important?

_____

_____

2. What is the purpose of a government?

_____

_____

3. What are the five themes of geography?

_____

_____

4. Why do the United States and Canada belong to the same culture region?

_____

_____

5. What are some rights and responsibilities of a citizen?

_____

_____

THINKING CRITICALLY

Answer the following questions on a separate sheet of paper.

1. What are some culture traits of the students at your school?

2. What could cause a culture region to change?

The Five Themes of Geography

BEFORE YOU READ

In the last chapter, you read about culture regions and the five fields of learning that make up social studies.

In this section, you will learn about the five themes of geography.

AS YOU READ

Use this chart to take notes about the five themes of geography.

The Five Themes of Geography				
Location				

TERMS & NAMES

absolute location the exact spot on Earth where a place can be found

latitude imaginary lines that run parallel to the Equator

longitude imaginary lines that run between the North and South Poles

relative location the location of one place in relation to another place

migrate to move from one area in order to settle in another

The Five Themes (page 35)

Which geography theme did Wegener explore?

In 1912, scientist Alfred Wegener proposed that the continents had once been joined together as one huge landmass. He called this supercontinent *Pangaea*. Wegener thought that over time, pieces of this landmass had broken away and drifted apart. People rejected his claim, saying that it was impossible for continents to move.

Eventually, the scientific community accepted Wegener's *theory*. Scientists discovered that giant slabs of Earth's surface, called tectonic plates, move, causing continents to drift. The movement of the plates also creates earthquakes, volcanoes, and mountains. *Geographers* study processes that cause changes like these. To understand how geographers think about the world, consider geography's five themes— location, place, region, movement, and human-environment interaction.

1. What do geographers study?

_____

_____

Location (pages 36–37)

How can location help you learn about a place?

Geography helps you understand where places are located and why they are located there.

Absolute location is the exact spot on Earth where a place can be found. Using imaginary lines drawn on Earth's surface, geographers can locate any place in the world. Lines that run parallel to the *Equator* are called **latitude** lines. They measure distance north and south of the Equator. Lines that run between the North and South Poles are called **longitude** lines. They measure distance east and west of the *Prime Meridian*.

Another way to define the location of a place is to describe its **relative location**, where it is in relation to other places. You might say your school's relative location is two blocks west of the pet store or close to the post office.

2. What is the difference between absolute location and relative location?

_____

_____

Place (page 37)
What physical features and human characteristics would you use to describe a place?
Another theme of geography is place. Every place on Earth has physical features, which include climate, landforms, bodies of water, and plant and animal life. Places can also have human characteristics, or features created by people, such as cities, governments, and cultural traditions.

Earth's physical features change. Some changes are dramatic, caused by volcanoes, earthquakes, or hurricanes. Others happen slowly, such as the movement of glaciers or the formation of a delta.

3. Why do places change?

_____

_____

Region (pages 37–38)
What is a region?
Geographers group places into regions. A region is a group of places that have physical features or human characteristics in common. A geographer interested in languages might divide the world into language regions. Geographers compare regions to understand the differences and similarities among them.

The world can be divided into ten natural regions. A *natural region*, such as a tropical rain forest, has unique plant and animal life and a unique climate.

4. Why are tropical rain forests examples of natural regions?

_____

_____

Movement (pages 38–39)
Why is movement one of geography's themes?
People, goods, and ideas move from one place to another. So do animals, plants, and other physical features of Earth. Sometimes, people move within a country. For example, vast numbers of people have migrated from farms

to cities. **Migrate** means to move from one area in order to settle in another.

Migration is a result of push and pull factors. Problems in one place, such as poverty, *prejudice*, and political oppression, push people out. Advantages in another place, such as employment and educational opportunities, freedom, and peace, pull people in.

Natural barriers, such as mountain ranges and rivers, make migration difficult. Oceans and flat land make it easier. Modern transportation also makes it easier.

5. What are push and pull factors?

_____

_____

Human-Environment Interaction
(pages 39–40)
Why does human-environment interaction occur?
Human-environment interaction occurs because humans depend on, adapt to, and change the world around them. Human society and the environment are shaped by each other.

An area may have open meadows because early settlers cleared the land for farming. Changes caused by humans, such as pollution, can hurt the environment. The environment can also harm people. Hurricanes wash away houses. Earthquakes cause destruction.

People adapt to the resources their environment provides. In the past, people who lived near oceans learned to fish. Those who lived near fertile soil learned to farm. People built homes using local materials and ate food grown nearby. Cultural differences in clothing styles and sports often reflected the environment.

People and the environment continually interact. When people use public transportation or ride bicycles rather than drive, less gasoline is burned and there is less air pollution.

6. In the past, how did people adapt their ways of life to the environment?

_____

_____

Name _____ Date _____

The Geographer's Tools

BEFORE YOU READ

In the last section, you read about the five themes of geography.

In this section, you will read about the tools geographers use to learn about and display the features of Earth.

AS YOU READ

Use this Venn diagram to compare and contrast maps and globes.

TERMS & NAMES

cartographer a mapmaker

thematic map a map that focuses on one idea or theme

map projections a flat map that shows Earth's curved surface in different ways

Maps   Similarities   Globes

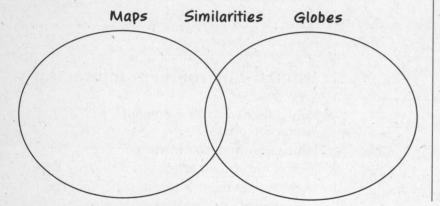

Maps and Globes (pages 45–48)

***What** are the tools that geographers use to represent the world?*

Geographers today have many tools to help them represent Earth. Increased knowledge and improved technology allow a **cartographer**, or mapmaker, to construct maps that give a much more detailed and accurate picture of the world.

Both maps and globes represent Earth and its features. A *globe* is an accurate model of the world because it has three dimensions and thus shows Earth's actual shape. Globes are difficult to carry around, however. Maps are more practical. They can be folded, carried, hung on a wall, or printed in a book or magazine. However, because maps show the world in two dimensions, they are not perfectly accurate.

General reference maps, which show natural and human-made features, are used to locate a place. **Thematic maps**, such as population maps, focus on one specific idea or theme. Pilots and

sailors use *nautical maps* to find their way through air and over water. A nautical map is sometimes called a chart.

The different ways of showing Earth's curved surface on a flat map are called **map projections**. All projections distort Earth. Some make places look bigger or smaller than they really are in relation to other places. Other projections distort shapes. For more than 400 years, the Mercator projection was most often used for maps of the world. Recently, the Robinson projection has come into common use because it gives a more accurate picture of the world.

1. How are the three main kinds of maps different from one another?

_____

_____

_____

Comparing Maps, Charts, and Graphs (page 49)

Why do geographers use charts and graphs?

Along with maps, geographers use charts and graphs to display and compare information. The graphs on this page contain information about the world's population. Notice how quickly and clearly they present facts that would otherwise take up many paragraphs of text.

2. According to the graphs below, which continent has the smallest population? How many people lived in the world in 1950?

_____

_____

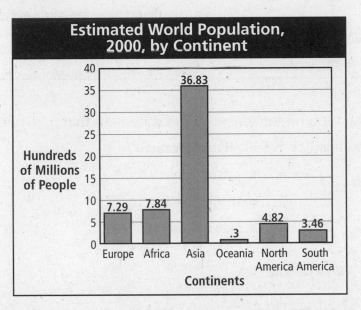

Estimated World Population, 2000, by Continent

Hundreds of Millions of People

Europe	Africa	Asia	Oceania	North America	South America
7.29	7.84	36.83	.3	4.82	3.46

Continents

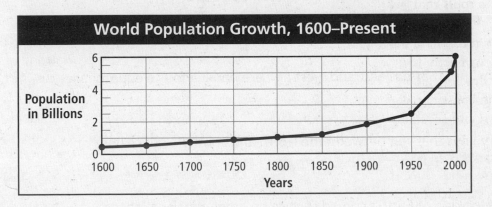

World Population Growth, 1600–Present

Population in Billions

Years: 1600, 1650, 1700, 1750, 1800, 1850, 1900, 1950, 2000

Glossary/After You Read

equator an imaginary line that separates Earth into Northern and Southern Hemispheres

general reference map a map showing natural and human-made features, used to locate a place

geographers scientists who study processes that cause changes in Earth

natural region a region that has unique plant and animal life and a unique climate

nautical map a map used by pilots and sailors

prejudice irrational hatred or dislike for a particular group, race, or religion

prime meridian an imaginary line that separates Earth into Eastern and Western Hemispheres

theory an explanation of events used to make predictions

TERMS & NAMES

Write the letter of the term or name next to the statement that matches the description.

a. absolute location   **e.** relative location

b. longitude   **f.** cartographer

c. latitude   **g.** thematic map

d. migrate   **h.** map projection

1. A population map is an example of a _____.

2. My school is located near the library. This is my school's _____.

3. The _____ of my house is its exact position on Earth.

4. Imaginary lines that run east and west and are parallel to the equator are called lines of _____.

5. Imaginary lines that run between the North and South Poles are lines of _____.

6. A way of looking at Earth's curved surface on a flat map is called a _____.

7. A _____ is someone who makes detailed maps of the world.

8. Sometimes people _____ from one area to another because of work opportunities.

MAIN IDEAS

1. What are the five themes of geography?

_____

_____

2. Why do places change over time?

_____

_____

3. What causes people to move from one place to another?

_____

_____

4. What is the difference between a map and a globe?

_____

_____

5. Explain the differences among the three kinds of maps.

_____

_____

THINKING CRITICALLY

Answer the following questions on a separate piece of paper.

1. How would you describe the relative location of your school?

2. Why do you think that graphs are sometimes used in newspapers?

Name _____   Date _____

From Coast to Coast

BEFORE YOU READ

In the last chapter, you read about the field of geography. In this section, you will read about the geographic features of the United States and Canada.

AS YOU READ

Copy this chart for taking notes on how each geographic feature contributes to the economies of the United States and Canada.

Economic Benefits of North America's Geography				
Climate & Soil	Oceans & Rivers	Plains and Lowlands	Canadian Shield	Mountain Ranges

TERMS & NAMES

Sacagawea Native American woman who guided explorers from 1804 to 1806

landforms features of Earth's surface, such as mountains, valleys, and plateaus

glacier thick sheet of ice that moves slowly across land

erosion process by which wind, rivers, and rain wear away soil and stone

river system network of major rivers and their tributaries

North America (pages 69–70)

What countries are located in North America?

Canada and the United States are in the northern part of the continent. Canada is the second largest country in area in the world. North America also includes Greenland, which is the world's largest island.

Mexico, the Central American countries, and the Caribbean island nations are part of the continent. These countries, along with South America, make up Latin America. Geographers study Latin America separately from the United States and Canada because the cultural heritage of the two areas is different.

Most of the United States and Canada is in the *middle latitudes* of the Northern Hemisphere, where a temperate climate and farming enable countries to feed large populations.

1. Why do geographers study Latin America separately from the United States and Canada?

_____

_____

An Isolated Continent (pages 70–71)

Why was North America once an isolated continent?

North America is almost completely surrounded by water, from the Arctic Ocean to the Gulf of Mexico and from the Pacific Ocean to the Atlantic Ocean.

At one time, oceans and seas isolated North America. The earliest settlers arrived 12,000 to 35,000 years ago. No other people reached this continent for thousands of years.

2. What are the names of the oceans that surround North America?

_____

_____

Crossing the Barriers (page 71)

Why did people begin to move to North America?

As people learned more about shipbuilding and navigation, the oceans became a travel route.

Copyright © McDougal Littell Inc.

Settlers arrived with plants and animals that at times replaced native plants and animals.

A Shoshone woman, **Sacagawea**, had a vital role in exploring the United States. From 1804 to 1806, she guided explorers Lewis and Clark into the Pacific Northwest.

In the 20th century, the distance from other countries helped protect Canada and the United States from wartime attack.

3. How did Sacagawea help explorers?

_____

_____

Regions of the United States and Canada (pages 72–73)

How are the regions of the United States and Canada alike?

The United States and Canada share many geographic regions.

The *Atlantic Coastal Plain* runs along the Gulf of Mexico and the east coast of North America. It has rich farmland and some wetlands.

The *Appalachian Mountains* are a 400-million-year-old mountain range west of the Atlantic Coastal Plain.

The *Central Lowlands* extend west of the Appalachians to the Great Plains. They are generally flat farmlands with rich soil.

The *Great Plains* have grasslands and few trees. Some areas have farms and cattle ranches.

The *Rocky Mountains and Coastal Ranges* in the west are North America's highest mountain ranges. These heavily forested ranges run from Mexico to Alaska.

The *Intermountain Region* lies between the Rocky Mountains and the western coastal mountains. This dry region contains plateaus, basins, and deserts. Ranchers raise cattle and sheep there.

The *Canadian Shield* is a rocky region that covers most of Greenland, curves around the Hudson Bay, and reaches into the United States. It is rich in iron and copper. Most of the land is not farmable and is sparsely populated.

4. What mountains run along the west coast of North America from Alaska to Mexico?

_____

_____

Physical Processes Shape the Land (pages 73–74)

How have natural processes shaped North America?

Some of the continent's most dramatic landforms were created by wind, water, ice, and moving slabs of Earth's crust. **Landforms** are features of Earth's surface, such as mountains, valleys, and plateaus.

A **glacier** is a thick sheet of ice that moves slowly across land. Thousands of years ago, glaciers covered much of North America. As they moved and melted, they smoothed out rough surfaces and piled up rock and dirt, creating new valleys, lakes, and hills.

Wind, rivers, and rain wear away soil and stone in a process called **erosion**. Erosion has created magnificent landforms, such as the Grand Canyon. Volcanoes and earthquakes have also created landforms across North America.

5. How does a glacier change landforms?

_____

_____

Waterways (page 74)

What is a river system?

North America has an extensive **river system,** or network of rivers and their *tributaries*. When snow melts and rain falls, water flows into creeks that become rivers. Rivers empty into oceans, lakes, and other rivers.

6. How does a river system work?

_____

_____

Name _____   Date _____

A Rich Diversity in Climate and Resources

BEFORE YOU READ

In the last section, you read about the regions and land-forms of the United States and Canada.

In this section, you will read about North America's climate, vegetation, and natural resources.

AS YOU READ

Copy this chart for taking notes about the vegetation zones of the United States and Canada.

TERMS & NAMES

weather the state of the atmosphere near Earth at a given time and place

precipitation moisture, such as rain or snow, that falls to Earth

climate typical weather in a region over a long period of time

vegetation trees, shrubs, grasses, and other plants

economy the way businesses use resources to provide the goods and services that people want

Vegetation Zones					
	Polar and Tundra	Forests	Rain Forests	Grasslands	Deserts
Climate					
Physical Features					

Climate and Vegetation/ Vegetation Zones (pages 75-76)

How do geography and climate affect a region's vegetation?

Weather includes temperature, wind, and **precipitation**, such as rain or snow. A region's typical weather, or **climate**, helps to determine what types of **vegetation** will grow there.

The climate and physical geography of each area determine North America's *vegetation zones*. Although it is usually warmer in the south and colder in the north, physical features such as mountains and oceans also affect the climate.

The polar and *tundra* regions of northern Canada and Alaska have cool summers and very cold winters. It is usually above freezing

(32°F/0°C) there for only two months a year. Much of the ground is frozen all year except for the surface, which thaws in summer.

Forests of conifer (evergreen) and broadleaf trees cover much of Canada and the northwestern, northeastern, and southeastern United States. Rainfall averages between 12 and 40 inches annually. Temperatures range from mild to cold in different areas.

Along the Pacific Coast, rainfall can reach 167 inches a year. Rain forests with trees 300 feet tall grow in these areas. The ground is covered in bushes, small trees, and other plants, such as moss and *lichen*. Temperatures are moderate even in the north, seldom falling below 32°F.

The center of North America is covered by grasslands. The prairie in the Mississippi Valley, where grasses are tall and thick, may get 30 inches or more of rain each year. Farther west, the land gets less rainfall and the grass is shorter. People grow grain and raise cattle in these areas.

The deserts of the American Southwest get less than 10 inches of precipitation a year. Desert plants must endure harsh sun, high temperatures, and little rain. Only the hardiest vegetation survives.

1. What is a vegetation zone?

_____

_____

_____

Natural Wealth (page 78)

How do natural resources affect economic development in the United States and Canada?

Rich natural resources have influenced the economic development of the United States and Canada. The farmlands of the midwestern United States and the prairies of central Canada have fertile soil. Western Canada and the northwestern, northeastern, and southeastern United States have valuable forests. There are oil fields in Alberta, Canada; in Texas, California, Louisiana, Oklahoma, and Alaska; and in the Gulf of Mexico. Coal is found in Canada's western provinces and in several U.S. states.

Water resources affect where people choose to live and work. Settlers in North America followed rivers to areas where fresh water and good soil encouraged farming. Businesses grew in the new communities. Rivers are still used to ship natural resources, such as timber and coal, and are used as trade and travel routes. Lakes and rivers provide food, water, power, and recreational opportunities.

2. What are three natural resources that play a role in economic development in the United States and Canada?

_____

_____

_____

Neighbors and Leaders (page 79)

How do the United States and Canada benefit from being neighbors?

Trade between the United States and Canada exceeds $1 billion a day. The two countries cooperate on issues as diverse as national security and defense, the environment, air traffic, and fishing regulations. More than 200 million people cross the U.S.-Canadian border every year.

Both countries have strong economies and are leaders in world trade. An **economy** is the way business owners use resources to provide the goods and services that people want.

3. Why is trade between Canada and the United States at such a high level?

_____

_____

_____

Glossary/After You Read

Appalachian Mountains mountain range in eastern North America extending from Quebec to Alabama

Atlantic Coastal Plain region along the Gulf of Mexico and the east coast of North America

Canadian Shield rocky, mineral-rich region extending from Greenland to the Great Lakes

Central Lowlands flat farmlands west of the Appalachians

Great Plains sloping region of grasslands in west central North America

Intermountain Region dry region between the Rocky Mountains and the western coastal mountains

lichen an organism that grows with algae on rocks or tree trunks

middle latitudes area between the Arctic Circle and the Tropic of Cancer; where most of the United States and Canada is located

Rocky Mountains and Coastal Ranges high, forested mountain ranges in western North America extending from Mexico to Alaska

tributaries rivers or streams that flow into larger rivers or streams

tundra treeless plains of the arctic regions

vegetation zone an area or region that has a similar climate and geography

---

TERMS & NAMES

A. If the statement is true, write "true" on the line. If it is false, change the underlined word or words to make it true.

_____ **1.** A thick sheet of ice that moves slowly across land is a <u>glacier</u>.

_____ **2.** Rain and snow are examples of <u>vegetation</u>.

_____ **3.** The process by which wind, rivers, and rain wear away stone and soil is called <u>weather</u>.

_____ **4.** A network of rivers and their tributaries is called a <u>river system</u>.

_____ **5.** The state of the atmosphere near Earth at a given time and place is called <u>climate</u>.

B. Write the term next to the description that matches it.

Sacagawea   climate   economy

landforms   vegetation

_____ **1.** features of Earth's surface, such as mountains and valleys

_____ **2.** trees, shrubs, grasses, and other plants

_____ **3.** typical weather in a region over a long period of time

_____ **4.** Native American woman who guided explorers Lewis and Clark

_____ **5.** how resources are used to provide goods and services

MAIN IDEAS

1. Describe North America's location on Earth and its climate. How do these factors affect farming in North America?

_____

_____

2. What were some barriers in the past that prevented people from moving to North America?

_____

_____

3. How have natural processes shaped the land of North America?

_____

_____

4. What is a vegetation zone?

_____

_____

5. What are some of North America's natural resources?

_____

_____

THINKING CRITICALLY

Answer the following questions on a separate sheet of paper.

1. Imagine that you are a rock climber looking for adventure. To which region of the United States and Canada would you go? Explain your thinking.

2. If you could live in any of North America's vegetation zones, which would you choose, and why?

We the People

BEFORE YOU READ

In the last chapter, you read about the physical geography of the United States and Canada.

In this section, you will read about the history of U.S. citizens.

AS YOU READ

Copy this chart to record main ideas about the history of U.S. citizens.

The United States Today	
History	
Government	
Economy	
Culture	

TERMS & NAMES

immigrant a person who chooses to move to another country

Anasazi early Native Americans who developed complex civilizations in the U.S. Southwest

equal opportunity guarantee that government or private institutions won't discriminate against people based on race, religion, age, or gender

citizenship the responsibilities and rights of a citizen

democracy a government that receives its power from the people

political process legal activities, such as voting, by which citizens influence government

patriotism love and support for one's country

One Country, Many Cultures
(pages 87–88)

Why do immigrants move to the United States?

People who choose to move to a new country are called **immigrants**. Immigrants bring unique contributions to the United States from all over the world. The United States is sometimes called a "melting pot" because it is a mix of many people with different cultural backgrounds.

Immigrants come to the United States for different reasons. Some are escaping from *discrimination*, persecution, or war. Others leave their homelands because of natural disasters. Often, people come in search of jobs or education.

1. Why is the United States considered a "melting pot?"

_____

_____

People from Many Lands
(pages 88–90)

What are some groups that moved to the land now known as the United States?

Millions of immigrants have come to North America over the past 500 years. However, this land was inhabited for thousands of years before they arrived. The first Americans came to North America from Eastern Asia, 12,000 to 35,000 years ago.

Groups such as the **Anasazi** developed complex civilizations before Europeans arrived.

European exploration of the Americas began in the late 1400s. Colonists soon followed. The British settled along the Atlantic coast. Spaniards settled in Florida. As the European population grew, competition for land grew keener. Europeans often took land from Native Americans without paying for it, which led to distrust and war.

European settlers began to farm, start businesses, and build towns. This activity created a demand for labor, so Europeans brought people to America by force.

Europeans had been buying people from slave traders in Africa for years. Beginning in 1619, slave traders shipped many enslaved Africans to the American colonies. Those who survived the journey were bought and sold as property and forced to work for nothing all their lives. *Indentured servants* from Europe also worked in exchange for passage to America.

In the second half of the 1800s, many Chinese entered the United States to work in mines or to help build the transcontinental railroad. In the 1880s and the 1920s, new laws limited the number of immigrants from specific countries. In 1952, legislation again allowed immigrants of all races to become citizens.

2. Why did Africans first come to the United States?

_____

_____

_____

Rights of Citizens (page 90)

What are some groups that have suffered from discrimination?

Although the United States is a world leader in protecting individual freedom, many U.S. citizens have had to struggle for their rights. Even after African Americans were legally freed from slavery in 1865, they were denied their rights. Women could not vote until 1920. Native Americans, as well as Hispanics, Asians, Jews, and other groups, have fought against discrimination. **Equal opportunity** in education, employment, and other areas of life has increased over the years. Today, it is illegal for the government or private institutions to discriminate on the basis of race, gender, religion, age, or disability.

3. What protects people from discrimination today?

_____

_____

Responsibilities of Citizenship
(page 90)

What does it mean to be a citizen?

Citizenship combines the duties and rights of a citizen. Good citizenship means doing more than is required by law for the good of the people. In a democracy, government receives its power from the people. **Democracy** is a Greek word that means "rule of the people." To make democracy work well, every citizen is responsible for taking an active role in the political process. The **political process** includes legal activities, such as voting, through which citizens can bring about change in public policy. By taking part in this process, U.S. citizens demonstrate their patriotism, or love for their country.

4. How can citizens participate in the political process?

_____

_____

Name _____ Date _____

A Constitutional Democracy

BEFORE YOU READ

In the last section, you read about the history of American citizens.

In this section, you will read about the government of the United States.

AS YOU READ

Copy this chart to take notes about the United States government.

The United States Today	
Government	

TERMS & NAMES

United States Constitution document that is the foundation for all laws and the framework for the U.S. government

limited government system that limits the power of government

unlimited government system that provides leaders with almost total power

constitutional amendment a change or addition to the Constitution

Bill of Rights the first ten amendments to the Constitution that list specific individual rights of every U.S. citizen

federal government national government

The Law of the Land/Limited and Unlimited Government (pages 94–95)

What is the United States Constitution?

After the American colonists gained independence from Great Britain, they established a nation called the United States of America. They set up a system of government for their new nation that was outlined in the **United States Constitution**, written in 1787.

This document has been the foundation for all laws and the framework for the U.S. government for more than 200 years. It was designed to protect people's rights and to establish a stable government.

The Constitution describes a government that receives its power from the people and whose leaders have a limited amount of control. It also defines the rights of citizens and their role in government.

The constitutional democracy of the United States is one example of a **limited government**. In other types of government, called **unlimited**

governments, the leaders have almost total power.

1. What were some of the goals of the leaders who wrote the Constitution?

_____

_____

_____

The Constitution Grows and Changes (page 96)

What was added to the Constitution in 1791?

The Constitution went into effect in 1789. A condition of ratifying, or approving, it in many states was the promise that a bill of rights would be added to guarantee individual rights of citizens. In 1791, a **Bill of Rights** was adopted. It listed specific freedoms, such as freedom of speech and religion, and the right to a fair trial. The Bill of Rights is made up of the first ten amendments to the Constitution. A **constitutional amendment** is a change or addition to the Constitution. In all, 27 amendments have adapted the Constitution to the country's changing needs. Amendments after the Bill of Rights include those ending slavery, and giving women the right to vote.

2. What is the purpose of the Bill of Rights?

_____

_____

Limiting Powers of Government
(pages 96–97)

What *kind of government did the writers of the Constitution want for the United States?*

Leaders of the new country wanted to limit government power and to preserve each state's right to govern itself. To accomplish these goals, they created a federal system in which power is divided between the **federal government**, or national government, and the state governments. Our federal government is a *republic* headed by our President.

The Constitution gives the federal government power to wage war, to raise money through taxes, and to make laws. All other powers are held by the states. The Constitution does not refer to local government, so each state determines the form of town or county government.

3. What are some of the powers of the federal government?

_____

_____

Three Branches of Government
(page 98)

What *are the three branches of the United States government?*

The Constitution separates the government into three branches: the executive, legislative, and judicial branches. This separation of powers is called a system of checks and balances. Each branch has its own job and checks the power of the other branches. All branches are located in Washington, D.C.

The President is elected to head the executive branch. The President enforces the laws, conducts foreign affairs, and is commander-in-chief of the armed forces. The Vice President is elected with the President. The President's *cabinet* includes the secretaries of the 14 executive departments and other key members of the executive branch.

The legislative branch is called Congress and is made up of two houses, or parts—the Senate and the House of Representatives. Congress creates national laws. Two senators are elected from each of the 50 states. The House of Representatives has 435 members, elected from each state according to the size of its population.

The judicial branch is the system of federal courts with the power to make sure that laws are constitutional—that they agree with the Constitution. The highest federal court, the Supreme Court, has nine judges, called justices, who serve for life.

4. Why does the Constitution separate the government into three branches?

_____

_____

The United States Economy

BEFORE YOU READ

In the last section, you read about U.S. government. In this section, you will read about U.S. economics.

AS YOU READ

Copy this chart to take notes about the U.S. economy.

The United States Today	
History	
Government	
Economy	
Culture	

TERMS & NAMES

factors of production elements needed for production to occur

GDP gross domestic product; total value of the goods and services that a country produces each year

free enterprise/market economy an economy in which business owners compete in the market with little government interference

consumers people who use goods and services

profit money that remains after the costs of producing a product are paid

competition rivalry among businesses to sell goods and services and make the greatest profit

The Study of Economics

(pages 102–103)

What factors can affect the state of the economy?

The American free market economy is always changing. As businesses start up and shut down, and the number of people without jobs rises and falls, people's confidence in the economy changes. The level of confidence affects choices made by investors, service providers, manufacturers, and consumers.

Economics involves the exchange of goods and services. A CD is an example of a good, or an object you can buy to satisfy a want. To earn money to buy a CD, you might provide a service, such as raking your neighbor's leaves. A service is an action that meets a want. Your neighbor buys your service to meet his or her want.

People are constantly deciding which goods and services to buy. They usually satisfy basic needs such as food, clothing, housing, and transportation first.

1. What is the difference between a good and a service?

_____

_____

_____

A Growing Economy (pages 103–104)

How do businesses meet the needs of consumers in a growing economy?

To meet the needs of consumers in a growing economy, business owners must keep production at a high level. Production is the making of goods and services. The four **factors of production** are the elements needed for production to occur. They include:

Natural Resources raw materials such as land, water, forests, and minerals

Labor Resources workers with skills and experience to make goods or provide services

Capital Resources machines, factories, and supplies

Entrepreneurs People who bring natural resources, labor resources, and capital resources together to produce goods and services

2. Explain the four factors of production.

_____

_____

The United States Economy
(pages 104–106)
What is a free enterprise/market economy?

One way to measure and compare a country's economy is to look at its **GDP**, or gross domestic product. This tells the total value of the goods and services that a country produces each year.

Industries such as health care and legal services, communications, finance, manufacturing, and electronics make the U.S. economy one of the wealthiest in the world.

U.S. citizens and businesses make most of their own economic decisions. The government does not set prices, tell businesses what to produce, or tell people where to work. These are qualities of a **free enterprise/market economy**. A market is a setting for exchanging goods and services. In a market economy, business owners compete in the market with little government regulation.

Consumers are the people who use goods and services in a market economy. They help decide what will be produced. Prices affect how many products are sold. The number of items offered at each price is the *supply*. The number of items that people will buy at each price is the *demand*.

For example, if a music company produces 1,000 CDs, but 1,100 people want to buy them, then there are not enough CDs to satisfy the wants of the consumers. Because demand for the good is greater than the supply, the seller is able to increase the price and make a larger profit. **Profit** is the money that remains after the costs of producing a product are paid.

When the supply of a good is greater than the demand, the seller usually lowers the price and, as a result, makes a smaller profit.

In a free market economy, many businesses produce similar goods or services. There is competition to attract consumers. Competition is the rivalry among businesses to sell goods to consumers and make the greatest profit. To achieve this, a company may offer an improved product, manufacture it more cheaply, or sell it at a better price.

3. What usually happens to the price of a good if the demand for it is higher than the supply available?

_____

_____

Other Economic Systems/The Global Economy (pages 106–107)
What are the differences between market, command, and traditional economies?

Most countries combine features from three types of economic systems: market, command, and traditional economies.

In a command economy, the government decides how many of which goods are produced and sets the prices.

In a traditional economy, social roles and culture determine prices, how goods and services are produced, and which consumers are allowed to buy certain goods. For instance, buying a tractor might depend on a family's social status.

Today, many countries have market economies. Countries trade with one another. The movement of people, goods, and ideas around the world has helped build a global, or worldwide, economy.

Sometimes countries establish trade barriers to restrict trade. Tariffs, or taxes on imported goods, raise the price to the consumer and make it more difficult for other countries to compete.

In 1994, the North American Free Trade Agreement reduced trade barriers among the United States, Canada, and Mexico.

4. What are some reasons why the global economy has grown?

_____

_____

United States Culture: Crossing Borders

BEFORE YOU READ

In the last section, you read about U.S. economics.
In this section, you will read about U.S. culture.

AS YOU READ

Copy this chart to take notes about U.S. culture.

The United States Today	
History	
Government	
Economy	
Culture	

TERMS & NAMES

values principles and ideals by which people live

globalization the spreading of an idea around the world

technology tools and equipment that apply new knowledge

American Way of Life (pages 110–111)

What are values?

People in the United States have brought various customs, traditions, and foods from their homelands, but they share many of the same values. **Values** are the principles and ideals by which people live. U.S. citizens care about individual freedoms; equal opportunities; fair treatment of people regardless of differences; and private ownership of property. Many of these values are part of the U.S. Constitution and help define American culture.

U.S. citizens believe they can improve their lives through education. State laws require that all children attend school until they are at least 16. More than 99 percent of U.S. children finish elementary school, and more than 85 percent finish high school.

About 70 percent of American citizens are members of religious groups. Many people originally came to America so that they could worship as they pleased. Our country now includes people of many different religions, such as Catholicism, Protestantism, Judaism,

Buddhism, Islam, Hinduism, and Native American religions.

1. What are some values that Americans share?

_____

_____

The Arts and Entertainment

(pages 111–112)

How has American culture been influenced by other cultures?

Leisure activities in the United States reflect the influence of other cultures. For example, tennis came from France, golf from Scotland, and soccer from England. Basketball was invented in the United States by a Canadian and later spread to other countries. Football is played chiefly in the United States and Canada.

The movies and television and certain musical forms, such as rock and roll, developed in the United States, although they were affected by other cultures. Jazz was influenced by the blues, which is rooted in spirituals once sung by enslaved Africans. Today, these musical styles are enjoyed around the world.

The international popularity of American music is an example of the globalization of culture. **Globalization** means spreading around the world. Today, cultural influences often cross national boundaries. People around the world enjoy blue jeans, sodas, and fast food from the United States. U.S. citizens eat Japanese sushi, listen to Italian operas, and drive South Korean cars. Literature from many nations is translated into different languages. Print and electronic communication provide rapid ways to share the products and creations of different cultures.

2. What is the globalization of culture?

_____

_____

U.S. Science and Technology
(pages 112–113)

How are U.S. scientists changing the world?

U.S. scientists are mapping DNA, discovering treatments and cures for diseases, and finding new energy sources. Once discoveries are made, inventors create **technology**, such as tools or equipment, to apply the new knowledge in practical ways. Modern technology enables U.S. scientists to work with other scientists from many countries.

Discoveries by U.S. scientists help people throughout the world. Polio was widespread, especially among children, in the 1940s and 1950s. Then, U.S. doctors Jonas Salk and Albert Sabin developed two *vaccines* against the disease. As a result, great progress has been made toward making the world free of polio.

Negative effects of technology include increased pollution of the environment and the loss of unique cultural features as countries share languages, foods, and customs. Poorer nations may lack the money and skilled labor to benefit from new applications of science.

3. How has technology helped and hurt the world?

_____

_____

Glossary/After You Read

cabinet group of advisers to the President, including heads of the 14 executive departments

demand the number of items that people will buy at a given price

discrimination unfair treatment of people on the basis of their race, religion, nationality, or gender

indentured servant immigrant who agreed to work for a number of years in exchange for passage to America

republic a nation in which citizens elect representatives to run the government

supply the number of items available at a given price

vaccine a preparation injected to prevent a disease

TERMS & NAMES

A. If the statement is true, write "true" on the line. If it is false, change the underlined word or words to make it true.

_____ **1.** A person who moves from one country to another is an <u>immigrant</u>.

_____ **2.** <u>Patriotism</u> is the guarantee that American citizens applying for jobs will not be discriminated against on the basis of their race, religion, age, or gender.

_____ **3.** <u>Citizenship</u> means the rights and responsibilities of a citizen.

_____ **4.** <u>Republic</u> is a Greek word that means "rule of the people."

_____ **5.** Citizens are taking part in the <u>Bill of Rights</u> when they are involved in legal activities that influence the government.

_____ **6.** The <u>Bill of Rights</u> is the document that is the foundation for all laws and the framework of the U.S. government.

_____ **7.** The United States is an example of an <u>unlimited government</u> because it is a constitutional democracy.

_____ **8.** In a <u>limited government</u>, leaders have almost total power.

_____ **9.** An addition to the Constitution is called a <u>political process</u>.

_____ **10.** The <u>Bill of Rights</u> guarantees individual rights of citizens and includes the first ten amendments to the Constitution.

B. Write the term next to the description that matches it.

| GDP | consumers | competition | technology | factors of production |
| Anasazi | profit | globalization | values | free enterprise/market economy |

_____ **1.** early Native Americans who built a civilization in the Southwest

_____ **2.** elements needed for the making of goods and services

_____ **3.** an economy that allows businesses to operate with little government regulation

_____ **4.** rivalry among businesses to make the greatest profit

_____ **5.** principles and ideals by which people live

_____ **6.** people who use goods and services

_____ **7.** total value of the goods and services produced in a year

_____ **8.** spreading of an idea around the world

_____ **9.** tools and equipment made by applying new knowledge

_____ **10.** money that remains after all costs of producing a product are paid

MAIN IDEAS

1. Why is the United States considered a "melting pot"?

_____

_____

2. What are some of the rights and responsibilities of being an American citizen?

_____

_____

3. What is the purpose of the United States Constitution?

_____

_____

4. What is a free enterprise/market economy?

_____

_____

5. How has the globalization of culture and science affected the United States?

_____

_____

THINKING CRITICALLY

Answer the following questions on a separate sheet of paper.

1. Why do you think the writers of the Constitution separated the government into three branches? How are powers separated at your school?

2. Suppose your town has a law that says your family cannot live in a certain section of town because of your religion. Is this law constitutional? Explain.

O Canada! Immigrant Roots

BEFORE YOU READ

In the last chapter, you read about the United States today.

In this section, you will read about the history of Canada's people.

AS YOU READ

Copy this chart to record historical facts about Canada's people that influenced the country's development. Make notes on the effects produced by the causes listed.

Causes		Effects
Early settlers were from enemy countries, France and Britain.	→	
French-speaking Canadians have kept their own language and culture.	→	
The people of First Nations and other culture groups want to preserve their traditions.	→	

TERMS & NAMES

First Nations the Canadian term for descendants of the first settlers who came to North America from Asia

multiculturalism an acceptance of many cultures instead of just one

refugees people who flee a country because of war, disaster, or persecution

Who Are the Canadians?/
The First Nations (pages 119–120)

Where do the Canadian people come from?

Over 50 ethnic groups make up the population of Canada. About 40 percent of them have British ancestry and 27 percent French. Other Canadians came from Germany, Italy, Ukraine, Africa, and Asia. Less than 5 percent are descendants of the first people to arrive there.

People have lived in North America for at least 12,000 years. At times in the past, the levels of the oceans were as much as 300 feet lower than they are today. At those times, the narrow water passage between Asia and North America—the Bering Strait—became dry land. Small bands of people crossed this land bridge into North America.

The Canadians of the **First Nations** are descendants of those first settlers from Asia. In the Arctic north, *Inuit* and other native people make up more than half the population. Large numbers of First Nations people, including Cree, Micmac, Abnaki, and Ojibwa, live in southern Canada near the U.S. border.

1. Who are the First Nations people?

_____

_____

European Immigrants (pages 120–121)

What European countries did immigrants come from?

The first wave of European settlement began in the 1600s, with both Britain and France establishing colonies in Canada. These two countries had a long history of conflict, and they continued their rivalry in North America. Between

1754 and 1763, they fought the French and Indian War for control of the new land.

France lost the war and surrendered most of its land to Great Britain. In 1791, the British government set up two areas in Canada. Upper Canada, now Ontario, had mostly British settlers. Lower Canada, now Quebec, remained largely French. In 1867 the two populations were united as the Dominion of Canada, along with Nova Scotia and New Brunswick. Canada became a self-governing nation, with the British monarch continuing as head of state.

In 1869, the Hudson Bay Company sold land to Canada that later became Manitoba, Alberta, and Saskatchewan. In 1871, British Columbia joined the Dominion. In 1931, Canada gained equal status with Britain and joined the *Commonwealth of Nations*. In 1982, the last legal connection between Canada and the British Parliament ended, although Canada remains a member of the Commonwealth.

Most of Canada's early immigrants were English, Scottish, Irish, and French, but after World War I, Italians and Ukrainians arrived. After World War II, Germans and Dutch arrived. In the 1960s, new immigration laws allowed people to migrate from Africa, Latin America, Asia, and the Pacific Islands.

2. What two countries did Canada's earliest European immigrants come from?

_____

_____

Canadian Citizens and Citizenship (pages 121–122)
How is Canadian citizenship similar to American citizenship?

Canadians of English or French descent have retained their separate languages and identities. Other immigrant groups have also kept the traditions of their homelands. Canada has adopted an official policy of **multiculturalism**— an acceptance of many cultures.

Canadian citizens have rights and responsibilities similar to those of U.S. citizens. They must obey Canada's laws. They have the option to vote and to participate in the political system. They are guaranteed freedom of speech, religion, and assembly, as well as equal protection for all under Canadian law.

3. How is Canada a multicultural country?

_____

_____

Where Do Most Canadians Live?
(pages 122–123)
Why is southern Canada a desirable place to live?

Canadians often live where geographic features and economic opportunities are favorable. Three-fourths of the population live in the cities and towns of southern Canada. In this region, the Great Lakes, the St. Lawrence Seaway, numerous rivers, and an excellent railway system provide transportation for people and goods.

Vancouver is Canada's largest port. Thousands of Chinese and Japanese arrived there at the end of the 20th century. In recent years, refugees have come from Vietnam, Laos, and Cambodia. **Refugees** are people who flee a country because of war, disaster, or persecution.

Toronto, Ontario's capital, is home to one-twelfth of Canada's population and one-fourth of its immigrants. More than 70,000 immigrants arrive each year from more than 100 countries. About 40 percent of Toronto's population is foreign-born, and 10 percent arrived after 1991. Toronto's location, with access to the Atlantic Ocean and the United States, has helped it become a center of industry and international trade.

4. Where do the majority of Canadian citizens live?

_____

_____

A Constitutional Monarchy

BEFORE YOU READ
In the last section, you read about the history of Canada's people.

In this section, you will read about Canada's government system.

AS YOU READ
Copy this chart to take notes on how Canada's government is organized.

Constitutional Monarchy	Head of State	Legislature	Judiciary

TERMS & NAMES
constitutional monarchy a government headed by a queen or king whose power is determined by the nation's constitution and laws

Parliament Canada's legislative branch

prime minister the head of government

Pierre Trudeau Canadian prime minister who worked for individual rights of citizens

separatists French-speaking Canadians who want Quebec to become a separate country.

A Nation of Provinces and Territories (page 124)
How is Canada's central government similar to the U.S. federal government?

Canada is a nation of ten provinces and three territories. The central government is responsible for national defense, trade and banking, immigration, criminal law, and the postal service. The provincial governments administer education, property rights, local government, hospitals, and provincial taxes. Territorial governments have fewer responsibilities but still have limited self-government.

1. How is Canada's provincial government similar to U.S. state government?

_____

_____

Organization of Canada's Government (pages 125–126)
What kind of government does Canada have?

Canada is a **constitutional monarchy**. It has a constitution to define the powers of the government, and it owes allegiance to a monarch, a queen or a king. The Canadian government consists of two branches: legislative and judicial. Executive duties are within the legislative branch.

The British monarch is Canada's head of state. Since the queen or king does not live in Canada, she or he selects a governor-general as representative. The monarch and governor-general have little real power in Canadian government. They represent Canada's historical traditions.

Canada's legislature, called **Parliament**, is made up of the House of Commons and the Senate. Together, they determine Canadian laws and policies. Citizens elect members of the House of Commons. The leader of the political party with the most elected members becomes the head of government, or prime minister, who runs the executive branch within the legislature.

The prime minister chooses senators from each of the ten provinces and three territories.

Canada's judiciary has both federal and provincial courts. The highest court is the federal Supreme Court. It is made up of the chief justice of Canada and eight other judges.

2. What role does Britain play in Canadian government?

_____

_____

_____

Equality and Justice (page 126)
What is the Charter of Rights and Freedoms?

Canada is a democracy. Its government is responsible for protecting people's rights. Prime Minister **Pierre Trudeau** led a drive to add a *Charter of Rights and Freedoms* to the Canadian Constitution in 1982. The Charter is similar to the U.S. Constitution's Bill of Rights. It guarantees freedom of speech, freedom of religion, and the right to vote. It says that Canadians are free to live and work anywhere in Canada. The Charter guarantees equal rights regardless of race, religion, gender, age, or national origin.

3. Why do you think Prime Minister Trudeau worked to add a Charter of Rights and Freedoms to the Canadian Constitution?

_____

_____

_____

Many Cultures, Many Needs
(page 127)
Why do many residents of Quebec want their province to become a separate country?

Canada's people come from different cultures, and many wish to protect their language and customs. Some French-speaking Canadians are **separatists**, or people who want the province of Quebec to become an independent country. In 1980 and in 1995, separatists called for a vote on whether Quebec should become independent. Both times the proposal was defeated, but the separatists intend to try again.

The federal government wants Quebec to remain part of Canada. Quebec is a major contributor to Canada's economy. It is responsible for half of Canada's aerospace production, half of its information technology, and 38 percent of its high-tech industry.

The Quebec provincial government has passed laws to preserve its citizens' French heritage. In an effort to satisfy the separatists, Canada's federal government passed the *Canadian Multicultural Act* in 1988. This act guarantees the right of all Canadians to preserve their cultural heritage. Finding ways to maintain a unified country is still a critical issue in Canada today.

4. Why does the federal government of Canada want Quebec to remain part of the country?

_____

_____

_____

Canada's Economy

BEFORE YOU READ

In the last section, you read about Canada's government. In this section, you will read about Canada's economy.

AS YOU READ

Copy this chart to take notes on different aspects of Canada's economy.

Contributions to Canada's Economy		
Natural Resources	Industries	Transportation

TERMS & NAMES

industry an area of economic activity

exports goods traded to other countries

imports goods brought into the country

transportation corridors paths that make transportation easier

transportation barriers geographic features that prevent or slow down transportation

Contributors to the Economy

(pages 128–130)

How are Canada's natural resources a source of wealth for the country?

Canada is rich in natural resources. Europeans first came to Canada because of its abundant fishing and fur-trading opportunities. In the 1800s, gold and other minerals were discovered. Today, most people work in service and manufacturing industries. Canada's skilled labor force, natural resources, and international trade all contribute to the economy.

The prairie provinces of central Canada have extensive grasslands and good soil that make them ideal for raising beef cattle and growing wheat. On the rich farmlands along the St. Lawrence River, farmers grow grains, vegetables, and fruit. People plant potatoes and raise dairy cattle on the east coast. The Grand Banks, located off the coast of Newfoundland, is one of the world's most productive fisheries. The salmon caught off Canada's Pacific coast enrich that area's economy.

Canada's vast forests make the timber industry important, especially in British Columbia. **Industry** refers to any area of economic activity. Mines in the northern territories yield iron ore, gold, silver, copper, and other metals.

Canada's active trade with other countries has contributed to the growth of its economy. Almost 80 percent of Canada's raw materials are shipped as exports around the world. **Exports** are goods traded to other countries. Canada's main exports are wood and paper products, fuel, minerals, aluminum, wheat, and oil. Manufactured goods are exported as well.

Canada and the United States have a valuable trade partnership. Most of Canada's exports go to the United States. Most of its **imports**, or goods brought into the country, are from the United States. In 1994, Canada, the United States, and Mexico signed the North American Free Trade Agreement (NAFTA), which lowered trade barriers among the three countries.

1. What are some of Canada's main exports?

_____

_____

_____

Industry and the Economy
(pages 130–131)

What are Canada's four types of industry?

Canada's well-educated work force is important to its economy. Since World War II, Canada has shifted from a mostly *rural economy* to a major industrial and *urban economy*. Canadians work in the following four types of industries:

Primary Industries prepare and process raw materials, such as timber, wheat, and iron ore. Examples: farms; mining companies; logging companies.

Secondary Industries manufacture raw materials into products that consumers or other businesses can use. Examples: bakeries; car manufacturers; furniture manufacturers.

Tertiary Industries include service industries and distributors. Examples: transportation companies; retailers of food, clothing, and other goods; health care; education; banking.

Quaternary Industries pass on information. Examples: communication companies, such as Internet providers and cable companies; research businesses that gather information and pass it on.

Service industries, such as health care, recreation, education, transportation, banking, and government, occupy about two-thirds of Canada's work force. About 30 percent of Canadians work in manufacturing industries. One of Canada's main products is transportation equipment, including automobiles, trucks, subway cars, and airplanes. Food processing, especially meat and poultry processing, is an important industry. Canada also makes chemicals, medicines, machinery, metal products, steel, and paper.

2. What type of industry do teachers work in?

_____

_____

Transportation (pages 130–131)

How does Canada's geography both help and hurt transportation?

Transportation is a major Canadian industry. Importing and exporting goods, and moving them across Canada's vast land, affects every consumer and business.

Canada's geography both helps and hinders transportation. Canada has natural **transportation corridors**, or paths that make transportation easier. Rivers and coastal waters, sometimes combined with canals and *locks*, provide convenient travel routes. The St. Lawrence Seaway, for example, allows oceangoing ships to travel between the Atlantic Ocean and the Great Lakes. Another important route is Canada's transcontinental railway system, which crosses the continent from coast to coast.

Canada also has **transportation barriers**, or geographic features that prevent or slow down transportation. In much of the north, snow and ice block travel by land or water. The Rocky Mountains in western Canada are also a major obstacle. Where transportation is difficult, industry develops slowly.

3. What is a transportation corridor? Name a few of Canada's transportation corridors.

_____

_____

A Multicultural Society

BEFORE YOU READ

In the last section, you read about Canada's economy.
In this section, you will read about Canada's diverse population.

AS YOU READ

Copy this spider web to take notes about Canada's multicultural population. Find main ideas by carefully reading the text under each heading.

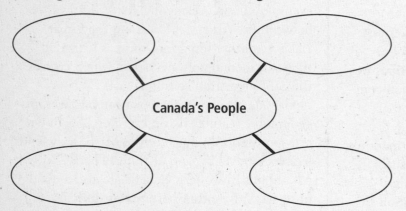

Canada's People

TERMS & NAMES

national identity sense of belonging to a nation

bilingual being able to speak two languages

Francophones French-speaking people

Canadian Identity (pages 132–134)

What are Canada's two official languages?

From 1994 to 2000, the United Nations rated Canada the best of 175 countries in a survey of the health, education, and wealth of each country's citizens. Yet, Canadians still seek a **national identity**, or sense of belonging to a nation, to unite its many immigrant cultures.

Many Canadians are **bilingual**, which means they speak two languages. Canada has two official languages, English and French. Literature, official documents, road signs, newspapers, and television broadcasts are in both languages.

French-speaking people are called **Francophones**. Canadian French, based on the French of the 1800s, is pronounced differently from the French spoken in modern France.

Canadian English uses some words, pronunciations, and spellings that differ from those used in the United States. Canadians use British spellings, such as *colour, theatre,* and *cheque*. The nation's first prime minister, Sir John A. Macdonald, ordered that all official Canadian documents use standards set by dictionaries written in England.

1. What does bilingual mean?

_____

_____

Arts and Entertainment (page 134)

How do Canadians and Americans show similar taste in the arts and in entertainment?

Canada's arts are actively supported by government funding. The Canada Council for the Arts gives money to more than 8,400 artists and art organizations each year. Provincial governments also support regional arts programs.

Canadians read many of the same magazines and watch many of the same television shows and movies as do people in the United States. Canadian musicians, such as Neil Young, Joni Mitchell, Buffy Ste. Marie, Céline Dion, and Shania Twain, are popular in both countries. So are comedian-actors Dan Aykroyd and Jim Carrey.

2. Who are some Canadian entertainers that are popular in the United States?

_____

_____

Religion (page 135)

What are some of the religions practiced in Canada?

Christianity is widely practiced in Canada, but many other religions are followed as well. Many First Nations people have their own religions, grounded in a spirituality based on respect for Earth and all forms of life. Other religions Canadians practice include Buddhism, Hinduism, Islam, and Judaism. People of every cultural group are free to worship as they please.

3. What are First Nations religions based on?

_____

_____

Culture Regions (pages 135–136)

What are some of Canada's culture regions?

Most Canadian immigrants during the 1600s, 1700s, and 1800s were European. Recently, more immigrants have come from Asia and South America. People who share the same language and background often settle in the same area. As a result, Canada has various culture regions, or areas where people belonging to one cultural group live together.

Quebec is home to many French-speaking Canadians. In *Nunavut*, more than 50 percent of the people are Inuit. Almost 16 percent of the people of Vancouver are Chinese, mostly from Hong Kong.

Getting different culture regions to agree on national issues can be difficult. The adoption of the Maple Leaf as Canada's flag in 1965 was one successful effort to unite all Canadians.

Languages, customs, and lifestyles differ among the cultural groups of Canada. Sometimes these differences cause conflict. For example, in the second half of the 20th century, some Canadians feared that the thousands of Chinese immigrants settling in the Vancouver area would change Canadian culture.

In 1975, the government began reviewing immigration policy. Chinese groups in Vancouver organized a Chinese-Canadian conference. They asked for continued support of multiculturalism and open immigration laws. The concerned groups solved the problem through human rights laws.

4. Why were Canadians once upset that thousands of Chinese immigrants were settling in Vancouver?

_____

_____

Glossary/After You Read

Canadian Multicultural Act guarantees the right of all Canadians to preserve their cultural heritage

Charter of Rights and Freedoms an addition to Canada's Constitution; similar to the U.S. Bill of Rights

Commonwealth of Nations an association of countries including the United Kingdom and many former British colonies that share a heritage of British law and government

Inuit native people of Arctic Canada

lock section of a canal or other waterway in which vessels are raised or lowered

Nunavut territory of northern Canada granted to the Inuit in 1999

rural economy economy that uses the resources of the countryside to produce goods and services

urban economy economy that uses the resources of the city to produce goods and services

TERMS & NAMES

A. Choose the term or name that best completes the sentence.

Pierre Trudeau	prime minister	refugees	multiculturalism
separatists	Parliament	Inuit	constitutional monarchy

1. In Canada's _____, the queen or king has little power, but represents the historical traditions of the country.

2. Canada's legislature is called _____ and is made up of the House of Commons and the Senate.

3. The _____ people are descendants of Canada's first settlers.

4. _____ worked hard to protect Canadians' civil rights.

5. _____ exists when a country is made up of diverse citizens who work to accept each other's differences.

6. _____ want Quebec to become an independent country.

7. Many _____ have migrated to Canada from Vietnam, Laos, and Cambodia.

8. The _____ of Canada runs the executive branch within the legislature.

B. Write the term next to the description that matches it best.

exports	refugees	imports	national identity	transportation barriers
industry	bilingual	First Nations	Francophones	transportation corridors

_____ **1.** goods brought into a country

_____ **2.** an area of economic activity

_____ **3.** able to speak two languages

_____ **4.** Canadians who speak French

_____ **5.** natural paths that make transportation easier

_____ **6.** goods sold to other countries

_____ **7.** geographic features that prevent or slow down transportation

_____ **8.** a sense of belonging to a nation

MAIN IDEAS

1. How did Great Britain divide up Canada after the French and Indian war?

_____

_____

2. Describe Canada's federal government system.

_____

_____

3. Why is the St. Lawrence Seaway a transportation corridor?

_____

_____

4. What are Canada's two official languages? Why are there two?

_____

_____

5. What aspects of Canada's government are similar to and different from the U.S. government?

_____

_____

THINKING CRITICALLY

Answer the following questions on a separate sheet of paper.

1. Suppose you are a reporter, working in 1982. Your assignment is to interview Pierre Trudeau. What questions would you ask him, and why?

2. Do you think that the separatists should be able to establish their own country? Explain your thinking.

CHAPTER 6

Section 1 (pages 153–159)

Latin America: Physical Geography

BEFORE YOU READ

In the last chapter, you read about the political, economic, and social structure of Canada.

In this section, you will learn about landforms, climate, and physical processes in the various regions of Latin America.

AS YOU READ

Use this chart to take notes on the area's physical features.

Region	Physical Features
Mexico	
Central America	
Caribbean Islands	
South America	

TERMS & NAMES

tributaries rivers or streams that flow into a larger body of water

deforestation the process of cutting and clearing away trees from a forest

Tropical Zone the area between the latitudes 23.27° north and 23.27° south, where the weather is typically hot

El Niño a warm ocean current linked to unusually high air pressure in the South Pacific and known for bringing heavy rains to Latin America

Defining Latin America (page 153)
How did Latin America get its name?

Latin America includes Mexico, Central America, the Caribbean Islands, and South America. Most of the Europeans who colonized these regions spoke Spanish or Portuguese. Because these languages are *derived* from Latin, this culture region is called Latin America.

1. What areas does Latin America include?

_____

_____

Mexico (page 154)
What are Mexico's major physical features?

Mexico is the farthest north of the Latin American countries. It has two mountain ranges, the Sierra Madre Occidental in the west and the Sierra Madre Oriental in the east. Between these two mountain ranges lies Mexico's central *plateau*.

South of the central plateau are the country's two highest mountain peaks, Orizaba and Popocatépetl, both of which are volcanoes.

Volcanic activity and earthquakes plague Mexico and many other Latin American nations. They are caused by the shifting of the five *tectonic plates* beneath Latin America.

Mexico City, the world's second most populous city, lies at the southern end of the central plateau. The surrounding mountains tend to trap air pollution over Mexico City. The soft, loose soil on which the city is built—a drained lakebed—makes earthquakes more destructive.

2. How do the physical features around Mexico City make the city more vulnerable to air pollution and earthquakes?

_____

_____

Central America and the Caribbean (page 156)
How have the landforms of Central America and the Caribbean been shaped by volcanic activity?

Central America is the landmass that forms a bridge between Mexico and South America.

About 80 percent of Central America is hilly or mountainous, and most of it is forested. More than 40 volcanoes line Central America's Pacific coast, making up the most active group of volcanoes in North or South America. Destructive earthquakes are also frequent in Central America.

East of Central America lie the island nations of the Caribbean Sea. Some of these islands, such as St. Kitts and Grenada, are the peaks of volcanic mountains that rise from the ocean floor. Others, such as the Bahamas, began as coral *reefs*, often encircling a volcanic island and then growing over it.

3. **What are the major physical features of Central America and the Caribbean?**

_____

_____

South America (pages 157–158)
***Describe** the largest river in South America.*

The continent of South America is linked to North America by the Isthmus of Panama. The Andes Mountains, the longest mountain range on Earth, stretch over 5,000 miles along South America's west coast. East of the Andes, in the southern part of South America, lie vast plains called the *Pampas*.

South America's largest rivers, including the Orinoco and the Amazon, begin in the Andes, drain the central plains, and flow into the Atlantic. The Amazon River carries the largest volume of water in the world. Its more than 1,000 **tributaries**—rivers or streams that flow into a larger body of water—drain water from Peru, Ecuador, Colombia, Bolivia, Venezuela, and Brazil.

On its more than 5,000-mile journey to the Atlantic, the Amazon River winds through a vast *rain forest*. The Amazon rain forest is a home for Native American tribes and for many species of animals. In recent years,

deforestation, or the process of cutting down and clearing away trees, has threatened the planet by releasing carbon dioxide that contributes to global warming.

4. **Describe what may be lost if deforestation continues in the Amazon rain forest.**

_____

_____

Climate (pages 158–159)
***Why** are the Caribbean Islands warm even in winter?*

Much of Latin America lies in the **Tropical Zone**, between the latitudes 23.27° north and 23.27° south. In the Tropical Zone, temperatures are generally high, and all *elevations* are warmer than they are elsewhere. The waters of the Caribbean stay warm most of the year and heat the air over them. This creates warm winds that keep the Caribbean Islands balmy even in winter.

At times, unusually high air pressure in the South Pacific quiets the *trade winds* that normally blow across the ocean. This allows a warm current known as *El Niño* to flow eastward toward North and South America. *El Niño* most often arrives around Christmas, and it can cause heavy rains and flooding in Latin America. At the same time, it can cause areas in the western Pacific to be drier than usual.

5. **How is Latin America's climate affected by location, elevation, wind patterns, and ocean currents?**

_____

_____

Ancient Latin America

BEFORE YOU READ

In the last section, you read about the geography of Latin America.

In this section, you will learn about the ancient peoples of Latin America, including the Maya, Aztec, and Inca civilizations.

AS YOU READ

Use this chart to take notes on these three ancient civilizations.

	Maya	Aztec	Inca
Location			
Achievements			

TERMS & NAMES

hieroglyphs symbols representing words or syllables in the Maya language

chinampas Aztec floating gardens

Machu Picchu stone city built by the Inca high in the Peruvian Andes

Hernán Cortés Spanish soldier who conquered the Aztec in 1521

Montezuma Aztec ruler who was conquered by the Spanish

Francisco Pizarro Spanish soldier who conquered the Inca in 1531

Atahualpa Inca ruler routed by the Spanish

Columbian Exchange the exchange of goods and ideas between Europe and its colonies in North and South America

Ancient Civilizations of Latin America (page 160)

What was unusual about the locations of the ancient Latin American civilizations?

The ancient Maya built cities in the jungles of Mexico and Central America. The Aztec established their capital on a marshy island in a Mexican lake. The Inca of South America built cities high in the Andes.

1. Where were the ancient civilizations located?

_____

_____

The Maya (pages 161–162)

What were the achievements of Maya civilization?

The Maya established one of ancient Latin America's most important civilizations in parts of present-day Mexico, Honduras, Guatemala, El Salvador, and Belize. Their civilization began

as early as 1600 B.C. and flourished from A.D. 250 to A.D. 900.

The Maya were among the first civilizations to understand the mathematical concept of zero. They developed a 365-day calendar based on the sun's movement and a 260-day calendar of sacred days. They had the best-developed system of writing in ancient Latin America. It used symbols called **hieroglyphs**.

Maya farmers often cut down and burned trees, planting crops in their place. They later allowed the forest to grow back to restore the soil's nutrients. The Maya also farmed rich floodplains, building up ridges of land on which to plant the crops.

Maya civilization declined for unknown reasons beginning around A.D. 900. Maya cities were abandoned, but the Maya people did not disappear. More than 2 million Maya still live in Guatemala and southern Mexico and speak dialects based on the languages of their Maya ancestors.

2. Describe some of the special knowledge and skills that prove how advanced the Maya were.

_____

_____

The Aztec (pages 162–163)

Why did all men have to serve in the Aztec army?

The capital of the Aztec Empire was an island city called Tenochtitlán. It sat in Lake Texcoco, and Mexico City was later built atop it. The Aztec were made up of a number of tribes of wandering warriors, including the Mexica, who gave Mexico its name. The Aztec controlled Mexico from the 1200s until the early 1500s.

The Aztec Empire centered on warfare. Military service was a religious duty, and the Aztec believed that anyone who died in battle was honoring Huitzilopochtli, the god of war.

The island location of the Aztec capital protected it from attack, but much of the island was *marsh*, making it difficult to farm. The Aztec raised crops on floating gardens called *chinampas*, which were anchored between the trunks of willow trees.

3. What was a benefit and a drawback of Tenochtitlán's location?

_____

_____

The Inca (pages 163–165)

What were the achievements of the Inca Empire?

The Inca people lived high in the Andes of Peru. Around 1400 they established an empire that included parts of what are now Colombia, Ecuador, Bolivia, northern Chile, and north-western Argentina. They ruled over this huge empire from Cuzco, their capital.

The Inca built stone terraces that allowed them to farm on steep mountainsides and prevented the *erosion* of the soil. In desert lands they built *irrigation canals* to water their crops, which included a grain called *quinoa*.

The Inca also built a huge system of stone roads. Relay teams carried verbal messages as far as 150 miles a day. This communication system was important because the Inca Empire covered thousands of miles, and the Inca had no written language and no knowledge of the wheel.

The most remarkable example of Inca stonework is the city of **Machu Picchu** in the Peruvian Andes. The walls of the city are surrounded by terraces, connected by stairways that run down the steep mountain slopes.

4. Why were roads so important to the Inca?

_____

_____

The Spanish in Latin America
(page 166)

How did the Spanish gain control of Latin America?

In the 1500s, the Spanish fought to take land from the Native Americans. **Hernán Cortés** captured the Aztec ruler **Montezuma II** in 1519. He claimed the Aztec Empire for Spain in 1521. In 1531, **Francisco Pizarro**, defeated the Inca ruler **Atahualpa** and claimed the Inca Empire for Spain.

The Spanish enslaved the Native Americans and forced them to do labor. They also converted many Native Americans to Christianity.

Latin America and Spain influenced each other's culture. Ships from Latin America brought to Europe new crops, such as corn, peppers, and tomatoes, that Spanish farmers soon began to plant. Spanish manufactured products, such as textiles, and foods and animals, such as peaches and pigs, were sent to Latin America. The exchange of goods and ideas between Europe and its colonies and North and South America is called the **Columbian Exchange**.

5. How did the Columbian Exchange affect Spanish and Latin American cultures?

_____

_____

Glossary/After You Read

derive to be traced to a source

plateau an elevated area of flat land

tectonic plate one of the gigantic slabs of rock that form Earth's crust and that shift to cause earthquakes

reef ridge of rock, coral, or sand near the surface of water

rain forest a dense tropical forest with abundant rainfall

elevation height above the surface of Earth

trade winds tropical winds that typically blow steadily from east to west and toward the equator

erosion the wearing away of land by running water

marsh an area of soft, wet, low-lying land, often forming a transition between land and water

irrigation canal artificial channel to carry water to crops

TERMS & NAMES

A. In each blank, write the term or name that best completes the meaning of the paragraph.

deforestation   *El Niño*

tributaries   **Tropical Zone**

The Amazon River is fed by more than 1,000 smaller rivers known as

(1) _____. In recent years, **(2)** _____,

or the cutting down and clearing away of trees, has threatened the Amazon

rain forest. The Amazon rain forest lies in the **(3)** _____,

between the latitudes 23.27° north and 23.27° south. The warm ocean

current called **(4)** _____, which is caused by unusually

high air pressure in the South Pacific, often brings heavy rains and flooding

to Latin America.

B. Write the letter of the term or name next to the description that explains it best.

a. *chinampas*   d. Francisco Pizarro

b. hieroglyphs   e. Montezuma II

c. Machu Picchu   f. Hernán Cortés

_____ **1.** symbols representing words or syllables

_____ **2.** Aztec ruler who was conquered by the Spanish

_____ **3.** floating gardens built by the Aztec

_____ **4.** Spanish soldier who claimed the Aztec Empire for Spain in 1521

_____ **5.** stone city built by the Inca high in the Peruvian Andes

_____ **6.** Spanish soldier who conquered the Inca

MAIN IDEAS

1. What problems has Mexico City's location created for the people who live there?

_____

_____

2. How may the destruction of the Amazon rain forest hurt the entire planet?

_____

_____

3. Why was warfare so important in Aztec culture?

_____

_____

4. How were the Inca able to maintain control over an empire that spread over thousands of miles?

_____

_____

5. How did the Columbian Exchange affect life in Europe and in the Americas?

_____

_____

THINKING CRITICALLY

Answer the following questions on a separate sheet of paper.

1. In what ways might people in other countries help to protect the Amazon rain forest?

2. Compare the methods of farming and communication of the Maya and Inca civilizations.

The Roots of Modern Mexico

BEFORE YOU READ

In the last chapter, you read about the geography and ancient history of Latin America. In this section, you will learn about the historical events that shaped modern Mexico.

AS YOU READ

Use this chart to take notes on events in Mexican history.

The Founding of New Spain	The War of Independence	The War with the United States

TERMS & NAMES

peninsulares ruling class of Mexican officials born in Spain

criollos people born in Mexico whose parents were born in Spain

mestizo person of mixed European and Native American ancestry

encomienda system in which Spaniards governed Native American villages and received tribute

Father Miguel Hidalgo Mexican priest who led a revolt in 1810 and began the independence movement

Treaty of Guadalupe Hidalgo treaty between Mexico and the United States ending the Mexican War

Gadsden Purchase Mexico sold land to the United States in this 1853 pact

The Arrival of the Spanish (page 173)

Why did Hernán Cortés come to Mexico?

In 1519, Hernán Cortés arrived in Mexico, hoping for lands for Spain as well as gold and glory for himself. He claimed Mexico for the king and queen, even though the land was already ruled by the Aztec king Montezuma.

1. What was the obstacle to Spanish rule in Mexico?

_____

_____

A Clash of Cultures (page 174)

How did the Spanish first enter Tenochtitlán?

Montezuma welcomed Cortés and allowed him to stay in the Aztec capital, Tenochtitlán. When Cortés made Montezuma his prisoner, Aztec warriors drove the Spanish from the city. During the fighting, Montezuma was killed.

Some of Montezuma's subjects wanted freedom from Aztec rule, so they helped the Spanish regain control of Tenochtitlán. The Spanish also had horses, armor, guns, and cannons against Native American war clubs, spears, and arrows.

2. What helped the Spanish to defeat the Aztecs?

_____

_____

The Founding of New Spain
(page 174)

What power shift did the fall of Tenochtitlán mark?

The fall of Tenochtitlán in 1521 marked the end of the Aztec Empire and the beginning of Spanish rule in Mexico. The Spanish called their empire "New Spain" and built their capital, Mexico City, on the site of Tenochtitlán.

The Spanish brought to Mexico new animals, such as horses, cattle, sheep, and pigs, and new trades, such as *ironsmithing* and shipbuilding.

They also brought Christianity to replace the Aztec religion.

3. How did the Spanish change life in Mexico?

_____

_____

The Influence of the Church
(page 175)
Why did the Catholic Church have so much power?

The Catholic Church was powerful in Spain. In New Spain its priests built churches, schools, and hospitals. Some Native Americans chose to convert to Christianity. Others were forced to. The new Spanish culture was blended with the Native American culture.

4. How did Christianity spread among Native Americans in New Spain?

_____

_____

Life in New Spain (pages 175–176)
What were the levels of society in New Spain?

The ruling class was made up of government officials called **_peninsulares_**, who were from the Iberian Peninsula in Europe. Next were the **_criollos_**, people born in Mexico whose parents were born in Spain. A person of mixed European and Native American ancestry was known as a **_mestizo_**. A fourth group consisted of enslaved Africans brought to New Spain by European slave ships.

Native Americans were the largest population group in New Spain, but they were powerless. Under the **_encomienda_** system, Spanish men controlled Native American villages. Villagers paid _tribute_ in goods, money, or labor.

5. How did the _encomienda_ system work?

_____

_____

The War of Independence
(pages 176–177)
How did the Mexican independence movement begin?

On September 16, 1810, **Father Miguel Hidalgo** urged people to throw off Spanish rule in a speech, known as the _Grito de Dolores_ (Cry of Dolores). Father Hidalgo gathered Native Americans and _mestizos_ and led them toward Mexico City. They were defeated, and Father Hidalgo was executed.

New leaders joined the fight for independence, and in 1821, after 11 years of fighting, Mexico became independent. However, the _peninsulares_ and _criollos_ still held all power, and little changed in the lives of the Native Americans and _mestizos_.

6. What part did Father Miguel Hidalgo play in the struggle for Mexican independence?

_____

_____

War with the United States
(pages 177–178)
Why did Mexico and the United States go to war?

When Mexico gained independence, it included lands that are now in the Southwestern United States. Mexico invited foreigners to move into Texas.

In 1835, settlers in Texas revolted against Mexican rule, won independence, and set up the Republic of Texas in 1836. Most Texans wanted to join the United States, and in 1845 the United States agreed. But Mexico and the United States argued about the Texas-Mexico boundary, which led to war in 1846. By 1848, the United States soldiers controlled northern Mexico. The **Treaty of Guadalupe Hidalgo** _ceded_ northern Mexican lands to the United States. In 1853, the United States bought more of Mexico's northern land in the **Gadsden Purchase**.

7. How did wars change Mexican boundaries?

_____

_____

Government in Mexico: Revolution and Reform

BEFORE YOU READ

In the last section, you read about the historic events that led to Mexico's independence.

In this section, you will learn about the revolution and reforms that shook Mexico as it struggled to establish a strong national government.

AS YOU READ

Use this chart to take notes on the 1857 and 1917 constitutions.

Constitution of 1857	Constitution of 1917

TERMS & NAMES

Benito Juárez reformer who became president of Mexico in 1858

Francisco Madero rancher who favored honest elections and was president of Mexico in 1911

hacienda huge farm or ranch that belonged to wealthy landowners

Emiliano Zapata rebel leader who fought for land reform

ejido community farm

Institutional Revolutionary Party (PRI) political party of all Mexican presidents from the 1920s until 2000

Vicente Fox Mexican president in 2000 who was not in the PRI

A Struggle for Power (pages 179–180)

What was happening in Mexico in the 1800s?

The 1800s were marked by warfare. In 1821, the Mexicans won independence from Spain. In the 1840s, they lost control of Texas, California, and other lands.

After independence, a power struggle occurred in Mexico. Army leaders periodically took over Mexico's government. Bandits attacked travelers, and Native Americans fought with Spanish landowners.

1. What conflicts inside and outside Mexico disrupted peace and order after independence?

_____

_____

Benito Juárez Brings Reform

(pages 180–181)

How did the French take control of Mexico in 1863?

By the 1850s, Mexicans wanted reform. Their hero and leader, **Benito Juárez**, rose from poverty to become president of Mexico in 1858.

His presidency gave control of the government to the reformers.

In 1857, the reformers wrote a new constitution, which gave Mexicans a *bill of rights* and promised freedom of speech and equality under the law. This constitution also ended slavery and forced labor and cut back the army's power. It did not promise freedom of religion, but church leaders were angry because it failed to name Catholicism as Mexico's official religion.

The reforms of the constitution of 1857 created controversy. The struggle between the reformers and their opponents from 1858 to 1860 was known as the War of the Reform.

The War of the Reform left Mexico weak and made it an easy target for foreign takeover. Spain, Great Britain, and France sent troops into Mexico. In 1863, the French marched into Mexico City and took control. They named Maximilian, a European nobleman, emperor of Mexico, but the Mexicans overthrew Maximilian and executed him in 1867.

Benito Juárez returned to power in 1867 and remained president until 1872. Later presidents cared less about reform, and wealth and power remained in the hands of the rich.

2. What changes did the reformers try to make?

_____

_____

The Mexican Revolution
(pages 181–182)
Why did revolution break out in Mexico in 1910?
At the start of the 20th century, only 800 families owned more than 90 percent of the land. Ten million of Mexico's 15 million people owned no land.

A renewed struggle for reforms led to the outbreak of the Mexican Revolution, which lasted from 1910 to 1920. One of the first revolutionary leaders was **Francisco Madero**, a wealthy rancher whose greatest concern was free elections.

Land reformers wanted the government to break up the *haciendas*, huge farms or ranches that belonged to wealthy landowners. Many *haciendas* included land that wealthy ranch owners took from village farmers in the 1880s and 1890s.

The revolutionary leader **Emiliano Zapata** became known for his *motto*, "Land and Liberty!" He gathered an army to fight for land reform and farmers' rights.

3. In what way was the *hacienda* system unfair?

_____

_____

A Continuing Revolution
(pages 182–183)
Why did the fighting among armies end in 1920?
Between 1910 and 1920, more than one million Mexicans died in the Revolution. Madero was murdered in 1913, and Zapata was killed in 1919. In 1920, a new government made peace among the many armies.

A new constitution in 1917 promised to distribute land among the Mexican people. Between 1920 and 1940, the government divided millions of acres among individual small

farmers and *ejidos*. An *ejido* is a community farm owned by all the villagers together.

The Revolution was so important to Mexicans that the most powerful political party called itself the party of the Revolution. Today it is known as the **Institutional Revolutionary Party** (Partido Revolucionario Institucional, or PRI). All Mexican presidents until 2000 were PRI members.

4. How did Mexican land reform finally occur?

_____

_____

Mexico's Government Today
(pages 183–184)
How would you describe Mexico's present system of government?
In 2000, **Vicente Fox** was elected president of Mexico, the first president in more than 70 years who did not belong to the PRI. The election of a president from outside the PRI showed that Mexico was entering a time of greater political freedom.

Mexico's official name is Estados Unidos Mexicanos, or the United Mexican States, and it is made up of 31 states. Mexico is a democracy, and all Mexicans 18 or older have the right to vote. Mexico has three branches of government: *executive*, *legislative*, and *judicial*.

Mexico has a federal system of government in which power is shared between the national and state governments. Voters in each state elect a governor, and each state has its own legislature.

Mexico's national government has some power over state and local governments. For example, the president and the national Senate can remove a state governor from office. Local governments provide public services to their towns and villages, but are dependent on money from the national government.

5. How are the governments of Mexico and the United States similar? How are they different?

_____

_____

Mexico's Changing Economy

BEFORE YOU READ

In the last section, you read about the Mexican Revolution and Mexico's government today.

In this section, you will learn how the Mexican economy changed during the 20th century.

AS YOU READ

Use this chart to take notes on privatization in Mexico during the 20th century.

Privatization of Land	Privatization of Business

TERMS & NAMES

Carlos Salinas de Gortari Mexican president who privatized land

privatization the process of replacing community ownership with individual, or private, ownership

distribution the process of moving products to their markets

maquiladora a factory that imports duty-free U.S. parts and then exports its products back across the border

nationalize to establish government control over

PEMEX government agency that runs the Mexican oil industry

tourism the business of helping people to travel on vacation

Farming in a Time of Change
(pages 185–186)

What are the benefits and possible disadvantages of dividing ejidos ***into individual farms?***

In 1938, the Mexican government decided to take control of the oil industry in Mexico. It was hoping to expand Mexico's economy, which relied almost entirely on farming. Since the 1950s, many Mexicans have found jobs in other industries, but farming is still important to Mexico's economy.

About one-fourth of Mexican workers are farmers. Many farmers still work on the *ejidos*, or community farms, that were set up during the Revolution. Although the *ejido* system gave land to many poor villagers, it did not lift them out of poverty. Because the land was owned by the community rather than by individuals, farmers could not use their land as *security* for bank loans. This meant they could not raise money for modern improvements such as tractors and

fertilizer. They continued to farm with hand tools on worn-out soil.

In 1992, Mexican president **Carlos Salinas de Gortari** helped change the laws of the *ejido* system. Under the new laws, farmers could divide their *ejido* into individual farms. Then each farm family could sell or rent its own land. This process of replacing community ownership with individual, or private, ownership is called **privatization**. Supporters hope that private farms will use modern techniques to grow such export crops as bananas, coffee, sugar cane, and strawberries.

Ejidos still hold about half the farmland in Mexico. Some farmers do not want to divide up community farms, fearing that Mexico's land will again fall into the hands of a few wealthy people.

1. What is farming's role in Mexico's economy?

_____

_____

Copyright © McDougal Littell Inc.

The Growth of Business and Industry (pages 187–188)

How did economic cooperation between the United States and Mexico increase during the 1990s?

During the mid-1900s, the Mexican government built new power plants and homes for factory workers. The government also lent new companies money, lowered their taxes, or helped them repay loans As a result, new factories made products such as steel, chemicals, paper, and *textiles*. The government also built highways, railroads, and airports to help companies with **distribution** of goods, or the process of moving products to markets.

In the 1990s, the Mexican government raised millions of dollars by selling businesses such as banks, mines, and steel mills to private companies. By 2000, only a few key industries, such as the oil industry, still belonged to the government.

During the 1990s, many of Mexico's fastest-growing companies, called *maquiladoras*, were located along the border with the United States. A *maquiladora imports* duty-free parts from the United States to make products that it then exports back across the border. The lack of a tax on the parts helps keep operating costs low. Most *maquiladoras* are owned by foreigners, who save money because wages are lower in Mexico than in the United States.

The North American Free Trade Agreement (NAFTA) aims to reduce taxes on items traded among Mexico, the United States, and Canada to encourage economic cooperation among North American countries. Although many Mexicans fear NAFTA will increase United States and Canadian influence over Mexico, the agreement has nearly doubled Mexico's trade with these countries.

2. How has the Mexican government encouraged the growth of industry?

_____

_____

_____

Mexico's Rich Resources (page 188)

What is Mexico's most important natural resource?

Mexico is rich in mineral resources. It produces more silver than any other country and mines lead, zinc, graphite, sulfur, and copper. Its most important natural resource is petroleum, or oil.

In 1938, the Mexican government decided to **nationalize**, or establish government control of, the oil industry. Today, when other businesses have been privatized, the oil industry is still government owned. A government agency called **PEMEX** (Petrólcos Mexicanos, or Mexican Petroleum) runs the oil industry. Oil is Mexico's biggest export, and the United States is its largest buyer.

3. How does the Mexican government control the oil industry?

_____

_____

Tourism Is Big Business (page 189)

Why did Cancún become a major tourist attraction?

Mexico's second largest industry is **tourism**. Tourists come to Mexico to enjoy its warm weather and sunny beaches as well as to visit ancient Native American ruins and experience Mexican culture.

One popular tourist attraction is Cancún, on Mexico's southeastern coast. Cancún was a small Maya village of about 100 people in 1970, when the government and businesses joined together to build hotels, roads, and an airport. Today, 2.5 million tourists visit Cancún each year, and the village has become a city of 300,000 people.

4. What part does tourism play in Mexico's economy?

_____

_____

Mexico's Culture Today

BEFORE YOU READ

In the last section, you read about Mexico's changing economy. In this section, you will learn about life and culture in modern Mexico.

AS YOU READ

Use this chart to take notes on the differences between urban and rural life in Mexico.

	Advantages	Disadvantages
Urban (City)		

TERMS & NAMES

Diego Rivera 20th-century mural painter whose work celebrated Mexican history

Frida Kahlo 20th-century Mexican painter known for her self-portraits

Octavio Paz Mexican poet who won the Nobel Prize in Literature in 1990

rural in the countryside

urban in the city

Day of the Dead November 1–2, when Mexicans remember and honor their loved ones who have died

fiesta a holiday celebrated with parades, games, and feasts

Mexico's Blend of Cultures
(pages 190–191)

How do the historical murals of artist Diego Rivera reflect the three cultures that are blended in Mexico today?

Mexican culture today is a blend of three influences: Native American culture, Spanish culture, and the distinctive Mexican culture that has developed over time. Near the center of Mexico City lies the Plaza of Three Cultures, which symbolizes these traditions. The plaza includes the stone ruins of an Aztec marketplace as well as a Catholic Church built by the Spanish. Just beyond these, skyscrapers stand as a monument to modern Mexico.

One of Mexico's most famous 20th-century artists, **Diego Rivera**, often painted scenes from Mexican history in his murals. His wife, **Frida Kahlo**, another important Mexican painter, is famous for her self-portraits. The Mexican poet **Octavio Paz**, who won the Nobel Prize in literature in 1990, has written about the connections between past and present in Mexico.

1. How does the Plaza of Three Cultures show the cultures that influence Mexico today?

_____

_____

Life in the City (pages 191–193)
How many people live in Mexico City?

With more than 18 million inhabitants, Mexico City is the largest city in Mexico and the second largest city in the world. About one in every five Mexicans lives in Mexico City, and thousands more arrive each year to study or work. Mexico City is the cultural center of Mexico. Its Palace of Fine Arts houses the national opera, theater, and symphony.

The rapid growth of Mexico City has led to heavy traffic, and the city has problems with air pollution created by car exhaust. Life there is also marked by sharp divisions between the city's rich and poor inhabitants.

2. Why does Mexico City continue to grow despite overcrowding and air pollution?

_____

_____

Life in the Countryside (page 193)

Why does life change more slowly in the countryside?

Mexico's traditional way of life can be seen in small villages and farming towns. At the center of each village is a *plaza*, where people gather to talk and visit with neighbors and to hold weekly markets. Most people speak Spanish, but many also speak Native American languages, such as those of the Aztec and Maya.

Many people in Mexico's **rural** areas—those in the countryside—live in poverty. Some homes have only one room and a dirt floor, and farmhouses often lack electricity and running water. These conditions have driven many Mexicans to leave the countryside for **urban**, or city, settings. Cities offer more opportunities for employment, services, and education than are available to people in the countryside.

3. Why do many Mexicans leave the countryside for the city?

_____

_____

Holidays (page 194)

How do Mexicans celebrate their independence?

Mexico's Independence Day is celebrated on September 16, when Mexicans reenact Father Hidalgo's call in 1810 to rise up against Spanish rule. People also watch fireworks, dance, and play music in the streets until late at night.

On November 1 and 2, Mexicans celebrate the **Day of the Dead** by remembering and honoring their loved ones who have died. They decorate graves with candles and flowers, and stores sell candy skulls and loaves of bread shaped like bones. Relatives gather for meals at cemeteries.

At least once a year, each village celebrates a **fiesta**, or a holiday with parades, games, and feasts. It usually takes place on a saint's day—a day set by the Catholic Church to honor the memory of a holy person. Although they have religious origins, fiestas are celebrated as big neighborhood parties.

4. What is the purpose of the Day of the Dead?

_____

_____

Sections 1–4 (pages 173–194)

Glossary/After You Read

ironsmithing forging objects such as tools out of iron

tribute forced payment or contribution

ceded surrendered possession of, especially by treaty

bill of rights list of basic rights and freedoms

motto a phrase that expresses the ideals of a group

executive branch the administrative arm of the government, including elected officials, such as the president

legislative branch the lawmaking arm of the government, or the legislature

judicial branch the arm of government that administers justice, including the courts

security something offered as a pledge of repayment

textiles cloth or fabric

import to bring goods into the country from another country in order to sell them

export to send goods out of the country to sell them

plaza a public square or marketplace in the center of a village

---

TERMS & NAMES

A. In each blank, write the term that best completes the meaning of the paragraph.

criollos   *peninsulares*

mestizos   *encomienda*

hacienda

Mexican officials who were born in Spain and made up the ruling class were

known as **(1)** _____. Next on the social scale were the

(2) _____, who were born in Mexico but whose parents were

born in Spain. People of mixed Native American and European ancestry were

called **(3)** _____. Under the **(4)** _____ system,

Spaniards governed Native American villages and received tribute. A huge ranch or

farm belonging to a wealthy landowner was known as a **(5)** _____.

B. Write the letter of the name next to the phrase that best describes the person.

    a. Francisco Madero   **c. Benito Juárez**   **e. Emiliano Zapata**

    b. Father Miguel Hidalgo   **d. Vicente Fox**

_____ **1.** reformer who became president of Mexico in 1858

_____ **2.** rebel leader who fought for land reform and was murdered in 1919

_____ **3.** Mexican priest who led a revolt in 1810

_____ **4.** wealthy rancher who became president of Mexico in 1911

_____ **5.** Mexican president elected in 2000 who did not belong to the PRI

MAIN IDEAS

1. How did the Spanish gain control of the Aztec Empire?

_____

_____

2. What event began the War of Independence in Mexico?

_____

_____

3. Why did war break out between Mexico and the United States in 1846?

_____

4. How was the *ejido* system changed during the 1990s?

_____

_____

5. What are the differences between urban and rural life in modern Mexico?

_____

_____

THINKING CRITICALLY

Answer the following questions on a separate sheet of paper.

1. What advantages made it possible for the greatly outnumbered Spanish soldiers to conquer the Aztecs?

2. Do you think privatization makes farming more efficient? Consider factors such as how hard people work on community land versus on private land and whether they can borrow money to make improvements.

Establishing Independence

BEFORE YOU READ

In the last chapter, you read about the history and culture of modern Mexico.

In this section, you will learn how countries in Central America and the Caribbean struggled to gain independence and establish democracies.

AS YOU READ

Use this chart to take notes on European rule and independence movements in Central America and the Caribbean Islands.

	European Rule	Independence Movements
Central America		
Caribbean Islands		

TERMS & NAMES

West Indies the islands in the Caribbean Sea

dependency a place governed by or closely connected with another country

mulattos people of mixed African and European ancestry

ladinos people of mixed European and Native American ancestry

dictator a person who has complete control over a country's government

Central America and the Caribbean (pages 203–205)

What is the ancestry of the Central American and Caribbean peoples?

Central America includes seven nations: Belize, Guatemala, Honduras, El Salvador, Nicaragua, Costa Rica, and Panama. The islands of the Caribbean Sea, called the **West Indies**, include 13 nations and 11 dependencies. A **dependency** is a place governed by or closely connected with another country.

When Christopher Columbus reached the West Indies in 1492, about 750,000 Native Americans lived on the islands. The European colonists forced Native Americans to work in mines and on *plantations*. Many Native Americans were killed by this harsh labor or by diseases that the colonists brought to the Americas. Within a few years, nearly all of the Native Americans in the Caribbean were dead.

The Spanish began bringing shiploads of slaves from Africa to the West Indies in the 1520s, to take on the work that had been done by the Native Americans. Other European

nations joined in the slave trade. From the 1500s to the mid-1800s, about 10 million enslaved Africans arrived in the West Indies. Today many people in the Caribbean are **mulattos**, or people of mixed African and European ancestry.

Many more Native Americans survived in Central America because they moved to inland mountains after the Spanish arrived in 1501. Therefore, they did not die from disease and mistreatment. Today, one-fifth of Central Americans are Native Americans.

Slave ships also brought Africans to Central America. As the years passed, the Spanish, Native Americans, and Africans intermarried. Today, about two-thirds of Central America's population are *ladinos*, or people of mixed European and Native American ancestry.

1. Why did many more Native Americans survive in Central America than in the Caribbean Islands?

_____

_____

From Colonies to Independence
(page 205)

Why did European countries colonize Central America and the West Indies?

From the 1500s to the 1800s, European nations ruled Central America and the West Indies as colonies. The Europeans hoped to discover gold. In addition to it, they found another source of wealth—sugar. They set up large sugar plantations, which depended on the labor of enslaved people who grew and cut the sugar cane.

By the 1800s, the people of Central America and the Caribbean Islands began to demand their independence. For example, in 1804, the French colony of St. Domingue (now Haiti) became the first nation in the region to win independence. In 1821, Guatemala, Honduras, Costa Rica, and Nicaragua declared independence from Spain.

2. When did the Central American nations gain independence?

_____

_____

Relations with the United States
(pages 205–206)

How have U.S. policies affected Central America and the West Indies?

Until the early 1900s, people who wanted to travel from one coast of North or South America could make the long, dangerous trip by land, or they could sail all the way around South America. The Isthmus of Panama—a land bridge linking Central America and South America—is only 50 miles wide. The United States wanted to build a canal across it to allow people to sail directly between the Atlantic and Pacific oceans.

At that time, Panama was part of Colombia. The United States offered to buy a strip of land on the isthmus, but Colombia refused to sell. The United States then encouraged a revolt in Panama, and in 1903, the newly independent nation of Panama agreed to *lease* land to the United States for a canal. Opened in 1914, the canal became one of the most important transportation routes in the world.

The people of Cuba and Puerto Rico rebelled against Spanish rule in the late 1800s, but they failed to gain independence. In 1898, the United States declared war on Spain to help Cubans and Puerto Ricans gain independence and also to protect the sugar cane plantations that U.S. businesses owned in the islands. The United States defeated Spanish forces in less than a year. Puerto Rico became a U.S. dependency. Cuba became independent, but the United States set up military bases there and kept control over the country.

3. What was the outcome of the Spanish-American War?

_____

_____

Dictatorships and Democracy
(page 207)

Why was democracy slow in coming to Central America and the West Indies?

Only Costa Rica has been a democracy since the beginning of the 20th century. Almost all of the other countries in Central America and the West Indies have spent many years under the rule of dictators. A **dictator** is a person who has complete control over a country's government. Dictators often use violence to gain and keep power.

Most countries in Central America and the West Indies now have democratically elected governments. The people of these countries overthrew their dictators one by one. Democracy remains fragile, but it is more widespread in the region than it was 50 years ago.

4. What political trend has been evident in Central America and the West Indies in the last half-century?

_____

_____

Building Economies and Cultures

BEFORE YOU READ

In the last section, you read about the struggle for independence in Central America and the Caribbean.

In this section, you will learn about the economies and cultures of this region.

AS YOU READ

Use these diagrams to take notes on the influences that have shaped modern Caribbean and Central American culture.

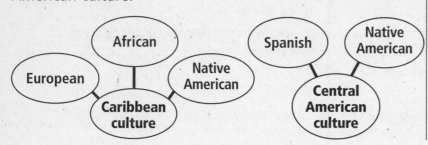

TERMS & NAMES

sugar cane plant grown throughout the Caribbean during the colonial period, whose sweet sap is used to make sugar and molasses

single-product economy an economic system that depends on one product to supply almost all jobs and income

diversify to invest in a variety of industries

The Economies of the Caribbean Islands (pages 208–210)

What was the basis of the Caribbean economy in the colonial period?

During the colonial period, the economy of the Caribbean Islands was based on growing **sugar cane**, a plant with sweet sap used to make sugar and molasses. From the 1600s to the 1800s, most islanders worked on sugar cane plantations, and many were enslaved. Although slavery ended by the late 1800s, few islanders had land of their own. They had little choice but to work on plantations owned by the wealthy.

During the colonial period, most islands traded only with the countries that ruled them. For example, Cuba sold its sugar to Spain and bought goods from Spain in return. After the colonial period ended, however, many of the islands traded mostly with the United States.

Sugar was so valuable that most plantation owners did not raise other crops. Since they didn't grow food, they had to buy it from other countries. A country that depends on just one

product for almost all its jobs and income has a **single-product economy**. Single-product economies are unstable, because if the market for that product fails, the economy of the entire country is ruined. By the late 1800s, the sugar business in the West Indies faced fierce competition from people raising sugar cane in other parts of the world. Steam-powered machines allowed these rivals to process sugar cane at lower prices.

The people of the West Indies needed to diversify their economies. To **diversify** means to invest in a variety of industries. They began to raise other crops, such as pineapples and bananas, and developed industries, such as textiles, medical supplies, and electronic equipment. Tourism became another important industry. On some of the smaller islands, such as Aruba and Antigua, tourism is now the major industry.

1. Why are single-product economies unstable?

_____

_____

Copyright © McDougal Littell Inc.

The Economies of Central America (pages 210–211)

What were the two major export crops in Central America in the late 1800s?

When the Spanish Central American countries became independent in the 1820s, they wanted to develop exports and increase trade with other nations. During the 1800s, coffee became a major export crop for Costa Rica, Guatemala, Honduras, El Salvador, and Nicaragua. In the late 1800s, U.S.-based United Fruit Company (UFCO) set up huge banana plantations in the lowlands of Central America. Bananas became another important Central American product.

The Central American economies came to depend heavily on bananas and coffee. Whenever the price of these two items fell, Central Americans faced economic hardship. Like the people of the Caribbean, Central Americans needed to diversify their economies. Seeking to become less dependent on agriculture, Central American countries have worked to build more factories that make products such as machinery, furniture, cloth, and medicine. Tourism has also become an important industry.

2. How and why have Central Americans tried to diversify their economies?

_____

_____

Caribbean Cultures (pages 211–212)

Why do Caribbean cultures differ from country to country?

Cultures vary from country to country in the Caribbean, as Native American, African, and European influences blend in different ways. People speak a variety of languages. The most widespread religion in the West Indies is Roman Catholicism. However, many islanders practice religions that combine Christian and African influences, such as voodoo (in Haiti) and Santeria (in Cuba). Music, too, often blends African and European influences to create

something entirely new—for example, salsa music in Cuba and reggae in Jamaica.

3. What aspects of Caribbean culture have been affected by both European and African influences?

_____

_____

Central American Cultures (pages 212–213)

How are Native American and Spanish influences blended in Central America?

The countries of Central America share a common history, and their cultures blend Native American and Spanish influences. The majority of people in Central America speak Spanish. Central Americans also speak about 80 Native American languages, nearly half of which are Maya languages.

Catholicism is the most widely practiced religion in Central America. In recent years, millions of Central Americans have become Protestants and Mormons. Some ancient Maya beliefs are still popular among Central Americans. For example, Maya people today believe that when each person is born, a companion spirit in the form of an animal is also born. The animal lives through the same experiences that the person does, and the person may learn about his or her companion spirit in dreams.

Traditional crafts such as weaving, embroidery, pottery, silversmithing, and basketmaking are still important in Central America. Many of the styles and methods used in these crafts originated with ancient Native Americans.

4. In what ways is Maya culture reflected in Central American culture today?

_____

_____

Cuba Today

BEFORE YOU READ

In the last section, you read about the economies and cultures of Central America and the Caribbean.

In this section, you will learn about the political events that have shaped life in modern Cuba.

AS YOU READ

Use this chart to take notes on Fidel Castro's actions as a revolutionary leader and as a dictator in Cuba.

	Castro's Actions
Cuban Revolution	
Cuba after 1958	

TERMS & NAMES

José Martí Cuban revolutionary who led the fight for independence from Spanish rule

Fidel Castro Cuban revolutionary who overthrew a corrupt government in 1959 but soon became a Communist dictator

communism economic and political system in which the government controls the economy and all property is shared by the community

malnutrition poor health caused by a lack of nourishing food

Carnival a Cuban holiday held at the end of July and celebrated with music and dancing

Independence and Revolution
(pages 215–218)

Who ruled Cuba after the country gained independence from Spain?

In 1895, under the leadership of **José Martí**, Cubans began to fight for independence from Spanish rule. Three years later, the country was caught up in the Spanish-American War. With U.S. aid, Cuba gained its independence from Spain. However, the United States maintained great influence over the new nation.

At the war's end, the United States appointed a governor for Cuba. From 1899 to 1902, U.S. Army forces remained in Cuba. They helped to set up a new government as well as to build roads, bridges, and schools. Most Cubans resented the U.S. presence in their country and wanted to rule themselves. In 1902, the U.S. Army withdrew from Cuba, which then became independent. However, the U.S. Navy kept a base for its ships at Guantanamo Bay.

After gaining independence, Cuba was ruled mostly by dictators. These dictators maintained friendly relations with the United States and welcomed U.S. businesses and tourists. Havana,

Cuba's capital, offered luxury hotels and casinos, but most Cubans lived in poverty.

Some Cubans, unhappy with the rule of the dictators, found a spokesman for their cause in the 1950s. **Fidel Castro** was a young lawyer with a deep interest in politics. By 1956, Castro and a few followers had begun a revolutionary movement. They set up their headquarters in the mountains of southeastern Cuba.

As Castro's small army grew, the rebels won several battles against government troops. At the beginning of 1959, Cuba's dictator, Fulgencio Batista, fled the country. On January 8, 1959, Castro and his followers marched into Havana. Castro, the new commander-in-chief of Cuba's army and head of the Cuban government, promised that the country would have no more dictators.

Castro took power in Cuba during the *Cold War*, when the United States and the Soviet Union were engaged in a worldwide struggle for power and influence. Eager to have Cuba as an ally, the Soviet Union established trade with the smaller country and provided it with weapons. The Soviet Union practiced **communism**, an economic and political system in which the government controls the economy. Castro soon began to adopt Communist economic policies. His government took over many businesses in Cuba that had been owned by U.S. companies, including large sugar cane plantations, banks, and oil refineries. In response, the United States cut off all trade with Cuba. Unable to sell their sugar crop to the United States, Cubans sold it to the Soviet Union instead. The Soviets sent weapons, farm machinery, food, and money to Cuba. In 1961, Castro declared that Cuba was a Communist country.

The poor usually supported Castro's policies, but many wealthier Cubans did not. They were especially angry when he *redistributed* land so that no family or farm owned more than a fixed amount. Castro also imprisoned people who spoke out against him. Cubans who opposed him began to flee to the United States and elsewhere, and hundreds of thousands of people eventually left Cuba.

Castro has ruled Cuba as a dictator for more than 40 years. He has served as head of state without ever being elected. His government controls all newspapers and radio and television stations, and criticism of the government is forbidden.

1. What part has Fidel Castro played in the history of Cuba?

_____

_____

Cuba's Economy (page 218)
What is Cuba's most important product in the world economy?

Soviet aid was the mainstay of Cuba's economy during the Cold War. Sugar is Cuba's most important product in the world economy, and with Soviet aid, Cuba was able to buy machinery to harvest sugar cane instead of cutting it by hand. Cuba then traded its sugar to the Soviet Union in return for necessary supplies, such as

oil, grain, and machinery. Since the collapse of the Soviet Union in 1991, Cuba has struggled to survive without Soviet aid.

2. How did the collapse of the Soviet Union in 1991 affect Cuba's economy?

_____

_____

Living in Cuba (pages 218–220)
How did Castro's government improve education and health care in Cuba?

After Castro took power, Cuba's government set up many new schools. In the 1960s, teachers and schoolchildren went into small villages in an effort to teach as many people as possible to read and write. Today, all Cuban children must go to public school from ages 6 to 12, and they may continue their education longer if they choose. All schools are free, including college.

All health care in Cuba is also paid for by the government, and every small village has a clinic. However, the worsening economic situation in the 1990s caused health problems among the Cuban people, including **malnutrition**, or poor health caused by the lack of nourishing food.

The Cuban government places strict limits on what artists, writers, and filmmakers can say in their work. Some artists have fled to other countries in search of freedom of expression. Still, certain art forms thrive in Cuba, including musical styles such as mambo and salsa, which combine African and Spanish influences.

Other popular activities include baseball, the national sport. One of Cuba's favorite holidays is **Carnival**, which takes place at the end of July. During this holiday, Cubans celebrate the end of the sugar harvest with festivals filled with music and dancing.

3. What are some of the disadvantages of life under Castro's regime?

_____

_____

Guatemala Today

BEFORE YOU READ

In the last section, you read about the political events that have shaped life in modern Cuba.

In this section, you will learn how Guatemala has struggled to establish a stable government.

AS YOU READ

Use this timeline to learn about important events in Guatemala's history. Identify an event for each date, and write a brief description in the box provided.

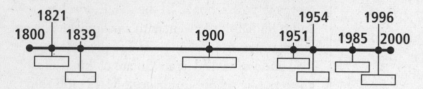

TERMS & NAMES

Rafael Carrera revolutionary leader who served as president of Guatemala from 1854 to 1865

Jacobo Arbenz Guzmán reformer who was president of Guatemala from 1951 to 1954

departamentos Guatemalan states

History of Government (pages 221–222)

How did Guatemala become an independent nation?

Guatemala gained independence from Spain in 1821 along with three other Central American states. Between 1821 and 1839, peasants in the mountains staged revolts against the government. In 1837, an uneducated farmer, **Rafael Carrera**, led a rebellion and became a new leader for Guatemala. In 1839, Guatemala left the union of Central American states to become its own nation. Carrera served as president from 1854 until his death in 1865.

After Carrera died, a series of dictators ruled Guatemala. In 1944, a group of military officers revolted and took control of the country. One of these officers, **Jacobo Arbenz Guzmán**, became president of Guatemala in 1951 and introduced social and political reforms. He worked to develop a *market economy* and to raise Guatemala's *standard of living*. He also redistributed 1.5 million acres of land in an effort to allow more people to earn their living as farmers.

Both United Fruit Company and the U.S. government owned land in Guatemala, and they strongly opposed Arbenz's redistribution program. The United States accused Arbenz of supporting communism, and in 1954 the U.S. Central Intelligence Agency (CIA) helped organize an invasion of Guatemala's capital, Guatemala City. The attack, led by a Guatemalan colonel, quickly overthrew Arbenz's government. A new U.S.-backed government took control of Guatemala.

After 1954, Guatemala's government was ruled mainly by military officers, and civil war raged throughout the country. Many people who opposed government policy were murdered. More than 100,000 Guatemalans were killed or kidnapped before a peace agreement was reached in 1996.

1. What events set off the civil war that began in 1954?

_____

_____

Guatemala's Government Today
(page 223)

How is power divided among Guatemala's federal, state, and local governments?

Guatemala's current constitution, written in 1985, established a representative democracy with three branches—executive, legislative, and judicial. The executive branch is headed by a president who is elected by the people every four years and can serve for only one term. Congress, the legislative branch, has only one chamber. Its 113 members are elected to four-year terms and may serve more than one term. The judicial branch has different levels of courts, somewhat like the United States. Its Supreme Court justices are elected by Congress to five-year terms.

Guatemala is a federal republic, so the national government shares power with state and local governments. The president appoints governors to head Guatemala's 22 states, or *departamentos*. Mayors elected by the people oversee the city governments.

2. Describe the government established by Guatemala's current constitution.

_____

_____

Guatemala's Economy (pages 223–224)

What is Guatemala's most important industry?

Guatemala has the largest *gross domestic product* in Central America. Its most important industry is agriculture, which employs more than half of the work force. Its economy relies on the export of agricultural products, including coffee, sugar, cardamom, and bananas. Coffee has been Guatemala's leading export since 1870. Bananas became an important export in the early 1900s, when U.S. companies established banana plantations in Guatemala and built railroads and ports in order to transport the crop to foreign markets.

The sale of manufactured products, such as processed foods, beverages, and clothing, contributes to the strong economy. The United States buys more of Guatemala's exports than any other country does. Many nontraditional agricultural products, such as cut flowers and winter fruits, have become popular in international markets. Tourism is also an important industry in Guatemala, which has many ancient Maya ruins.

3. The sale of what products has contributed to Guatemala's strong economy?

_____

_____

Living in Guatemala (pages 224–225)

How do urban and rural life differ in Guatemala?

More than half of Guatemala's people are Maya. The rest are ladinos, who are of mixed Maya and Spanish ancestry or who are of Maya ancestry but no longer practice Maya culture. Like the ancient Maya, most Maya today work in agriculture and live in small rural villages. They speak Maya languages, although many also speak Spanish. They wear traditional clothing, often woven by hand.

Guatemalan children are required to go to school from ages 7 through 13. However, about one-third do not, usually because they live in rural areas that have no schools. Only 15 percent of Guatemalans attend high school.

Rural Guatemalans often live without bathrooms, running water, or electricity. Most homes in rural villages are very small, and many have dirt floors. On the other hand, urban Guatemalans live in homes with modern conveniences, attend schools and universities, and go to theaters, museums, and restaurants. Their cultural influences, such as movies, magazines, and clothing styles, often come from foreign countries, while cultural influences for rural Guatemalans are often local in origin.

4. In what ways does Maya culture influence Guatemalan life today?

_____

_____

Glossary/After You Read

plantation a large farm cultivated by workers living there

lease to allow use of lands and property for a fixed fee

salsa Latin American dance music of African and Cuban origin, influenced by jazz and rock music

reggae Jamaican popular music that is marked by a strong rhythm and influenced by calypso and rock music

Cold War the period of rivalry and tension between the United States and the Soviet Union after World War II

redistribute to take away from original owners and give to others, so as to spread wealth more evenly among people

market economy an economic system in which prices, wages, and production are determined by the forces of supply and demand and not by the government

standard of living the level of material comfort in daily life

gross domestic product the total value of the goods and services produced by a nation in one year

TERMS & NAMES

A. In each blank, write the term or name that best completes the meaning of the paragraph.

single-product economy　　　West Indies　　　diversify

sugar cane　　　communism

The islands in the Caribbean Sea, known as the **(1)** _____,

had excellent conditions for growing **(2)** _____, a plant

with sap used to make sugar and molasses. The economy of each Caribbean

island was a **(3)** _____, depending on just one product for

most jobs and income. The instability of the market for sugar later caused the

islanders to **(4)** _____, or invest in a variety of industries.

The big plantations in Cuba were taken over by the government when Fidel

Castro embraced **(5)** _____, an economic and political

system in which the government controls the economy.

B. Write the letter of the term or name next to the description that explains it best.

a. dependency　　　**c. José Martí**　　　**e. Rafael Carrera**

b. Fidel Castro　　　**d. dictator**

_____ **1.** Cuban revolutionary who led the fight for independence from Spanish rule

_____ **2.** Revolutionary leader who was president of Guatemala from 1854 to 1865

_____ **3.** a place governed by or closely connected with another country

_____ **4.** Cuban revolutionary who became a Communist dictator

_____ **5.** a person who has complete control over a country's government

MAIN IDEAS

1. Why did the United States want to build a canal in Panama?

_____

_____

2. What were the causes of the Spanish-American War?

_____

_____

3. What were the two most important crops in Central America, and why did the Central American countries need to diversify their economies?

_____

_____

4. How has Cuba changed under Fidel Castro's leadership?

_____

_____

5. Why did civil war break out in Guatemala in 1954?

_____

_____

THINKING CRITICALLY

Answer the following questions on a separate sheet of paper.

1. Do the Caribbean Islands that rely on tourism as their major industry suffer the same disadvantages as a single-product economy that relies on a crop such as sugar cane? Think about whether tourism is a stable source of income and how it might be affected by changing political events, the world economy, or the weather.

2. Why do you think Maya culture is so much stronger in rural Guatemala than in urban Guatemala?

Establishing Independence

BEFORE YOU READ

In the last chapter, you read about Central America and the islands of the Caribbean.

In this section, you will read about how South America became independent from European rule.

AS YOU READ

Use the diagram to record facts you read that support each generalization.

Generalizations	Facts
Independence led to different types of governments in South America.	
South American countries are trying to cooperate with one another and with the United States.	
Geography and politics affect the economies of South America.	

TERMS & NAMES

Simón Bolívar general who led the fight for independence in northern South America

José de San Martín general who led the fight for independence in southern South America

Pan-American term meaning "all of the Americas"

Organization of American States (OAS) international organization made up of the United States and Latin American countries that promotes economic cooperation and social justice

Europeans Arrive in South America (pages 231–232)

Which two European countries took over South America?

Spanish explorer Francisco Pizarro came to South America in 1531. He conquered the Inca kingdom in what is now Peru. Peru is in western South America. Pizarro claimed the land for Spain.

About the same time, Portugal claimed land in what is now Brazil. Brazil is in eastern South America.

Spain and Portugal ended up colonizing much of South America. Many Native Americans died as a result. To replace them as workers, Spain and Portugal imported enslaved Africans.

Spain and Portugal ruled much of South America for 300 years, until the early 1800s.

Both countries became wealthy from their South American colonies.

1. What two European countries colonized much of South America?

_____

_____

Independence (pages 232–233)

Who led South Americans in their fight for independence?

By the early 1800s, many people who lived in South America wanted to become independent from Spain and Portugal. These groups included people with Spanish or Portuguese ancestors, but who were born in South America. It also included *mestizos* and *mulattos*, who were poorly treated.

Beginning in 1810, two generals led wars for independence in South America. These generals were named **Simón Bolívar** and **José de San Martín.** Almost all of South America was independent by 1825.

Brazil did not have to fight a war to become independent from Portugal. The Portuguese governor of Brazil agreed to independence. He then became emperor of Brazil.

2. Who were Simón Bolívar and José de San Martín, and what did they do?

_____

_____

Governments of South America
(page 234)
What kinds of government have there been in South America?

South Americans hoped that winning their independence would lead to fair governments. They wanted governments that did not have too much power. They wanted limited governments, or governments in which a *constitution* limited the government's power.

But the former colonial officials in South America wanted to keep their money and power. They used their influence to turn control of the new governments over to military officials, who would help them keep their wealth. In some cases, the military took over the governments on their own. In any case, they established unlimited governments, or governments in which one person or group held all the power.

By the 1990s, however, most governments in South America were democratic.

In the late 1800s, the United States began encouraging the governments of Latin America to work together. This idea is called Pan-American unity. Pan means "all," so **Pan-American** means "all of the Americas."

One way to cooperate is through the **Organization of American States** (OAS). It was founded in 1948. The OAS includes the United States and Latin American coun-

tries. The goals of the OAS are to promote economic cooperation, social justice, equality, and democracy.

3. What type of government is most common in South America today?

_____

_____

The People of South America
(page 235)
What groups of people live in South America?

Until the 1800s, most immigrants to South America came from Spain and Portugal. During the 1880s, immigrants came from other European countries.

All of these immigrants influenced societies in South America. They helped build South America's economy by starting industries. They also brought their customs with them. For example, immigrants from Great Britain introduced football (which we call soccer) to South America. Today, soccer is popular all over South America.

There are many different ethnic groups in South America. These *ethnic groups* include Native Americans, descendants of Europeans, descendants of enslaved Africans, and people with mixed ancestry. Some of these groups live in particular places. Others live all over South America.

The majority of South Americans are either mestizos or mulattos.

4. What two groups do most people of South America belong to?

_____

_____

Building Economies and Cultures

BEFORE YOU READ

In the last section, you read about how South American countries became independent from European countries.

In this section, you will read about how the newly independent countries of South America built their own economies and cultures.

AS YOU READ

Use the diagram to record facts you read that support each generalization.

TERMS & NAMES

free-trade zone area where people and goods move across borders without being taxed

economic indicators measurements that show how a country's economy is doing

urbanization the movement of many people from the countryside to the cities

Generalizations	Facts
Geography and politics affect the economies of South America.	
Urban growth presents serious problems for some South America countries.	
South Ameria's different cultures contribute to world culture.	

Geography and Trade in South America (pages 238–239)

***What** are South America's transportation barriers and transportation corridors?*

The physical geography, or landscape, of South America gives the region both transportation barriers and transportation corridors.

Transportation barriers are parts of the landscape that interfere with transportation. South America's transportation barriers include the Amazon rain forest and the Andes Mountains.

Transportation corridors are parts of the landscape that are easy to move through. South America's transportation corridors include the Amazon River and its *tributaries*. Today, ships carrying many different products sail along these transportation corridors.

1. Name one transportation barrier and one transportation corridor in South America.

_____

_____

Products and Industries of South America (pages 240-241)

What products does South America produce?

South America has many *natural resources*. These include minerals and fertile land. But many of these resources have not yet been used.

Mineral resources in South America include gold, iron ore, lead, petroleum, tin, copper, and emeralds.

South America is home to some of the largest farms in the world. These farms produce beef, grain, sugar, wool, bananas, and coffee. These farm products are often exported.

However, most farms in South America are small. Manufacturing is important in South America. The three South American countries with the most industry are Chile, Argentina, and Brazil. Brazil is one of the most important industrial countries in the world. Brazil manufacturers cars, trucks, computers, televisions, and airplanes. Other countries manufacture such goods as shoes, furniture, beverages, and textiles.

Many countries in South America cooperate to develop their economies. At the Summit of the Americas in 1994, they agreed to create the Free-Trade Zone of the Americas. A **free-trade zone** is an area where people and goods move across borders without being taxed. Many people believe the Free-Trade Zone of the Americas will improve many countries' economies.

Economic indicators are measurements that show how a country's economy is doing. Economic indicators include the literacy rate of a country and the life expectancy. The literacy rate shows the percentage of a country's people who can read and write at an elementary school level. Life expectancy is the average age to which people in a country live.

2. What are the three most important industrial countries in South America?

_____

_____

Daily Life in South America
(page 241–242)

What is daily like life in South America?

South America is home to both urban and rural areas. In the urban areas, many people are wealthy, but millions more are very poor.

Over the last 50 years, urbanization has occurred in South America. **Urbanization** means that many people have moved from the countryside to the cities. There are many reasons for urbanization in South America. Mostly, poor people from the country moved to the cities to get jobs and a chance at better lives.

Urbanization in South America has created some of the biggest cities in the world. São Paolo, Brazil, is home to almost 18 million people. Buenos Aires, Argentina, is home to almost 13 million people. Unfortunately, not all of the people live in good homes. Big cities are surrounded by slums. In the slums, people live in shacks made of cardboard, wood scraps, or tin. They often don't have electricity or running water. Millions of people live in poverty.

The arts, such as literature and music, are very important to the people of South America. Three South Americans have won the Nobel Prize for Literature. Their names are Gabriela Mistral, Pablo Neruda, and Gabriel García Márquez. There are many kinds of South American music. *Huayno* is the traditional music of the Andean regions. *Salsa* is a kind of music that has African roots. Musicians in the cities combine such traditional music with rock.

3. What are some effects of urbanization?

_____

_____

CHAPTER 9

Brazil Today

BEFORE YOU READ

In the last section, you read about how South American countries built their economies and cultures.

In this section, you will read more about one particular country: Brazil.

AS YOU READ

Use the diagram to record facts you read that support each generalization.

Generalizations	Facts
Brazil is a regional leader.	
Many different peoples live in Brazil.	

TERMS & NAMES

inflation a general increase in the price of goods or services

São Paulo one of the two largest cities in Brazil

Rio de Janeiro one of the two largest cities in Brazil

Brasília the capital of Brazil

Carnival a famous Brazilian holiday

Brazil: Regional Leader (page 243)
***What* makes Brazil a leader in the South American region?**

Brazil is the largest country in South America. It covers almost half of the continent. Almost half of the people of South America live in Brazil. Brazil has the best economy in South America.

1. What fraction of South Americans live in Brazil?

_____

_____

The Government of Brazil (page 244)
***What* kinds of government has Brazil had?**

Brazil became an independent country in 1822. At first, it was ruled by emperors. In 1889, it became a *republic* with a *constitution*. Then, beginning in 1930, it was ruled by dictators and military leaders. In 1995, Brazil again became a democracy.

2. What type of government does Brazil have today?

_____

_____

_____

The Economy of Brazil (pages 244–245)
***What* products does Brazil export?**

Brazil has the largest economy in South America.

The government of Brazil helps certain industries in order to help the economy. In the 1950s, it started helping the automobile industry. The government wanted to decrease the number of cars that were imported. By the late 1980s, Brazil was building more than 1 million cars and trucks a year. This was enough for Brazil to export cars, instead of importing them.

Only the United States exports more crops than Brazil. Brazil produces more coffee than any other country. It also produces oranges, bananas, and corn.

Brazil has a strong economy, but it has problems. Many people do not have jobs, and so unemployment is a problem. Inflation is another economic problem. **Inflation** is a general increase in the price of goods or services. Unemployment and inflation have created much poverty in Brazil.

3. What two problems does the economy of Brazil face?

_____

_____

The People of Brazil (pages 245–246)
Where in Brazil do most Brazilians live?

Portugal took over Brazil in the 1500s. They built sugar cane plantations and made Native Americans work on them. But Native Americans died of disease. So the plantation owners brought enslaved Africans to work on the plantations. Brazil brought more enslaved Africans to Brazil than any other country in North or South America.

Today, many people in Brazil are descended from enslaved Africans. Many Brazilians have both European and African ancestors. Less than 1 percent are Native Americans.

Today, four out of five people in Brazil live in cities. Brazil's two largest cities are **São Paulo** and **Rio de Janeiro.** The population of these cities and the whole country is increasing. By 2025, the population of Brazil might reach 210 million.

The government of Brazil has encouraged people to move inland and away from the coast to make the coast less crowded. To help encourage this movement, they built a new capital city, **Brasília,** far inland.

4. What are three important Brazilian cities?

_____

_____

The Culture of Brazil (pages 246–247)
How is Brazilian culture a mix of other cultures?

Brazil's culture is a mix of the cultures of the many people who have lived there. Brazil's official language is Portuguese. But the people also use many Native American words.

Most Brazilians are Catholic. More Catholics live in Brazil than in any other country. However, the percentage of non-Catholics has increased. Many Brazilians practice African religions and enjoy music with African roots, such as *samba.*

Carnival is a famous Brazilian holiday. It is celebrated every year four days before *Lent.* Carnival is celebrated with huge parades and parties.

The most popular sport in Brazil is football, which we call soccer. Millions of Brazilians watch and play the game.

5. What religion are most of the people in Brazil?

_____

_____

Peru Today

BEFORE YOU READ
In the last section, you read about the South American country of Brazil.

In this section, you will read about another country in South America: Peru.

AS YOU READ
Use the diagram to record facts you read that support each generalization.

Generalizations	Facts
Peru is a rugged land.	
Peru faces economic challenges.	

TERMS & NAMES
oasis a fertile region in a desert that formed around a river or spring

guerrilla warfare warfare characterized by small groups using surprise attacks

Alberto Fujimori a president of Peru

Quechua people who live in the Andes highlands and speak the Inca language Quechua

The Land of Peru (pages 250–251)
What is the land of Peru like?

Peru has many resources, such as *guano*. But the land also presents problems. The three types of landforms in Peru—mountains, rain forest, and desert—are transportation barriers.

The steep Andes Mountains divide the country in two. To the east of the mountains grows the rain forest, or selva. To the west of the mountains is the Atacama Desert. Most of Peru's cities, large farms, and factories are located at oases in the desert. An **oasis** is a fertile region in a desert that formed around a river or spring.

1. What are the three major landforms of Peru?

_____

_____

_____

The Economy of Peru (pages 251–252)
What does Peru produce?

Peru's harsh landscape causes economic problems. For example, mountains and desert cover so much land that there is not enough *arable* land for farming. Peru must import some food. However, it does export sugar cane, cotton, and coffee. Peru also has a large dairy industry. Peru produces meat from cattle, sheep, *alpaca*, and goats.

Peru borders the Pacific Ocean. Peruvians fish the ocean for sardines and anchovies. These are made into fishmeal, which is used as cattle food. Peru exports fishmeal.

Peru produces metals such as silver, copper, and *bismuth*. It contains oil and gold deposits. But these deposits are located in hard-to-get-at places, such as the rain forest or the mountains, so they have not brought Peru much wealth.

2. Why does Peru have to import food?

_____

_____

The Government of Peru
(pages 252–253)
What problems have faced governments in Peru?

Peru declared its independence in 1821. It won its independence under Simón Bolívar in 1824. From then until the late 20th century, military and civilian leaders struggled with each other for control of the government.

In the early 1980s, *Communist* groups rose up against the government. The most powerful Communist group was Sendero Luminoso, which means "Shining Path." Shining Path used guerilla warfare to fight for communism. **Guerilla warfare** is warfare characterized by small groups using surprise attacks. Shining Path's leader was imprisoned in 1992, and the *civil war* ended.

From 1990 to 2000, the president of Peru was **Alberto Fujimori.** He was the son of a Japanese immigrant. In 2000, he was accused of *corruption* and left the country. The new president tried to get the people of Peru to trust the government again.

3. What is guerilla warfare?

_____

_____

Peruvian People and Culture
(pages 253–254)
From whom are many Peruvians descended?

Today, more Native Americans live in Peru than in any other South American country. Forty-five percent of Peruvians—almost half—are Native Americans. They are descended from the Inca people. Many of these people are Quechua. The **Quechua** are people who live in the Andes highlands and speak the Inca language Quechua.

The second-largest group of Peruvians are mestizos. Other Peruvians have European, African, or Asian ancestors.

Most Peruvians live in cities. The largest city and capital of Peru is Lima. There are many poor neighborhoods in Lima that don't have electricity or running water.

Many farmers live in the country. Most of them are Native American and are very poor. They often move to the city in search of better lives, but they have a hard time finding jobs because they don't speak Spanish or have much education.

Catholicism is the national religion of Peru. Nine-tenths of Peruvians are Catholic. Many Native Americans follow Inca religious practices. Sometimes the two religions mix.

Two famous Peruvian writers are Mario Vargas Llosa and César Vallejo, who is a *mestizo.*

4. What is the major religion in Peru?

_____

_____

Glossary/After You Read

alpaca an animal similar to a llama

arable land that is good for farming

bismuth a white or pinkish metallic mineral with many uses

civil war a war within a country

Communist believing that the government should control the economy and society

constitution a written plan of government

corruption misbehavior while in office

ethnic group people of the same race or nationality who share a culture

guano natural waste, often from sea birds, collected and used for fertilizer

Lent period of time before Easter observed by some Christians

mestizo a person with both European and Native American ancestors

mulatto a person with both European and African ancestors

natural resources materials found in nature that people can use

republic a government in which people elect leaders to represent them

tributary a smaller stream that flows into a larger river

TERMS & NAMES

Write the letter of the correct term on each line.

a. Alberto Fujimori

b. Brasília

c. Carnival

d. economic indicators

e. free-trade zone

f. guerrilla warfare

g. inflation

h. José de San Martin

i. oasis

j. Organization of American States (OAS)

k. Pan-American

l. Quechua

m. Rio de Janeiro

n. São Paulo

o. Simón Bolívar

p. urbanization

_____ **1.** a famous Brazilian holiday

_____ **2.** a fertile region in a desert that formed around a river or spring

_____ **3.** a general increase in the price of goods or services

_____ **4.** a president of Peru

_____ **5.** area where people and goods move across borders without being taxed

_____ **6.** general who led the fight for independence in northern South America

_____ **7.** general who led the fight for independence in southern South America

_____ **8.** international organization made up of the United States and Latin American countries that promotes economic cooperation and social justice

_____ **9.** measurements that show how a country's economy is doing

_____ **10.** one of the two largest cities in Brazil

_____ **11.** one of the two largest cities in Brazil

_____ **12.** people who live in the Andes highlands and speak the Inca language Quechua

_____ **13.** term meaning "all of the Americas"

_____ **14.** the capital of Brazil

_____ **15.** the movement of many people from the countryside to the cities

_____ **16.** warfare characterized by small groups using surprise attacks

MAIN IDEAS

1. From which two European countries did most countries in South America gain their independence?

_____

_____

2. What are several ethnic groups that make up South America's population?

_____

_____

3. How does geography influence the economy in South America?

_____

_____

4. How has urbanization affected South America?

_____

_____

5. What is the major religion in Brazil and Peru?

_____

_____

THINKING CRITICALLY

Answer the following questions on a separate sheet of paper.

1. If you could go to just one place in South America, where would it be? A huge city? A steep mountain? The rain forest? Explain the reasons for your choice.

2. Imagine you are the president of Brazil. What would you do to help the poor people of the slums of São Paulo and Rio de Janeiro? Explain how your actions would help.

A Land of Varied Riches

BEFORE YOU READ

In the last chapter, you read about the conditions that helped to shape the countries of South America.

In this section, you will learn how Europe's diverse geography has shaped its diverse cultures.

AS YOU READ

Use this chart to take notes on the geography, climate, and natural resources of Europe.

Geography	
Climate	
Natural Resources	

TERMS & NAMES

Mediterranean Sea inland sea that borders Europe, Southwest Asia, and Africa

peninsula a body of land surrounded by water on three sides

fjord a long, narrow, deep inlet of the sea located between steep cliffs

Ural Mountains a mountain range along Europe's eastern border that divides the continent from Asia

plain a large, flat area of land, usually without many trees

The Geography of Europe
(pages 273–275)

What are some important geographic features of Europe?

Europe is a **peninsula,** surrounded by water on the north, south, and west. The European continent also has smaller peninsulas, as well as important inland waterways. Mountain ranges are among the natural landforms found in Europe. In addition, the continent contains a vast **plain** that is used for agriculture.

Among Europe's inland waterways are a number of rivers, including the Rhine, the Danube, and the Volga. These waterways and the seas on three sides of the continent have enabled people and goods to move both within Europe and to other parts of the world.

Two of Europe's smaller peninsulas are the Scandinavian and Iberian Peninsulas. Northern Europe's Scandinavian Peninsula, home to Norway and Sweden, has the deep sea inlets known as **fjords.** Western Europe's Iberian Peninsula, containing Portugal and Spain, is separated from the rest of the continent by the *Pyrenees* mountains.

Other mountain ranges found in Europe are the *Alps* and the **Ural Mountains.** The Urals run along Europe's eastern border and divide the continent from Asia. The mountain ranges of Europe separated groups of people as they settled the land. This is one reason why different cultures developed.

Rich farmland is found in the large, flat area of Europe known as the Great European Plain. The ancient trading centers of this plain, which stretches from the coast of France to the Ural Mountains, drew many settlers. It now includes large cities such as Paris, Berlin, Warsaw, and Moscow.

1. How did Europe's seas and waterways help in its settlement by people from diverse cultures?

_____

_____

_____

Climate (pages 275–276)

How does the climate vary within Europe?

The Gulf Stream's warm water and warm, moist air help to give much of Europe a mild climate. However, cold winds from the Arctic Circle can cause harsh winters in Northern Europe and in mountainous regions. In these areas, the average January temperature can fall below 0°F. Southern areas that border the **Mediterranean Sea** are warmer, protected from Arctic winds by the Alps and the Pyrenees mountain ranges. Here, January temperatures tend to stay above 50°F.

Vacationers enjoy the Mediterranean coast's hot, dry summers, where July temperatures average about 80°F. In more northerly parts of Europe, except in the far north and in the coldest mountain regions, July temperatures range from 50°F to 60°F.

2. How do the Gulf Stream and Arctic winds affect Europe's climate?

_____

_____

Natural Resources (pages 276–277)

What natural resources does Europe have?

Minerals, rich soil, and plentiful rainfall are some of Europe's natural resources. Mineral resources include the coal deposits of Germany's Ruhr Valley, which help to make that area an industrial center. Large deposits of iron ore are found in Russia and Ukraine.

Because of its rich soil and abundant precipitation, Europe is also a world leader in crop production. In fact, most areas of the continent support some form of agriculture. Among the crops grown in Europe are wheat, rye, and potatoes. Europe also has large expanses of dairy and grazing land, and regions planted with orchards and vineyards.

3. What are the two main uses of Europe's natural resources?

_____

_____

Ancient Greece

BEFORE YOU READ

In the last section, you read about the geography, climate, and natural resources of Europe.

In this section, you will learn about the achievements of the ancient Greeks in government, learning, and the arts and sciences.

AS YOU READ

Use this chart to take notes on this section about ancient Greece.

Land and Early History	Government	Colonization	Learning and the Arts	The Spread of Greek Culture

TERMS & NAMES

city-state a community made up of a central city and surrounding villages

polis the Greek term for a central city

Aegean Sea a branch of the Mediterranean Sea, lying between Greece and Turkey

oligarchy a system of government in which a few powerful individuals rule

Athens the capital of Greece and once one of the largest ancient city-states

philosopher a person who studies and thinks about why the world is the way it is

Aristotle a brilliant Greek philosopher of the third century B.C. who taught Alexander the Great

Alexander the Great a ruler of ancient Greece whose conquest of new lands led to the spread of Greek culture

The Land and Early History of Greece (pages 278–280)

What were some of the reasons for the spread of Greek culture?

Greece is a rocky, mountainous peninsula on which few crops will grow. However, it is surrounded by water, its greatest natural resource. The ancient Greeks depended on the sea for fishing and trade.

As their population grew, the ancient Greeks formed city-states. Each **city-state** consisted of a central city, or **polis,** and its outlying villages. Each city-state had its own laws and form of government, but all shared a common language, religion, and way of life.

Although Greece's early settlers could grow olives and grapes on their rocky land, they needed access to a wider variety of crops and resources. About the mid-eighth century B.C., the Greeks began to *colonize* the islands and

eastern coastline of the **Aegean Sea.** These distant Greek colonies traded with one another as well as with communities on the Greek Peninsula. The Greeks could now obtain goods such as wheat, timber, and iron ore. As new colonies were settled, Greek culture spread.

Three forms of government were common in the Greek city-states. One city-state might be an **oligarchy,** in which a few powerful, wealthy individuals ruled. Another might be ruled by a *tyrant*. Still another might be a democracy, in which citizens took part in their own government.

1. What were two of the main accomplishments of the ancient Greeks?

_____

_____

Copyright © McDougal Littell Inc.

Athens and Sparta (page 280)

What were the two most important city-states in ancient Greece?

Athens and *Sparta* were two large, powerful Greek city-states. Athens, located in the central part of the Greek Peninsula, was a democracy. Sparta, in the southernmost part of the peninsula, was an oligarchy ruled by two kings.

Although Athens had a democratic form of government, not everyone had citizenship rights. Only free adult males whose fathers had been citizens could engage in politics and vote. Women, slaves, and foreigners had no role in government.

Athens and Sparta were rivals. Each had a large army that protected the city-state from slave rebellions, attacks by other city-states, and foreign invasions.

2. How were Athens and Sparta alike?

_____

_____

Learning and the Arts (pages 280–282)

What were some achievements of the ancient Greeks in learning and the arts?

The ancient Greeks made great contributions to literature, learning, and architecture. Many of their achievements date from their defeat of a Persian invasion of the Greek Peninsula in 480 B.C.

Plays are among the finest works of literature from ancient Greece. These plays were tragedies, serious plays that ended unhappily, and comedies, plays that poked fun at important citizens. Sophocles, Aeschylus, and Euripides wrote tragedies, and Aristophanes wrote comedies. Some modern operas and films are based on these plays.

There were several important ancient Greek thinkers. Socrates was a noted **philosopher,** or person who studies and thinks about why the world is the way it is. In the fifth century B.C., he taught about knowledge, friendship, and jus-

tice. His student Plato wrote about human behavior, government, mathematics, and astronomy. **Aristotle**, a student of Plato, was another brilliant thinker. He wrote about government, astronomy, and poetry. His work still influences scientists and philosophers today.

Among the architectural achievements of ancient Greece were beautiful temples, including the *Parthenon* in Athens. Greek architectural styles are often used today for government buildings.

The city-states of ancient Greece, weakened by war with each other, were conquered by King Philip II of Macedonia in 338 B.C. When Philip's son **Alexander the Great** took control, he conquered vast new regions. During the rule of Alexander, who had been Aristotle's student, Greek culture, language, and ideas spread throughout the Mediterranean region and to the east. The empire collapsed, however, after Alexander's death.

3. In what ways are Greek achievements in arts and learning still important today?

_____

_____

Ancient Rome

BEFORE YOU READ

In the last section, you read about the achievements of the ancient Greeks in government, the arts and learning, and the sciences.

In this section, you will learn how ancient Rome expanded, becoming first a city, then a republic, and finally an empire.

AS YOU READ

Use this chart to take notes on ancient Rome's culture and its contributions to government, law, and engineering.

From Villages to Republic	Expansion of the Roman World	From Republic to Empire	Christianity and Constantine

TERMS & NAMES

republic a nation in which power belongs to the citizens, who govern through elected representatives

senate an assembly of elected representatives

patrician in ancient Rome, a member of a wealthy, landowning family

plebeian an ordinary, working male citizen of ancient Rome

Julius Caesar a general who became dictator of the Roman world in the first century B.C.

empire a nation or group of territories ruled by a powerful leader, or emperor

Augustus Caesar's adopted son and first emperor of Rome in 27 B.C.

Constantine first Christian emperor of Rome; ruled from A.D. 306 to 337

The Beginnings of Ancient Rome
(pages 284–285)

How was ancient Rome governed in its earliest stages?

Rome began as a group of villages along Italy's Tiber River. About 750 B.C. the villages united to form the city of Rome. It was governed by kings for more than 200 years and then became a **republic**—a nation governed by its citizens through their elected representatives.

Representatives elected by the people formed the republic's ruling body, called the Senate. Every year the **Senate** elected two leaders, or *consuls*, to head the government and the military.

Early on, most senators were patricians. A **patrician** was a member of a wealthy, landowning family who claimed family roots dating back to Rome's founding. Patricians controlled the law.

A **plebeian,** in contrast to a patrician, was an ordinary, working male citizen of Rome. Until they gained equality with patricians in 287 B.C., plebeians could vote but could not hold public office.

1. Who were the people responsible for the government of the Roman Republic?

_____

_____

The Expansion of the Roman World (pages 285–286)

How was the expansion of the Roman world accomplished?

As the republic and its army grew, Rome conquered new lands. It had gained control of most of the Italian Peninsula, and, therefore, of the central Mediterranean, by the third century B.C. Then, through a victory over the city-state of

Carthage, Rome gained control of North Africa, southern Spain, and the western Mediterranean.

Rome's culture and language spread farther into Spain and eastward into Greece. By the end of the second century B.C., Romans were calling the Mediterranean Sea *mare nostrum* ("our sea") because they controlled most of the land around it.

2. What were the three steps in Rome's expansion throughout the Mediterranean region?

_____

_____

From Republic to Empire
(pages 286–288)

What roles did Julius Caesar and Augustus play in the early days of the Roman Empire?

Julius Caesar was an ambitious Roman general and governor. He brought Rome's republican government to an end by becoming its dictator. Later, his relative Augustus became the first emperor of Rome. Caesar's rule was marked by strife and followed by civil war, but the rule of **Augustus** was a time of peaceful prosperity.

Before he became Rome's dictator, Caesar was the governor of Gaul. Today, this ancient Roman territory includes France, Belgium, and northern parts of Italy. The Roman Senate, fearful that Caesar was becoming too powerful, ordered him to resign. Caesar refused and gained control of the Roman world in 46 B.C. Not long after, on March 15 in 44 B.C., he was stabbed to death by senators on the floor of the Roman Senate. A civil war resulted.

In 27 B.C. Rome became an **empire**, a nation or group of territories ruled by one powerful leader. The first emperor was Caesar's adopted son, who ruled under the name Augustus. During the 40 years of his rule, called the Augustan Age, Rome prospered. Its army kept peace throughout Rome's vast lands. Shipments of goods across the Mediterranean grew. Engineers built many public buildings. Lighthouses were built to help ships locate ports.

Great Roman literature, including Virgil's long poem, the *Aeneid,* was written. In all, the period of cultural growth and peace that Augustus began—known as the *Pax Romana,* or Roman Peace—lasted 200 years.

3. How did the periods following the rules of Julius Caesar and Augustus differ?

_____

_____

The Rise of Christianity (page 289)
What was the early history of Christianity in the Roman Empire?

Christianity began to take hold after Augustus died in A.D. 14. This new religion spread from the Middle East into the eastern half of the Roman Empire. Moving along Roman transportation routes, it had reached the entire empire by the third century A.D. Then, although they had earlier allowed a variety of religions, Roman leaders became suspicious of Christianity. Christians began to be punished or killed for their beliefs.

4. How did the attitude of Roman leaders toward Christians change as Christianity spread?

_____

_____

The First Christian Emperor
(page 289)

What promise did Emperor Constantine make?

In A.D. 306, **Constantine** became Rome's emperor. Later, just before a battle, he had a vision of a cross in the sky. Constantine promised to become a Christian if he won the battle, and he did both. Christianity became the empire's official religion. Today, there are nearly two billion Christians around the world.

5. What came about as a result of Emperor Constantine's promise?

_____

_____

Time of Change: The Middle Ages

BEFORE YOU READ
In the last section, you read about the establishment and growth of the Roman Empire.

In this section, you will learn about the changes in Western Europe after the collapse of the Roman Empire.

AS YOU READ
Use this chart to take notes on the developments in Western Europe during the Middle Ages.

Effects of the Empire's Collapse	Charlemagne and the Church	Political and Social Systems	Medieval Life

TERMS & NAMES
medieval of or about the Middle Ages

Charlemagne Germanic king; crowned Holy Roman Emperor in A.D. 800

feudalism system in which nobles gave land to lesser nobles in return for services

manorialism system in which a lord received food and work from peasants in exchange for his protection

guild association set up by trades-people to protect their common interests

Magna Carta document of 1215 that limited the English king's power

Western Europe in Collapse
(pages 290–291)
How do we define the Middle Ages?

The Middle Ages, or **medieval** era, is the period between the fall of the Roman Empire and the beginning of the modern world.

By A.D. 476, the weak Roman army could no longer fight off invaders from the north and east. Gradually, the city of Rome, smaller villages and towns, and even whole territories were overtaken.

The empire's central government collapsed. Buildings, roads, and water systems were not maintained. People fled from towns and cities. Travel and trade became unsafe. Advances and inventions of the ancient world were lost. People turned to military leaders and the Catholic Church for guidance.

1. What was the main cause of Western Europe's problems during the Middle Ages?

_____

_____

Charlemagne and the Christian Church (page 291)
Who was Charlemagne?

Charlemagne was a Germanic king and warrior who ruled the northwestern edge of the former Roman Empire. Rome was the center of the Catholic Church by the late 700s. The Pope, seeking more power for the Church, decided to join forces with Charlemagne. In 800, the Pope declared Charlemagne to be the new Holy Roman Emperor.

During Charlemagne's rule, order was established and the government grew stronger. Education was improved, cultural advances were made, and Catholicism spread. After Charlemagne died, though, Western Europe was again without a strong leader.

2. How did the Catholic Church benefit from Charlemagne's rule as emperor?

_____

_____

The Role of the Church
(pages 291–292)

What services did medieval churches provide?

Medieval communities centered around a church that held religious services, and cared for orphans and the sick, poor, and elderly.

Monks and nuns devoted their lives to the church. Monks were men who lived together in *monasteries*. They prayed, studied, and copied holy books by hand. Many monasteries came to be centers of learning. Nuns were women who lived together in *convents*. In their *secluded* communities, they prayed, taught girls, sewed, cared for the poor, and also copied books.

3. How did monasteries and convents help to maintain learning in the Middle Ages?

_____

_____

Two Medieval Systems (pages 292–293)

What two systems did nobles develop?

Members of the nobility and the church owned most of the land. They began feudalism and manorialism to protect their property.

Feudalism was a system in which lords gave land to lesser nobles, called vassals, in return for services. A vassal supplied knights, foot soldiers, and arms. A vassal's land was called a *fief*. At its center was a manor, consisting of a large house or castle, farmland, villages, and a church. Some fiefs included manors owned by the vassals of the fief-owner.

Under **manorialism,** peasants lived on and farmed the manor, trading their labor and some crops for the lord's protection. Serfs were peasants who belonged to fiefs and could not leave without permission.

4. How did lords benefit from feudalism and manorialism?

_____

_____

Medieval Ways of Life/The Growth of Medieval Towns
(pages 293–294)

What caused the growth of medieval towns?

During the Middle Ages, both rich and poor lived uncomfortably. Manor houses and castles, built for defense, had thick walls and few windows. They were dark, cold, damp, and smoky from fires. Lice and other pests were common, and indoor plumbing was absent.

The peasants' small homes had dirt floors and straw roofs. They kept farm animals in their homes. Their time was divided between working for their lord and farming their own plots.

By the middle of the 11th century, new farming methods had increased Western Europe's crop production, and fewer farmers were needed. People moved to towns, bought property, and started businesses. Business competition grew, and guilds were formed. A **guild** was an association to protect workers' rights, set wages and prices, and settle disputes.

5. How was a guild like a modern trade union?

_____

_____

The Late Middle Ages (pages 294–295)

What were two challenges to authority?

As medieval towns grew, citizens set up local governments. Their leaders began to challenge the authority of the Pope and of their rulers.

Kings and other leaders struggled for power with the Pope, who claimed authority over Christian lands. Nobles also rebelled against their rulers. England's nobles forced King John to sign the **Magna Carta** in 1215. This document gave nobles a larger role in government and limited the king's power.

6. What were the goals of the nobles who drafted the Magna Carta?

_____

_____

Glossary/After You Read

Alps crescent-shaped mountain system of south central Europe, extending from the Mediterranean Sea through France, Italy, Switzerland, Austria, and beyond

colonize to form or establish a colony or settlement

consul either of two chief officers of the Roman Republic, elected by the Senate for a term of one year

convents communities of nuns, women who have vowed to lead religious lives

fief parcel of land granted to a vassal by his lord

monasteries communities of monks, men who have vowed to lead religious lives

Parthenon temple built at Athens between 442 and 437 B.C.

Pax Romana "Roman Peace"; the terms of peace imposed by ancient Rome on its empire

Pyrenees mountain range along the border between France and Spain

secluded shut off or set apart; hidden away

serf a peasant bound to the land owned by a lord

Sparta a powerful military city-state of ancient Greece

tyrant an absolute ruler in ancient Greece, especially one who seized power

TERMS & NAMES

A. Write the letter of the name or term next to the statement that describes it best.

a. fjord   **c.** feudalism   **e.** peninsula

b. plebeian   **d.** oligarchy

_____ **1.** a form of government in which a few powerful, wealthy individuals rule

_____ **2.** an ordinary, working male citizen of ancient Rome

_____ **3.** a body of land surrounded by water on three sides

_____ **4.** a medieval system in which nobles gave land to less powerful nobles in return for services

_____ **5.** a long, narrow, deep inlet of the sea located between steep cliffs

B. Write the letter of the name or term next to the statement that describes it best.

a. Julius Caesar   **d.** patrician   **f.** Augustus

b. Magna Carta   **e.** Aristotle   **g.** Charlemagne

c. Constantine

_____ **1.** I was the teacher of Alexander the Great.

_____ **2.** I was signed by King John of England in 1215.

_____ **3.** I was crowned Holy Roman Emperor by the Pope in 800.

_____ **4.** I was killed on the floor of the Roman Senate in 44 B.C.

_____ **5.** I became a Christian after having a vision of a cross in the sky.

_____ **6.** I became Rome's first emperor in 27 B.C.

_____ **7.** I was a member of a wealthy, landowning family that claimed to be able to trace its roots back to the founding of Rome.

MAIN IDEAS

1. How did the fact that Europe is a peninsula affect its development?

_____

_____

2. Why is Europe able to produce such an abundant supply of crops?

_____

_____

3. What were the three most common forms of government in ancient Greece?

_____

_____

4. What were the stages of the city of Rome's expansion into an empire?

_____

_____

5. How did the Church come to play such an important role in medieval society?

_____

_____

THINKING CRITICALLY

Answer the following questions on a separate sheet of paper.

1. Ancient Greece and Rome made great achievements in literature, architecture, philosophy, government, engineering, and the sciences. Which of those achievements do you think was the biggest influence on the world today? Why?

2. Do you think that the church should have had an active role in government during the Middle Ages? Why or why not?

Renaissance Connections

BEFORE YOU READ

In the last chapter, you learned about the physical geography of Europe as well as its ancient history.

In this section, you will learn about the Renaissance in Europe. You will also learn about the Reformation and the emergence of Protestantism in Northern Europe.

AS YOU READ

Copy this chart to take notes about the Renaissance in Europe.

Influences	New Ideas	People/ Achievements	Events/ Effects
The Renaissance			

TERMS & NAMES

Crusades a series of military expeditions led by Western European Christians in the 11th, 12th, and 13th centuries to reclaim control of the Holy Lands from the Muslims

Renaissance an era of creativity and learning in Western Europe from the 14th to the 16th century

Florence a city in Italy that was a bustling center of banking, trade, and manufacturing during the 14th century

Leonardo da Vinci a famous Renaissance artist and scientist

William Shakespeare a famous English playwright whose works are still performed today

Reformation a 16th-century movement to change practices within the Roman Catholic Church

Martin Luther a German monk who criticized corrupt practices and later translated the Bible from Latin into German

Protestant a person who follows Martin Luther's ideas about Christianity

Europeans Encounter New Cultures/The Rebirth of Europe
(pages 301–303)

How did the Crusades create favorable conditions for the Renaissance to develop?

During the 11th, 12th, and 13th centuries, Christians from Western Europe led a series of military *expeditions* to Asia and Northern Africa. These **Crusades** were an attempt to recover the Holy Lands from the Muslims. During the Crusades, the Europeans rediscovered ancient Greek and Roman culture.

Interest in these ancient cultures grew. Between the 14th and 16th centuries, Western Europe experienced a rebirth of creativity and learning that came to be known as the **Renaissance.**

Artists, writers, scholars, and architects created many important works during the Renaissance. Their new ideas and achievements spread. Eventually, they changed the way people saw the world.

The Italian Peninsula was the birthplace of the Renaissance. In the mid-14th century, *city-states* like **Florence** were centers of banking, manufacturing, and trade. Many wealthy people lived in these cities. Aristocratic families lived luxurious lives and placed a high value on education and the arts.

1. What conditions encouraged the development of Renaissance ideas?

_____

_____

Learning and the Arts Flourish/ The Northern Renaissance

(pages 303–304)

What did Renaissance artists create?

The wealthy people of Italy's city-states were *patrons* of the arts. They supported artists and scholars and funded architectural projects. City-states competed with each other to attract the most talented scholars and artists.

Artists continued to create religious art. They also began to depict other subjects. Some painted portraits of their patrons, while others illustrated stories from history or mythology.

Leonardo da Vinci (1452–1519) was one of the Renaissance's most famous artists and scientists. His paintings include the *Mona Lisa* and *The Last Supper*. A scientist, engineer, and inventor, he sketched thousands of discoveries and inventions.

Artists and writers in Northern Europe were inspired by the new Renaissance ideas about art and religion. Two writers were especially important. Desiderius Erasmus (1466–1536) was a Dutch philosopher and writer who was critical of the church. **William Shakespeare** was a popular English playwright. His plays, written during the late 16th and early 17th century, are still widely performed and read today.

2. Name two famous writers or artists who created great works during the Renaissance.

_____

_____

The Reformation/A Conflict over Religious Beliefs (page 305–306)

Why was Martin Luther a major figure of the Reformation?

The **Reformation** was a 16th-century movement to reform the Roman Catholic Church. **Martin Luther** was a German monk and a critic of the church. He was disturbed by the corruption of many church officials. Luther criticized the church for selling *indulgences*—forgiving sins in exchange for money. He was *excommunicated* in 1517 after publishing his ideas. He later translated the Bible into German from Latin. His ideas spread throughout Europe.

The **Protestants** were followers of Martin Luther. They protested against the church's intolerance of their beliefs. The conflict between these two groups led to religious wars. In 1555, these wars ended with the Peace of Augsburg. German rulers could now choose the official religion of their state.

By 1600, Protestantism had spread beyond Germany to England and Scandinavia. Protestants pushed for wider education.

The Roman Catholic Church began the Counter Reformation in the mid-16th century. First, the church ended its practice of selling indulgences. Then it established a new religious order called the Society of Jesus, or Jesuits.

3. How did the Protestants put Martin Luther's ideas into practice?

_____

_____

Traders, Explorers, and Colonists

BEFORE YOU READ

In the last section, you read about the Renaissance, the Reformation, and Protestantism in Europe.

In this section, you will read about the spice trade and how it inspired exploration. You will learn what European explorers discovered and how they influenced people's lives in the newly discovered lands.

AS YOU READ

Copy this chart to take notes on details about European traders, colonists, and explorers.

Influences	New Ideas	People/ Achievements	Events/ Effects
European Exploration and Conquest			

TERMS & NAMES

Prince Henry the Navigator a Portuguese prince who sent explorers down the coast of Africa to find a shortcut to Asia

Christopher Columbus an Italian explorer who sailed west from Spain in 1492 in order to find a direct route to Asia and who eventually landed on a Caribbean island

Ferdinand Magellan a Portuguese explorer who sailed west from Spain in 1519 and who eventually arrived in the Philippines

circumnavigate to sail completely around the world

imperialism the practice of one country controlling the government and economy of another country or territory

Trade Between Europe and Asia
(pages 307–308)

Why were spices so expensive in Europe?

Before the Renaissance, merchants traveled to North Africa and to the eastern Mediterranean in search of spices like pepper, cinnamon, nutmeg, and cloves. Europeans wanted these spices because they could use them both to preserve food and improve its flavor.

Merchants from Genoa and Venice had controlled the spice trade for centuries. These spices sold for very high prices in Europe because it was so expensive to transport them. Merchants knew that their profits would be higher if they could trade directly with Asia. In the 15th century, European explorers began looking for a new route to Asia.

1. Why did European traders want to find a new route to Asia?

_____

_____

Leaders in Exploration (pages 308–309)

How did the Portuguese discover a sea route to Asia?

By the early 1400s, the Portuguese had already sailed from Europe south to Africa and west to the Azores, the Canary Islands, and Madeira. Hoping to find a shortcut to Asia, **Prince Henry the Navigator** decided to send explorers even farther down the African coast. By the time he died in 1460, the Portuguese had traveled as far as present-day Sierra Leone.

Copyright © McDougal Littell Inc.

The Portuguese continued to explore the African coast. In 1488, explorer Bartolomeu Dias rounded Africa's southern tip, the Cape of Good Hope. Within the next ten years, explorer Vasco da Gama traveled 13,500 miles from Portugal to India. Portugal established trading posts along the Indian Ocean coast. Now spices and other goods could be brought directly to Europe.

2. How did Vasco da Gama make the dream of Prince Henry the Navigator come true?

_____

_____

Europe Enters a New Age
(pages 309–310)

What did Spanish and English explorers discover?

England and Spain both tried to find their own routes to Asia. Some thought that explorers could reach Asia by sailing to the west. Spain's Queen Isabella funded such an expedition. It was led by **Christopher Columbus,** an Italian explorer.

Columbus left Spain in 1492 with three ships—the *Santa Maria,* the *Pinta,* and the *Niña.* After several weeks, a crew member finally spotted land. They had not reached Asia, as Columbus first believed, but an island in the Caribbean Sea.

The Portuguese explorer Ferdinand Magellan, also funded by Spain, set sail in 1519. He had five ships and more than 200 sailors. Eighteen months later, the crew finally reached the Philippines, but the journey had been difficult. Rough storms, a shortage of food, and disease killed many sailors. Magellan and several members of his crew were killed in the Philippines. One boat and 18 sailors finally returned to Spain, three years after departing. They had successfully **circumnavigated** the globe.

King Henry VII of England sent explorer John Cabot to search for another route to Asia. Cabot traveled west through the northern Atlantic. When they discovered land, Cabot thought he had reached Asia. In fact, he had probably reached Canada's present-day Newfoundland.

3. What lands did explorers discover while trying to reach Asia?

_____

_____

The Outcomes of Exploration
(pages 310–311)

How did Europeans affect the new lands they discovered and explored?

Most European explorers did not reach Asia, but they took advantage of what they found. European countries established colonies along the coasts of Africa and North and South America. The practice of **imperialism** involved controlling the economy and government of these conquered lands.

The arrival of the Europeans had many effects on *indigenous* peoples. European missionaries worked hard to convert them to Christianity. Unfortunately, the missionaries also spread diseases such as measles, smallpox, and malaria. Tens of thousands of indigenous people died.

Exploration caused the slave trade to expand. The Portuguese bought West Coast Africans to work as slaves in Portugal. In Mexico and other colonies in South America, conquered peoples were forced to work the land.

4. How were people in Africa and the Americas affected by European exploration?

_____

_____

The Age of Revolution

BEFORE YOU READ

In the last section, you learned about European trade, exploration, and colonization.

In this section, you will read about the Scientific and Industrial Revolutions and the French Revolution.

AS YOU READ

Copy this chart to take notes about the Scientific and Industrial Revolutions and the French Revolution.

Influences	New Ideas	People/ Achievements	Events/ Effects
Scientific and Industrial Revolution			
Political Revolution			

TERMS & NAMES

Scientific Revolution a period of great scientific change and discovery during the 15th through 17th centuries

Industrial Revolution a period of change in the 18th century during which goods began to be manufactured by industry and machines

labor force a pool of available workers

capitalism an economic system in which the factories and businesses that make and sell goods are privately owned, and the owners make the decisions about what goods to produce

French Revolution a revolution that began on July 14, 1789, and that led to France becoming a republic

Reign of Terror the period between 1793 and 1794 during which France's new leaders executed thousands of its citizens

Napoleon Bonaparte a French general who took control of France in 1799, thus ending the French Revolution

Changes in Science and Industry

(pages 313–314)

What scientific discoveries and inventions influenced the growth of modern societies?

In the 1600s, scientists and inventors began to make many new discoveries. The scientist Galileo Galilei explored the stars and planets with a telescope, and Antoni van Leeuwenhoek used a microscope to explore the invisible world. A system for naming and classifying all living things on Earth was developed.

Modern societies grew from the **Scientific Revolution.** For example, new inventions changed how Europeans worked. Machines now did much of the work that had been done by humans and animals. Eventually, these inventions changed how goods were produced. The **Industrial Revolution** had begun.

Early factories were built outside the cities. Since the factories were powered by water, they needed to be near streams and rivers. Steam engines began to be used to power machinery in the late 1700s. More factories could now be built in cities. People began moving to the cities from the countryside to find work.

1. How was life changed by the discoveries and inventions of the 17th and 18th centuries?

_____

_____

The Workshop of the World
(pages 314–315)

Who were the employees of the "Workshop of the World"?

In the late 1700s, English factories made *textiles,* or cloth. Steam-powered machines made it possible to produce large amounts of goods quickly and cheaply. During the Industrial Revolution, so many factories were built in English cities that England was called "The Workshop of the World." Workers could earn more money in the cities than on farms, but life was hard. Long hours and low pay were common. In 1838, three fourths of the **labor force** was made up of women and children.

England's early textile industry was part of the development of **capitalism.** In this system, factories and other businesses that make and sell goods are not owned or controlled by the government. Instead, private business owners decide what goods to produce. They sell these goods at a price that will earn a profit.

Industrialization spread to other countries in Europe and to the United States. Cities in these countries grew rapidly. Deadly diseases spread, and air and water pollution became extensive.

2. How did the changes that took place in the Industrial Revolution affect the lives of workers?

_____

_____

_____

The French Revolution (pages 316–317)

What were the main causes of the French Revolution?

New ideas about government followed changes in science and industry. By the late 18th century, more citizens began fighting for political rights.

The French economy was in terrible shape. Hunger and high taxes made life miserable for common working people. Meanwhile, the French king, Louis XVI, and his queen, Marie Antoinette, continued to live a life of luxury.

The **French Revolution** began on July 14, 1789, when mobs attacked a Paris prison called the Bastille. Revolts spread from Paris to the countryside. By 1791, France had a new constitution that made all French citizens equal under the law. France finally became a republic in 1792.

King Louis XVI and Marie Antoinette were sentenced to death in 1793. But there was no peace in France. During the next two years, called the **Reign of Terror,** the new revolutionary leaders executed 17,000 citizens.

General **Napoleon Bonaparte** took control of France in 1799, ending the French Revolution. Ideas about equality and feelings of *nationalism* spread throughout Europe. Citizens of other European nations began to fight for more political rights and political power.

3. How did the French Revolution and the reign of Napoleon influence other European countries?

_____

_____

The Russian Empire

BEFORE YOU READ

In the last section, you read about the Scientific and Industrial Revolutions and the French Revolution.

In this section, you will learn about the Russian Empire from the early days of Ivan the Terrible to the Russian Revolution.

AS YOU READ

Copy this chart to take notes about the Russian Empire.

Influences	New Ideas	People/ Achievements	Events/ Effects
The Russian Empire			

TERMS & NAMES

czar in Russia, the title for emperor

Ivan the Terrible the first czar of Russia, crowned in 1547, whose rule of 37 years was marked by constant war

Peter the Great ruler of Russia from 1682 to 1725, who brought many improvements from Europe

Catherine the Great ruler of Russia from 1762 to 1796, who made Russia one of Europe's most powerful nations

Russian Revolution the 1917 revolution that removed the Russian monarchy from power after it had ruled for 400 years

Russia Rules Itself (pages 318–319)
Who were the early rulers of Russia?

Russia's huge landmass is located in both Europe and Asia. It is the world's largest nation. The continents of Europe and Asia have helped shape Russia's history.

Russia was conquered in the 13th century by Mongols from eastern Asia. The Mongols ruled for about 200 years until Russia broke free. The western city of Moscow was the most important urban center in Russia at this time.

Ivan IV, nicknamed **Ivan the Terrible,** was Russia's first **czar,** or emperor. He was crowned in 1547 at the age of 16. He had a reputation for cruelty, especially toward Russia's enemies. Russia was constantly at war during the 37 years of his rule.

Beginning with the reign of Ivan the Terrible, Russia had an *unlimited government.* The czars were often in conflict with the Russian nobles, whom they viewed as a threat to their control. Many Russian nobles and church leaders who opposed Ivan the Terrible were killed.

Russia's peasants also suffered under the first czars. They were forced to become *serfs* and could not leave the farms where they worked.

1. What was Russia like when it was ruled by Ivan the Terrible?

_____

_____

The Expansion of Russia
(pages 319–320)
How did Peter the Great and Catherine the Great change Russia?

Russia expanded greatly during the 17th and 18th century, under the rule of Peter the Great and Catherine the Great. These rulers gained new territory by conquering neighboring peoples.

Peter the Great ruled Russia from 1682 to 1725. He built a new capital on the Baltic Sea on land he had won from a war with Sweden. He called the city St. Petersburg. He thought of this new capital as Russia's "window on the west."

Peter wanted to have closer ties with Western Europe. He was interested in the Scientific Revolution and wanted to modernize and strengthen Russia by using its ideas and inventions. Peter made several reforms of the army and the government. He built new schools. He required Russians to adopt European styles of dress. These reforms helped Russia, but life for the Russian peasants remained unchanged.

Catherine the Great ruled from 1762 until 1796. Under her rule, the present-day countries of Ukraine and Belarus were added to Russia's empire. Like Peter the Great, Catherine was also interested in the culture of Western Europe. She built new schools and new towns. She expanded trade and encouraged art, science, and literature.

Russia became a powerful nation during Catherine's reign. The peasants, however, continued in their misery. When they rebelled in the 1770s, Catherine crushed their revolt.

2. What two things did Peter the Great and Catherine the Great have in common?

A Divided Russia (pages 320–321)
What caused conflict within 19th century Russia?

Russia entered the 19th century as a divided nation. The many peasants were poor, and the few nobles were wealthy. Conflict and political revolution would eventually arise from this division.

Western Europe was a strong influence in Russia. Many Russian nobles spoke French at home, and they sent their children to schools in Germany and France. Russians were exposed to the idea that a nation's government should reflect the wishes of its citizens.

Most Russian nobles supported the czar and were army officers or government officials. In 1825, however, one group of nobles tried to gain more power and replace the government. Their attempt failed.

The Russian serfs were still very poor, without land or money of their own. In 1861, Czar Alexander II decided to free the serfs. He hoped

that this would help his country compete with Western Europe. The serfs were heavily taxed, however. Often, the land they were given was not good for farming.

Other Russians, including university students, artists, and writers, were unhappy as well. They protested the government's treatment of the serfs. Some tried to overthrow the government. Also, workers in the cities complained about low pay and poor working conditions. In 1905, government troops shot a group of workers who had marched to the royal palace in St. Petersburg with a list of demands. As news of "Bloody Sunday" spread, Russians became even angrier with the government and czar.

3. What did Russia's serfs and workers in the cities have in common?

The End of the Russian Empire
(page 322)
What caused the end of czarist Russia?

Nicholas II was the czar of Russia when World War I began in 1914. Nicholas did not want war, but he could not keep his country out of the battle. Russia fought with the United Kingdom and France against Germany and its allies. It suffered terrible losses.

The **Russian Revolution** began when food shortages in the cities led to strikes by workers. Revolutionaries organized the workers. The Russian army revolted as well, and Nicholas was forced from power in 1917.

The revolutionaries held Nicholas II and his family (the Romanovs) in prison. The Romanovs had ruled for more than 300 years, and czars had ruled Russia for nearly 400 years. When, on July 17, 1918, the Romanovs were all shot to death, czarist Russia was no more.

4. How did the Russian Revolution begin?

Glossary/After You Read

city-states independent cities

expeditions journeys with a special purpose

excommunicated removal from church membership

indulgences forgiveness of sins, sold by the church

indigenous native to a place or region

nationalism loyalty to a particular country

patrons people who support or protect someone else

serfs peasants under the control of a rich landowner

textiles cloth products

unlimited government a government whose power rests in one ruler

TERMS & NAMES

A. In each blank, write the place or term that best completes the meaning of the paragraph.

Renaissance	Reformation	William Shakespeare
Florence	Martin Luther	

The period from the 14th to the 16th centuries was a prosperous, culturally alive time in Europe. Many famous examples of the **(1)** _____ period are found in **(2)** _____. In London, **(3)** _____ was writing plays, which are still famous today. The **(4)** _____, begun by **(5)** _____'s actions, was responsible for many changes in the Roman Catholic Church.

B. Write the letter of the name or term next to the description that explains it best.

a. imperialism   **d.** Crusades

b. capitalism   **e.** Protestants

c. czar

_____ **1.** system where businesses decide what to make, and to sell it at a profit

_____ **2.** the Russian word for emperor

_____ **3.** one nation extending its power or influence over another

_____ **4.** people who followed Martin Luther in disagreeing with the church

_____ **5.** Christian military expeditions in the 11th, 12th, and 13th centuries

MAIN IDEAS

1. Who are three important figures of the European Renaissance
and Reformation?

_____

_____

2. In the 15th century, European explorers tried to find a new route to Asia
in order to get what kinds of products?

_____

_____

3. What negative effects did the arrival of Europeans have on the
indigenous people?

_____

_____

_____

4. How did the Industrial Revolution change the ways in which products
were manufactured?

_____

_____

_____

5. What attitude toward the West did Peter the Great and Catherine the
Great share?

_____

_____

THINKING CRITICALLY

Answer the following questions on a separate sheet of paper.

1. Christopher Columbus set out to discover a better route to India, and he
failed. In what sense, however, could his voyages be considered successful?

2. It is clear that the Scientific Revolution and the Industrial Revolution caused
major changes in Europe. Many would argue that some of these changes
were for the better. In what ways might these changes have not been for
the better?

European Empires

BEFORE YOU READ

In the last chapter, you read about the history of Europe from the Crusades through the Russian Revolution.

In this section, you will learn about the growth of nationalism before World War I.

AS YOU READ

Copy this chart to take notes about Europe before World War I.

Term	Definition
constitutional monarchy	
colonial empires	
dual monarchy	

TERMS & NAMES

nationalism strong pride in one's nation or ethnic group

colonialism a system by which a country maintains colonies elsewhere

Austria-Hungary the largest empire in Eastern Europe in 1900

dual monarchy a form of government in which one ruler governs two nations

The Spread of Nationalism
(pages 329–332)

What caused the growth of nationalism in Europe?

During the late nineteenth century and early twentieth century, new ideas were sweeping across Europe. **Nationalism,** or strong pride in one's nation or *ethnic group,* was one of these ideas. An ethnic group includes people with similar languages and traditions, who are not necessarily ruled by a common government.

In part, the spread of nationalism was fueled by the fact that more Europeans than ever before could vote. Monarchs held unlimited power for centuries. In country after country, more and more Europeans demanded the right to vote for their lawmakers, who would represent them and limit the monarch's power. This kind of government is called a *constitutional monarchy.* A constitutional monarchy not only has a king or queen, but also a ruling body of elected officials. One example of a constitutional monarchy is the United Kingdom, which has a ruling body of elected officials as well as a monarch.

Many Western European countries had become constitutional monarchies by the end of the nineteenth century. Citizens who had elected their own lawmakers identified with and supported their countries. They were willing to go to any lengths, including fighting a war, to defend their countries.

At the beginning of the twentieth century, many Western European countries had *colonies* in Asia and Africa. These countries included France, Italy, the United Kingdom, Germany, and Belgium. Colonies supplied *raw materials* that the ruling countries needed to produce goods in their factories back home. Goods manufactured in Europe were then sold to people in the colonies.

During this period of **colonialism,** Western European nations spent much of their wealth on building strong armies and navies. Although this was expensive, it was necessary for them to protect their interests. Military forces helped defend their borders at home as well as colonies in other parts of the world. Ruling countries sometimes fought one another for control of the colonies. They also struggled to extend their territories.

Most nations of Western and Northern Europe had become *industrialized* by the late 1800s. In contrast, the majority of Eastern European countries, including Russia, remained agricultural. These countries *imported* most of their manufactured goods from Western and Northern Europe.

At this time, the largest empire in Eastern Europe was **Austria-Hungary.** The empire was a **dual monarchy,** in which one ruler governs two nations. Austria-Hungary also included parts of many other present-day countries, including Romania, the Czech Republic, and portions of Poland.

1. What were the three main developments in Western and Northern Europe during the nineteenth century?

_____

_____

Europe at War

BEFORE YOU READ

In the last section, you read about the growth of nationalism before World War I.

In this section, you will learn about World War I and World War II.

AS YOU READ

Copy this chart to take notes about World War I and World War II.

Causes	Event	Effects
	World War I	
	World War II	

TERMS & NAMES

World War I a war from 1914 to 1918 between the Allies (Russia, France, the United Kingdom, Italy, and the United States) and the Central Powers (Austria-Hungary, Germany, Turkey, and Bulgaria)

alliance an agreement among people or nations to unite for a common cause and help one another if one is attacked

Adolf Hitler leader of the German Nazi Party, elected in 1933

fascism a philosophy that supports a strong, central government controlled by the military and led by a powerful dictator

Holocaust the organized killing of European Jews and others by the Nazis during World War II

World War II a war from 1939 to 1945 between the Axis powers (Germany, Italy, and Japan) and the Allies (the United Kingdom, France, the Soviet Union, and the United States)

NATO North American Treaty Organization, a defense alliance signed in 1949 to join the countries of Western Europe, Canada, and the United States under the agreement that they would defend one another if attacked

The World at War/Europe After World War I (pages 333–336)

Which countries fought each other during World War I?

The emperor of Austria-Hungary declared war on Serbia in 1914 after the murder of Archduke Franz Ferdinand. Russia responded by sending troops to defend Serbia. Germany then declared war on Russia. **World War I** had begun.

European rulers worried about other countries declaring war on them. For self-defense, several countries joined alliances.

An **alliance** unites people or nations in a common cause.

France joined forces with Russia when Germany entered the war to support Austria-Hungary. Germany then invaded *neutral* Belgium in order to attack France. Since Great Britain had promised to protect Belgium, it also declared war on Germany. The United States joined the side of Russia, France, and Great Britain after German submarines sank four American merchant ships. Italy joined the Allies after the war began, although it had originally

Copyright © McDougal Littell Inc.

supported Germany and Austria-Hungary. Russia dropped out of the war completely in 1917 after the Russian Revolution.

The Allies won World War I, but Europe was devastated. Nearly 22 million civilians and soldiers on both sides had been killed.

More people died in World War I than in all the wars of the nineteenth century combined. The suffering did not end when the war was over. People in many countries on both sides were poor, homeless, and without work.

The Allies blamed Germany for the devastation of the war. The Treaty of Versailles, which Germany and the Allies signed in 1919, forced Germany to give up valuable territory. The treaty also required Germany to pay for the damage done to the Allied countries.

The political boundaries of many European countries were altered by additional treaties. Austria-Hungary became two separate countries.

1. What happened to Germany and Austria-Hungary after the war?

_____

_____

World War II/Europe After World War II (pages 336–338)

How did World War II begin?

By the 1930s, the German economy was in ruins. The Germans wanted to rebuild their own country, but they were still paying for the damage done to the Allied countries during World War I. **Adolf Hitler** and the National Socialist, or Nazi, Party came to power in 1933. Supporters of Hitler and the Nazis believed that they would help Germany recover.

Members of the Nazi Party believed in **fascism.** This philosophy supports a government that is both strong and centralized. The government is controlled by the military and led by a *dictator.*

These fascists were extremely patriotic and nationalistic. They also had racist beliefs. The Jewish citizens of Germany and other groups were unjustly blamed for Germany's problems. The Nazis seized Jewish property. Then they began sending the Jews, disabled people, and others, to concentration camps. During this **Holocaust,** millions of people were killed. Others died from starvation or disease.

Hitler took command of the armed forces in 1934. **World War II** began in 1939, when Hitler's army invaded Poland. By June 1940, the Germans had conquered Belgium, the Netherlands, Luxembourg, France, Denmark, and Norway. The Soviet Union was invaded a year later.

The United States tried to stay uninvolved. It had no choice but to enter the war, however, after Japan bombed U.S. military bases at Pearl Harbor in Hawaii, on December 7, 1941.

Europe was a battleground during World War II. By the end of the war, Western Europe was occupied by the United States, France, and the United Kingdom. Eastern Europe, including the eastern part of Germany, was occupied by the Soviet Union.

The Allies helped to establish free governments in Western Europe. In 1949, the countries of Western Europe joined Canada and the United States to form **NATO,** or the North Atlantic Treaty Organization. The members of this alliance agreed to defend one another if they were attacked. Because of political differences, the Soviet Union became separated from Western Europe and the United States.

The Marshall Plan was also known as the Economic Cooperation Act. It was created in 1948 by the United States Secretary of State, George C. Marshall. The plan offered assistance from the United States to the countries of Western Europe. The Marshall Plan helped Europe recover from the war's devastation. It may also have kept economies and governments from weakening or collapsing.

2. What alliances and plans were formed after the war?

_____

_____

The Soviet Union

BEFORE YOU READ

In the last section, you read about some causes and effects of World War I and World War II.

In this section, you will learn about the growth of the Soviet Union.

AS YOU READ

Copy this chart to take notes about the Soviet Union.

Causes	Event	Effects
	Growth of Soviet Union	

TERMS & NAMES

Iron Curtain an invisible barrier between the people of Eastern and Western Europe after World War II that reflected their being restricted from traveling outside their respective countries

puppet government a government that is controlled by an outside force

one-party system a system in which there is only one political party to choose from when voting and only one candidate to choose from for each government position

Joseph Stalin ruler of the Soviet Union from 1928 to 1953

collective farm a government-owned farm that employs large numbers of workers

Warsaw Pact a treaty signed in 1955 that established an alliance among the Soviet Union, Albania, Bulgaria, Czechoslovakia, East Germany, Hungary, Poland, and Romania

Cold War after World War II, a period of political non-cooperation between the members of NATO and the Warsaw Pact nations, during which these countries refused to trade or cooperate with each other

East Against West (pages 342–343)

How did the Soviet Union become the strongest nation in Europe?

The countries of Western Europe were separated from the Soviet-controlled countries of Eastern Europe after World War II. An invisible wall known as the **Iron Curtain** was erected. This meant that people could no longer pass freely from the West to the East.

The Union of Soviet Socialist Republics, or USSR, included 15 republics. Russia was the largest republic. When Germany invaded

in 1941, the Soviet Union entered World War II. The Soviet Union nearly collapsed after the invasion. The Germans destroyed much of the western Soviet Union. Millions of people were killed. After the defeat of Germany in the war, however, the Soviet Union became the most powerful nation in Europe.

The Soviet Union established Communist governments in Eastern Europe after World War II. Force or politics were sometimes used to keep the governments in line.

The Soviet Union used puppet governments to control the countries of Eastern Europe. Members of a **puppet government** do what they are told by an outside force. In this case, that outside force was the Soviet leadership in Moscow.

Most Eastern Europeans could vote, but elections gave them no choices. The only party to choose from was the Communist Party, since all other parties were outlawed. Only one candidate was on the *ballot* for each government position. Soviet citizens could not complain about this **one-party system.** They could be thrown in jail for expressing their opinions.

1. What was the relationship between the Soviet Union and Eastern European countries after World War II?

_____

_____

Joseph Stalin (pages 344–346)
What methods did Joseph Stalin use to rule the Soviet Union?

Joseph Stalin came to power after the death of Vladimir Lenin, a Communist leader who had helped overthrow the czar in 1917. Stalin ruled the Soviet Union during World War II. He continued to control the government until his death in 1953.

The government controlled every aspect of Soviet life. Stalin hoped to make the country stronger. He created *five-year plans,* which were sets of economic goals. For example, many new factories were built upon Stalin's orders. The Soviet government made all the decisions about these factories.

Stalin believed that agriculture could be used to strengthen the Soviet Union. Therefore, in the 1930s, peasants were forced to move to collective farms. A **collective farm** was owned by the government, which distributed all the crops the farms produced. Sometimes there was not enough food left over to feed the large numbers of workers who lived on the farms.

Russians who did not support the government were arrested by the secret police. The

police also arrested citizens whom Stalin did not trust. Millions of these prisoners were sent to Siberia to live and work in slave-labor camps. Siberia, in northeastern Russia, is remote and bitterly cold. Many prisoners died there.

2. What was life like for most Russians during Stalin's rule?

_____

_____

The Cold War (pages 346–347)
What were the causes of the Cold War?

The United Kingdom, the United States, and the Soviet Union were allies against the Axis powers during World War II. After the war there was little reason for these countries to remain allies. They no longer had a common enemy.

The governments of most Western European countries were either constitutional monarchies or democracies. The governments of Eastern Europe were Communist and largely Soviet-controlled.

For many years after World War II, the members of NATO and the nations in the **Warsaw Pact**—the Eastern European alliance—refused to trade or cooperate with each other. This period is called the **Cold War.** The war stayed "cold" because neither side wanted to start an actual war. Such a war might involve the use of nuclear weapons. These weapons could cause massive destruction to the planet.

The United States and Western Europe worried about Soviet influence in other countries. At the same time, the Soviet Union wanted to protect itself against invasion. Countries on opposite sides of the Iron Curtain were suspicious of each other. For almost 40 years, the tension caused by the Cold War would continue.

3. What did both sides in the Cold War want?

_____

_____

CAPÍTULO 12

Glossary/After You Read

ethnic group people with similar languages and traditions

constitutional monarchy a form of government with elected officials and a king or queen with limited powers

colonies territories or countries settled by people from another country; often a source of labor and raw materials

raw materials products such as minerals and timber, before they are used in manufacturing

industrialized having factories and other advanced ways of making products and energy

imported brought in from an outside place

neutral not supporting either side in a dispute or war

dictator a ruler that has total power

ballot a piece of paper or a card used in marking a vote

five-year plans sets of economic goals meant to be accomplished within five years

TERMS & NAMES

A. Fill in the blanks with the letter of the term that best completes the sentence.

    a. alliance   **c.** one-party system   **e.** colonialism

    b. fascism   **d.** Cold War

1. During World War I, Russia, France, the United Kingdom, Italy, and the United States formed an _____ against Austria-Hungary, Germany, Turkey, and Bulgaria.

2. Although the _____ was a period of hostility between NATO and the Warsaw Pact countries, it did not actually involve fighting.

3. The period of widespread _____ was a time when some countries expanded their territory.

4. _____ is a philosophy of government based on military control and a powerful dictator.

5. Elections held by a government with a _____ do not offer choices to voters.

B. Write the letter of the name or term next to the description that explains it best.

    a. nationalism   **c.** Holocaust   **e.** puppet government

    b. dual monarchy   **d.** Iron Curtain

_____ **1.** leaders who are controlled from outside the country

_____ **2.** strong pride in one's nation or ethnic group

_____ **3.** the organized murder of a large number of civilians during World War II

_____ **4.** an imaginary line dividing Eastern Europe and Western Europe after World War II

_____ **5.** when one ruler governs two nations

MAIN IDEAS

1. What advantages did a country with colonies have?

_____

_____

2. In times of war, why is it an advantage for a country to be part of an alliance?

_____

_____

3. What kind of government did the Soviet Union support in Eastern Europe after World War II?

_____

_____

4. With the spread of colonialism, European governments felt they needed to strengthen their armies and navies. Why?

_____

_____

5. In gaining power in Germany prior to World War II, Adolph Hitler took advantage of which one of the results of World War I?

_____

_____

THINKING CRITICALLY

Answer the following on a separate sheet of paper.

1. Nuclear weapons were first used at the end of World War II. Do you think the existence of nuclear weapons today makes the world safer or more dangerous?

2. How did the ideas of nationalism shape the world in the 20th century?

Eastern Europe Under Communism

BEFORE YOU READ

In the last section, you read about war and change in Western Europe, from World War I through the Cold War.

In this section, you will learn about Eastern Europe, Russia, and the European Union.

AS YOU READ

Copy this chart to take notes about Eastern Europe under Communism.

Aspect	Under Communism
Government	
Economy	
Culture	

TERMS & NAMES

propaganda material designed to spread certain beliefs

private property rights the right of individuals to own land or industry

Nikita Khrushchev ruler of the Soviet Union from 1958 until 1964

deposed removed from power

détente lessening of tension

Soviet Culture (pages 353–355)

How did the Soviet Union treat its various ethnic groups?

The Soviet Union received international attention for its space program during the 1950s and 1960s. However, most of the people of the Soviet Union and the Eastern European countries it controlled had no say in their government. They were very poor, and daily life was difficult.

To keep some ethnic groups from breaking away from the Soviet Union, Soviet leaders tried to create a strong *national identity*. For example, they did not want people in the republic of Latvia to think of themselves as Latvians. They wanted the Latvians to think of themselves as Soviets.

The government created and distributed **propaganda,** material designed to spread certain beliefs. This propaganda praised the Soviet Union, its leaders, and communism. It included pamphlets, posters, artwork, statues, songs, and films.

The Soviet government prohibited many cultural celebrations. It wanted the nation's many

ethnic groups to identify with the nation rather than with their individual cultures. Thousands of religious leaders were killed. Churches and religious buildings were destroyed. Members of some ethnic groups were not allowed to speak their native languages, and they could not celebrate certain holidays.

Most Soviets knew little about what was happening around the world. The government controlled newspapers, books, and radio, along with other *communications media*.

During the Soviet era, the works of many writers, poets, and other artists were often banned or *censored*. These artists were forced to join unions run by the government. They could not choose their own subjects for their art. Those who disobeyed were punished, imprisoned, or killed.

The Soviet Union wanted more status in the world. To achieve this goal, it decided to become a strong competitor in the Olympics and in other international sports competitions. The government supported the nation's top athletes. All their basic needs were provided for. The Soviet government paid for their training. It even hired and paid for the coaches. The Soviet Union's hockey teams and gymnasts became some of the world's best.

1. How did the Soviet Union try to create a strong national identity?

_____

_____

The Soviet Economy (pages 355–356)

Who controlled the Soviet economy after World War II?

Soviet leaders ran the economies as well as the governments of the Soviet Union and the Eastern European countries. The Soviets had promised the Eastern Europeans that communism would improve industry and give all citizens enough to meet their needs. This promise was broken.

The Communist Soviet Union did not support **private property rights**, or the right of individuals to own land or an industry. The Soviet leaders wanted the government to own all major industries. So the government took over factories, railroads, and businesses.

The government made all decisions about production. It decided what would be produced and how it would be produced and distributed. These choices were not based on the needs or interests of the republics or of individuals. As a result, people in Eastern Europe often did not have enough bread, meat, and clothing.

2. How successful was the Soviet economy in meeting the needs of its people?

_____

_____

Attempts at Change (pages 356–358)

How did the Soviet Union begin to change in the 1950s?

Eastern Europeans finally began making their own demands. They demanded more goods of better quality. They also wanted their governments to change. In 1956, Hungary and

Poland made unsuccessful attempts at independence. The Communist army put down these rebellions.

Nikita Khrushchev ruled the Soviet Union from 1958 until 1964. This period is called "The Thaw," because citizens and artists began to have more freedoms. Khruschev visited the United States. The thaw was short-lived. The Soviet economy was growing weaker. In 1964, Khrushchev was **deposed,** or removed from power.

Alexander Dubček became the First Secretary of the Czechoslovak Communist Party in January 1968. He wanted the Soviet Union to have less control over Czechoslovakia. Briefly, there was a period of improvement called the *"Prague Spring."* Czech citizens had more contact with Western Europe and had other freedoms as well. In August, however, Soviet troops forced Czechoslovakians under strict Communist control.

NATO's member nations wanted to avoid war with the Soviet Union. As a result, they could not stop the Soviet control of Eastern Europe. In the 1970s, however, a period of **détente,** or lessening tension, began. Leaders of the Soviet Union and the United States began to have more contact with each other. There was more contact between the members of NATO and the Warsaw Pact nations.

Economic conditions in the Soviet Union and Eastern Europe continued to grow worse. The Soviet government spent most of its money on its armed forces and nuclear weapons. People who lived in the non-Russian republics of the Soviet Union began to resist the government. They wanted more control over their lives. Many citizens began to reject communism. The Soviet leaders still refused to give up any of their power or control.

3. What did those who rebelled against the Soviet Union demand?

_____

_____

Eastern Europe and Russia

BEFORE YOU READ

In the last section, you read about Eastern Europe under Communism.

In this section, you will learn about Eastern Europe and Russia after the breakup of the Soviet Union.

AS YOU READ

Copy this chart to take notes about Eastern Europe and Russia after the breakup of the Soviet Union.

Aspect	After Communism
Government	
Economy	
Culture	

TERMS & NAMES

Mikhail Gorbachev leader of the Soviet Union who, in 1985, began reducing Cold War tensions with the United States

parliamentary republic a republic whose head of state, usually a prime minister, is the leader of the political party that has the most members in parliament

coalition government a government formed by small political parties joining together

ethnic cleansing the organized killing of members of minority ethnic groups

Duma one of the two houses of the Russian legislature

The Breakup of the Soviet Union/Modern Eastern Europe

(pages 360–364)

What happened when the Soviet Union broke up?

Mikhail Gorbachev made reforms in Russia, but problems remained. The economy got worse. Communists were unhappy when Gorbachev relaxed control in Eastern Europe. A group of traditional leaders tried to overthrow the Soviet government in 1991. This *coup d'état* failed. Then the Soviet republics began to declare their independence. By the end of 1991, the nation had become 15 different nations. The Soviet Union no longer existed.

The Soviet republics established their own non-Communist governments. Many Eastern European countries wrote or revised their *constitutions.* They held democratic elections.

Former Communists could not take important government posts in some countries. In other countries, they created new political parties and won elections. Many ethnic groups tried to create new states, or re-establish old ones, within a nation.

Most Eastern European countries today are parliamentary republics. A **parliamentary republic** is led by the head of the political party with the most members in parliament. A prime minister usually leads the government.

Coalition governments have been created in some countries. These are formed when small political parties work together.

Life was very hard under Soviet rule. Freedoms were restricted. The economies of Eastern Europe were not prosperous. Today, Eastern Europeans have gained their freedom. However, they still face problems such as inflation and unemployment.

The countries of Eastern Europe are shifting from *command economies* to *free-market economies,* some more quickly than others.

The economies of several former Soviet republics are in bad shape. Violence and civil war have broken out. Pollution has caused serious health problems. Yet, some republics are making progress, including Ukraine, Latvia, Lithuania, and Estonia.

Eastern European nations no longer needed the Soviet government to defend them. Many wanted to become members of NATO to receive protection from invasion. In 1999, Poland, Hungary, and the Czech Republic joined NATO. Other countries, including the *Baltic States* of Estonia, Latvia, and Lithuania, were also working to become NATO members.

1. What are the post-Communist economies of the former Soviet republics and Eastern Europe like?

_____

_____

War in the Balkan Peninsula
(pages 363–364)

What was the basic cause of conflict in the Balkan Peninsula after Tito's death in 1980?

Turmoil and struggle have been constant in Eastern Europe since the late 1980s, especially in Yugoslavia. The dictator Marshal Tito governed Yugoslavia after World War II until his death in 1980. Then, after years of turmoil, Slobodan Milosevic became Yugoslavia's president in 1997.

Milosevic was a Serb, and he wanted the Serbs to rule Yugoslavia. The Serbs began fighting the Croats and Muslims living in Bosnia. They murdered many Muslims. The Serbs called these killings of members of minority ethnic groups **ethnic cleansing.** The war finally ended when NATO launched an air war against Yugoslavia.

The Serbs, Croats, and Muslims of Bosnia signed a peace treaty in 1995. Then, in 1999, Milosevic began to use ethnic cleansing against the Albanians in Kosovo, a region of Serbia. Milosevic was removed from power in 2000. He was tried for war crimes by the United Nations.

2. How did Milosevic practice ethnic cleansing in Bosnia and Kosovo?

_____

_____

Modern Russia (pages 364–366)
How has life improved for the Russians since the breakup of the Soviet Union?

Since the breakup of the Soviet Union, life in Russia is better. Russia still faces serious problems, however. Dishonest leaders and an economic system that is being reformed too slowly make some unhappy. Many Russians are still poor. The crime rate is growing. A war in the region of Chechnya has caused much suffering.

Most Russians are now free to follow their cultural practices. They can practice the religion of their choice. They can buy and read books once banned. Writers and other artists have more freedom of expression. New magazines, newspapers, and history books are telling more of the truth about the Soviet Union.

Russia's government is democratic. The people elect the president. They also elect members of the **Duma,** which is part of the legislature. Democracy is still new to the Russian people.

Russia has many natural resources. It produces much of the world's oil. It has the world's largest forests. Some factories produce steel. Other factories make tractors and other machines. Russia has a large fishing industry.

Russia has been moving toward a free-market economy. Citizens can own land. Foreign companies are encouraged to do business in Russia. These changes have created both opportunities and difficulties. For example, the government no longer controls prices, and companies can make a profit. However, people's wages have not risen as fast as prices.

Some Russians have done well in the new economy. Others with less education have not done as well. Most new businesses and jobs are in the cities, which means that people in rural areas have fewer opportunities.

3. What improvements have been occurring in Russia's economy?

_____

_____

The European Union

BEFORE YOU READ

In the last section, you read about Eastern Europe and Russia after communism.

In this section, you will learn about the European Union and the region's cultural diversity.

AS YOU READ

Copy this chart to take notes about Europe today.

Aspect	Europe Today
Government	
Economy	
Culture	

TERMS & NAMES

European Union an economic and political grouping of countries in Western Europe

currency a system of money

euro the currency of the European Union

tariff a duty or fee that must be paid on imported or exported goods

standard of living a measure of quality of life

Court of Justice the European Union court that protects the rights of all its citizens in whichever member country they live

Western Europe Today (pages 367–368)

What is the European Union?

Western Europe's national leaders and elected lawmakers share power. Citizens can vote. They can belong to one of several political parties.

Many countries of Western Europe belong to the **European Union** (EU). At first, these countries joined to encourage trade. Membership in the EU, however, has political advantages as well.

Many Eastern European countries want to join the European Union. They cannot join the EU automatically. Many must first make improvements to their legal and economic systems and to their environments. Eventually, these countries will belong to the EU. The EU could have more than 20 member nations by 2003. Peace and prosperity in Europe may depend on the European Union.

Each nation in Western Europe also has regional governments. These are similar to the individual states that make up the United States. These governments are growing more powerful. Western Europeans enjoy increased *self-rule* and are active participants in the political process.

1. **What are the advantages of membership in the European Union?**

_____

_____

EU Economies (pages 369–370)

How has the European Union helped its member nations?

Each European nation has had its own system of money, or **currency.** The EU intends to simplify international trade. Europeans using the **euro**, the European Union currency, will no longer have to exchange currency when payments cross borders within the region.

Tariffs on goods traded by member nations with each other no longer exist. A **tariff** is a duty or fee paid on exported goods. Border controls between EU member nations have also been lifted. Goods, services, and people now flow freely among these nations.

In the pursuit of economic equality, EU members are sharing their wealth with each other. For example, poorer countries such as Ireland receive help for their businesses.

A higher standard of living is an important goal of the EU. A person's **standard of living,** or quality of life, is based on the availability of goods and services. By increasing trade and sharing wealth, member nations hope that all citizens of the EU will have a high standard of living.

A high standard of living guarantees enough food and housing, good transportation and communications, and access to education and health care. There is also a high rate of *literacy.* This means that most adults can read.

The EU is helping the countries of Eastern Europe improve their environments. For example, the EU will pay up to 75 percent of the cost for a new waste treatment system in Romania. The system includes recycling centers for paper, glass, and plastics. Old dumping grounds leaking pollution will be cleaned up.

The EU also runs job-training programs. Citizens of member nations may work in any part of the EU. They can vote in local elections wherever they live. The EU's **Court of Justice** protects citizens' rights in all member countries.

2. What are three goals of the European Union?

_____

_____

Cultural Diversity (pages 370–371)

In what ways is Europe culturally diverse?

The European nations that belong to the EU still have their own cultures and traditions. Many of their traditions developed over hundreds of years. They may include different languages, foods, ways of doing business, special games, and celebrations.

Some nations blend several cultures. For example, Flemings live in the north of Belgium and speak Dutch. The Walloons, who speak French, live in southern Belgium. A third group of German-speaking Belgians lives in the eastern part of the country. Many Belgian cities include people from all three groups.

Western Europe contains some of the world's most fascinating cities. These include London, Madrid, Paris, Amsterdam, and Rome, which are major centers for the arts, business, and education. Europeans are working hard to preserve these beautiful old cities.

Urban areas offer many conveniences. Excellent public transportation includes subways, buses, and trains. People meet friends, eat, and relax at popular sidewalk cafés.

The European countryside is also popular. Tuscany in Italy and Provence in France are two of the best-known examples of the many beautiful rural areas.

The residents of some small European villages have been farming or raising animals on the same land for generations. They relax in the town square and in the village's cafés. Some live in houses that have been owned by their families for hundreds of years.

3. How do European cities differ from rural areas?

_____

_____

Glossary/After You Read

Baltic States the countries of Estonia, Latvia, and Lithuania

censored when ideas and information are limited by the government

command economies economies controlled by the government

communications media means of communication, such as radio, television, and newspapers

constitutions rules for a government, usually written

coup d'etat sudden overthrow of a government by a small group

free-market economies economies not controlled by the government

literacy the ability to read and write

Prague Spring a brief period of freedom in Czechoslovakia in 1968

self-rule when the people of an area have the right to govern themselves

PLACES & TERMS

A. If the statement is true, write "true" on the line. If it is false, change the underlined word or words to make it true.

1. <u>Propaganda</u> is information created by a government to spread beliefs. _____

2. <u>Gorbachev</u> began in 1985 to reduce tensions with the United States. _____

3. During a period of <u>détente</u>, tensions between countries are lessened. _____

4. A <u>coalition government</u> is a republic whose head of state, usually a prime minister, is the leader of the party with the most members in parliament.

_____

5. The <u>Duma</u> is part of the legislature of Russia. _____

6. A <u>tariff</u> is a measure of a country's quality of life. _____

7. The <u>euro</u> is used by many people in Western Europe.

_____

8. In 1964, Soviet leader <u>Krushchev</u> was deposed, or removed from power. _____

9. The <u>European Union</u> is an organization that protects the rights of all citizens in whichever member country they live. _____

10. <u>Ethnic cleansing</u> is the organized killing of minority groups by a government. _____

B. Write the letter of the name or term next to the description that explains it best.

_____ **1.** taxes paid on imported goods

_____ **2.** money of the European Union

_____ **3.** ability of citizens to own land and businesses

_____ **4.** medium of exchange

_____ **5.** for example, a newspaper that praises communism

a. propaganda

b. tariff

c. currency

d. euro

e. private property rights

MAIN IDEAS

1. What was life like in the Soviet Union for journalists, writers, and other artists?

_____

_____

2. Who was responsible for the period in Soviet history known as "The Thaw," and what did it consist of?

_____

_____

3. What happened to the governments of Eastern European countries when the Soviet Union let go of its control?

_____

_____

4. What kinds of changes have Eastern European countries been making in their economies?

_____

_____

5. What have many countries done in Western Europe to improve their economies and encourage trade?

_____

_____

THINKING CRITICALLY

Answer the following questions on a separate sheet of paper.

1. The European Union encourages the sharing of wealth, the development of business, and free trade among its members in order to raise everyone's standard of living. Why do you think these conditions go along with a high rate of literacy?

2. The relationship between the United States and Russia is better today than it was during the Cold War. Why?

Name _____ Date _____

CHAPTER 14

Section 1 (pages 379–383)

Reading Study Guide

The United Kingdom

BEFORE YOU READ

In the last chapter, you read about post-war Eastern Europe and the Soviet Union, as well as changes in Europe since the end of the Cold War.

In this section, you will learn about the United Kingdom.

AS YOU READ

Copy this chart to take notes about the United Kingdom today.

Country	Physical Geography	Government	Economy	Culture	Interesting Facts
United Kingdom					

TERMS & NAMES

London the capital city of England

secede to leave a political union, such as a nation

Good Friday Accord an agreement signed in 1998 by Ireland's Protestants and Catholics that established the Northern Ireland Assembly to represent voters from both groups

Charles Dickens a popular author of the nineteenth century

A Kingdom of Four Regions
(pages 379–381)

What are the four regions of the United Kingdom?

Although it is a small island nation, the United Kingdom has had a huge impact on the world. Its official name is the United Kingdom of Great Britain and Northern Ireland. **London** is the capital city.

The United Kingdom is made up of four regions: Scotland, England, Wales, and Northern Ireland. The British *monarchy* has ruled these regions for centuries.

The government is a constitutional monarchy. Today, the British king or queen is merely a symbol of power. **Parliament** is the national lawmaking body. It has the actual power of government.

The British Parliament is made up of the House of Lords and the House of Commons. The Lords are nobles and the Commons are elected representatives. The House of Commons is the more powerful of the two groups.

The *prime minister* is the head of government. His or her political party wins the most seats in the House of Commons. The role of the other political parties is to question government policies.

Some regions of the United Kingdom have been returned to self-rule. For example, Welsh voters created their own *assembly* in the 1990s. Also at this time, the Scots voted to create their own parliament. These lawmaking bodies met for the first time in 1999.

Northern Ireland has long been an area of conflict between Irish Catholic nationalists and Irish Protestants. During the 1960s, many Irish Catholics wanted Northern Ireland to **secede,** or withdraw from, the United Kingdom. They hoped to unite Northern Ireland with the Republic of Ireland. Irish Protestants supported the government of the United Kingdom.

The British government sent troops to stop riots that broke out in 1969. Violence continued for almost 30 years. Finally, in 1998, Catholic and Protestant representatives signed the **Good**

Copyright © McDougal Littell Inc.

Friday Accord. This agreement established the Northern Ireland Assembly, which represents both Catholic and Protestant voters. For this new government to succeed, the former enemies will need to work together.

1. How did the government of the United Kingdom change in the 1990s?

_____

_____

Cultural Heritage (pages 382–383)

How has the United Kingdom's culture affected the United States and Canada?

As an *imperial* power, the United Kingdom has been exporting its culture around the world for centuries. For example, the governments of India, the United States, and the former British colonies were modeled on Britain's parliamentary system. British culture has set trends in sports, music, and literature of various nations.

The former British colonies of Canada and the United States were influenced by British music. Americans know the tune "God Save the Queen" as "My Country, 'Tis of Thee." British groups, including the Beatles and the Rolling Stones, were popular throughout the world during the 1960s. British singers like Elton John, Sting, and Dido became popular in the years to come.

Aside from the English language, literature is the best-known cultural export of the United Kingdom. Mary Shelley and Sir Arthur Conan Doyle created Frankenstein's monster and Sherlock Holmes in the nineteenth century. **Charles Dickens,** who wrote *Oliver Twist* and *A Christmas Carol,* was another popular author.

British writers of the early twentieth century include Virginia Woolf and George Orwell. Some modern authors have written popular books for young people. These include C. S. Lewis's *The Chronicles of Narnia* and J. K. Rowling's Harry Potter books.

2. What kinds of culture has the United Kingdom exported?

_____

_____

The British Economy (page 383)

What goods are produced in the United Kingdom?

Trade and finance are central to the economy of the United Kingdom. Mining and manufacturing are also important activities. Factories turn out a variety of products. The nation has few natural resources, although there is enough coal, natural gas, and oil to fuel its factories.

Trade is a major industry. The United Kingdom needs to import raw materials used in manufacturing. It also has to import food, because the small nation's farms cannot feed such a large population.

3. What does the United Kingdom need to import?

_____

_____

Sweden

BEFORE YOU READ

In the last section, you read about the United Kingdom.

In this section, you will read about the government, economy, and culture of Sweden.

AS YOU READ

Copy this chart to take notes about Sweden today.

Country	Physical Geography	Government	Economy	Culture	Interesting Facts
Sweden					

TERMS & NAMES

Riksdag Sweden's parliament

ombudsmen Swedish officials who protect citizens' rights and ensure that the courts and civil service follow the law

armed neutrality a policy by which a country maintains military forces but does not take sides in the conflicts of other nations

hydroelectricity power generated by water

acid rain rain or snow that carries air pollutants back to Earth

skerries small islands

Sweden's Government (pages 384–385)

How does the government of Sweden work?

Sweden is one of Europe's most prosperous and beautiful countries. Located in Northern Europe, it shares the Scandinavian Peninsula with Norway. Sweden is a constitutional monarchy. The Swedish monarch has only ceremonial duties and cannot make laws. The people elect representatives to the Swedish parliament, or **Riksdag.**

The Riksdag's 349 members nominate Sweden's prime minister. The Riksdag also appoints **ombudsmen.** These officials protect citizens' rights. They make sure that the Swedish courts and civil service follow the law.

Voters decide how many mem-bers of each political party serve in the Riksdag. The Social Democratic Labour Party was in power for nearly 44 years before 1976. Today the government includes other parties as well.

Sweden's foreign policy is **armed neutrality.** This has been its policy since World War I. It has a military but does not fight for or against other nations. The country will not become involved in war unless it is directly attacked.

Sweden is a strong supporter of the United Nations.

1. What is the function of the Riksdag?

_____

_____

The Economy and the Environment (pages 385–386)

What makes Sweden's economy so strong?

Sweden's economy relies on privately owned businesses and international trade. It exports many goods, including metals, minerals, and wood. Automobiles, engineering, and communications are major industries.

More than 80 percent of the population live in the urban areas of southern Sweden. Most workers are highly educated and have a high standard of living.

Most of Sweden's electrical power comes from **hydroelectricity,** or power generated by water. Another source is nuclear power. Other sources of energy, including solar- and wind-powered energy, are being explored.

Sweden and its neighbors share environmental problems. One major problem is acid rain. **Acid rain** occurs when air pollutants come back to Earth in the form of rain or snow. These pollutants poison trees. Sweden and other countries are trying to control air pollutants produced by cars and factories.

2. What environmental issues concern Sweden today?

_____

_____

Daily Life and Culture (pages 386–387)
How do most Swedes live?

For the most part, Sweden is a *homogeneous* country. Ninety percent of the population are native Swedes and belong to the Lutheran Church. Most people speak Swedish.

Immigrants have brought some diversity to Sweden since World War II. Many have come from Turkey, Greece, and other countries, bringing their cultures with them. Today, immigrants make up about 10 percent of Sweden's population.

Among their many benefits, Swedish workers get long vacations. Winter and summer sports are popular. These include cross-country and downhill skiing, skating, hockey, and ice fishing.

Small islands, called **skerries,** are found along the Swedish coast. Many people visit these islands in the summer to hike, camp, and fish. Other popular activities are tennis, soccer, and outdoor performances such as concerts.

Sweden is well known for its contributions to drama, literature, and film. The plays of August Strindberg, Astrid Lindgren's children's books, and Ingmar Bergman's films are popular around the world.

3. What recreational activities do the Swedes enjoy?

_____

_____

France

BEFORE YOU READ

In the last section, you read about Sweden.

In this section, you will learn about the government, economy, and culture of France.

AS YOU READ

Copy this chart to take notes about France.

Country	Physical Geography	Government	Economy	Culture	Interesting Facts
France					

TERMS & NAMES

Charles de Gaulle a member of the French Resistance who became president of France in 1959

French Resistance an anti-German movement in France during World War II

Jean Monnet established the Planning Board in 1946

socialism an economic system in which some businesses and industries are owned collectively or by the government

European Community an association developed after World War II to promote unity among the countries of Western Europe

impressionism an art style that uses light to create an impression rather than a strictly realistic picture

The Fifth Republic (pages 390–391)

What were Charles de Gaulle's contributions to the history of France?

Charles de Gaulle was a general in the French army. He fled to Britain after Germany conquered France. In exile, de Gaulle was in contact with the French Resistance. The **French Resistance** helped the Allied forces. It established communications and spied on German activity. Sometimes it *assassinated* German officers.

In 1958, Charles de Gaulle was elected France's president. He instituted the Fifth Republic of France and reorganized the constitution.

France is a *parliamentary republic*. The president and the parliament share power. The president is elected to a seven-year term; in 2002, it becomes a five-year term. The president protects the constitution. He or she makes sure that other authorities function properly.

The Senate and the National Assembly make up parliament. A prime minister chosen by the president heads parliament. The internal workings of the government are the responsibility of the prime minister. The government is very active in France's economy.

1. What is the relationship between France's president and parliament?

_____

_____

A Centralized Economy

(pages 391–392)

What steps did France take to improve its economy after World War II?

France was poor when World War II ended. Much of the country needed to be rebuilt. **Jean Monnet**'s Planning Board started a series of five-year plans after the war. The board planned to modernize France. It set economic goals for the country.

A *mixed economy,* with both public and private sectors, was the result. Many industries were *nationalized,* or taken over by the French government. These included banks; insurance companies; the electric, coal, and steel industries; schools; universities; hospitals; railroads; airlines; and even an automobile company.

Nationalized industry was a form of **socialism**. A socialist government also provides benefits such as health care, housing, and unemployment insurance. Today, private companies are slowly taking more control of the economy in France.

After 1946, the French economy grew rapidly. In the 1970s, however, the French economy suffered when oil prices rose. The country turned to nuclear power in the 1980s. France wanted its economy to be less dependent on oil. Today nuclear power provides 75 percent of France's power, more than in any other country.

France is famous for its wines. The country also exports grains, automobiles, electrical machinery, and chemicals. It exports more agricultural products than any other nation in the European Community, though only 7 percent of the labor force works on farms.

The **European Community** was developed after World War II. Its members wanted the countries of Western Europe to help each other economically. Its success gave rise to more political and economic unity in the European Union.

2. How has France's government influenced its economy?

_____

_____

The Culture of Paris (pages 392–393)

Which artists and writers made Paris famous?

Paris is France's capital city. It is famous for its culture. Paris has inspired most European artists, whether they lived there or not.

Edouard Manet was an important painter who helped influence the impressionist art movement. **Impressionism** is an art style that uses light to create an impression of a scene rather than a strictly realistic picture. Manet inspired the artists Claude Monet, Pierre Renoir, and Paul Cézanne. All of them lived in Paris.

Two of the greatest collections of fine art in the world can be found in Paris's Orsay Museum and the Louvre. The School of Fine Arts has produced artists such as Pierre Bonnard and Balthus.

France has a rich tradition of literature as well. Marcel Proust, author of *Remembrance of Things Past,* was influential in the early twentieth century. Other significant French writers include Albert Camus and Simone de Beauvoir.

3. Who were the impressionist painters?

_____

_____

Germany

BEFORE YOU READ
In the last section, you read about France.
In this section, you will learn about the government, economy, and culture of Germany.

AS YOU READ
Copy this chart to take notes about Germany.

Country	Physical Geography	Government	Economy	Culture	Interesting Facts
Germany					

TERMS & NAMES

Berlin Wall a wire and concrete wall that divided Germany's East Berlin and West Berlin from 1961 to 1989

reunification the uniting again of parts

Ludwig van Beethoven one of Germany's best-known composers (1770–1827)

Rainer Maria Rilke a German writer (1875–1926)

A Divided Germany (pages 394–396)
Why was Germany divided at the end of World War II?

Today, Germany is one of the largest countries in Europe. The country was divided, however, when World War II ended in 1945. U.S. and British soldiers occupied West Germany. Soviet soldiers occupied the eastern part of the country.

West Germany, with the help of the United States, set up a democratic government. Germany was located between the Communist countries of Eastern Europe and the rest of Western Europe. This is one reason why the United States supported Germany.

West Germany also received U.S. loans. Within 20 years, it rebuilt its factories and became one of the world's richest nations. Its strong economy later became the driving force behind the European Union.

East Germany remained poor. Most East Germans knew that people in West Germany and Western Europe had better lives. The Communist government of East Germany prevented them from having contact with the west.

By 1989, the Soviet Union was growing weaker and losing control of Eastern Europe. Hungary, an ally of the Soviet Union, loosened its borders with Western Europe. East Germans began crossing the Hungarian border. Eventually they came into West Germany. The **Berlin Wall** came down in 1989, and even more East Germans moved to the west.

1. How did the economies of East and West Germany differ after World War II?

_____

_____

Reunified Germany (page 396)
How has the German government tried to rebuild the country?

The **reunification** of East and West Germany took place in 1990. The German government has worked hard and spent a lot of money to rebuild the eastern part of the country. It has rebuilt roads, factories, housing, and hospitals. The capital city of Berlin, once divided, was also rebuilt, as was the Reichstag. The Reichstag is where the Federal Assembly meets.

Reunification has also caused tensions between former West and East Germans. There are few jobs in the east, and housing is very expensive. People in the western part of the country have to pay heavy taxes to rebuild the nation.

2. What problems have been caused by reunification?

_____

_____

German Culture (pages 396–397)
Who are Germany's most famous composers and writers?

Germany has rich cultural traditions. Its people are especially proud of their music and literature. Germans are also famous for designing high-quality cars, appliances, and other complex machinery.

Johann Sebastian Bach, George Frederick Handel, and **Ludwig van Beethoven** are three of Germany's best-known composers. The German composer Richard Wagner wrote many operas. These included the Ring Cycle, a series of operas based on German myths and legends.

Rainer Maria Rilke was one of Germany's greatest writers. His poems are still admired and studied today. Other important German authors include Günter Grass and Thomas Mann. Grass set his novel *The Tin Drum* in World War II. Both writers received the Nobel Prize in Literature—Mann in 1929 and Grass in 1999.

3. In what cultural areas has Germany been especially strong?

_____

_____

Poland

BEFORE YOU READ

In the last section, you read about Germany.

In this section, you will learn about the government, economy, and culture of Poland.

AS YOU READ

Copy this chart to take notes about Poland.

Country	Physical Geography	Government	Economy	Culture	Interesting Facts
Poland					

TERMS & NAMES

Solidarity a trade union in Poland whose original goal was to increase pay and improve working conditions

Lech Walesa leader of Solidarity who became Poland's president in 1990

Czeslaw Milosz a well known Polish writer (b. 1911)

censorship the outlawing of certain information

dissident a person who openly disagrees with a government's policies

Political and Economic Struggles
(pages 399–400)

Why were Polish workers dissatisfied?

Poland had a tradition of struggle long before the 1970s and 1980s. In 1956, for example, Polish workers rioted to protest their low wages. Communists had taken over the government and set strict wage and price controls.

Lech Walesa, an electrical worker from the shipyards of Gdansk, led a trade union called **Solidarity** in the 1980s. Labor unions throughout Poland joined Solidarity.

Solidarity began by pushing for increased pay and better working conditions. Before long, the organization had bigger goals. In 1981, members of Solidarity called for free elections and an end to Communist rule. At that time, Solidarity had about ten million members. Still, the government fought back. It suspended Solidarity and arrested thousands of members.

1. What were the goals of Solidarity?

_____

_____

_____

A Free Poland (page 401)

What two groups cooperated to form a new Polish government?

In the late 1980s, economic conditions in Poland grew worse. The leaders of Solidarity were asked to help the government solve Poland's economic difficulties. The Communists finally agreed to Solidarity's demand for free elections.

When the elections were held, the Communists lost power. Many Solidarity candidates were elected. Lech Walesa became president in 1990.

Poland is a parliamentary republic. A new constitution guarantees *civil rights,* such as free speech. The constitution also helps to balance the powers held by the president, the prime minister, and parliament.

The parliament has two houses. The upper house has 100 members. The lower house, which chooses the prime minister, has 460 members. The prime minister is usually a member of the largest party or alliance of parties within parliament.

Some parties represent the small German and

Ukrainian ethnic groups living in Poland. They are also represented in parliament. All Polish citizens have a voice in their government.

2. What kind of government does Poland have today?

_____

_____

A Changing Economy (pages 401–402)
What problems did Poland have with its new free-market economy?

The Poles have had to deal with a changing economy as well as a new government. Within a very short time, Poland switched from a command economy to a free-market economy. The government no longer controlled prices. Trade suddenly faced international competition.

More goods became available, but prices rose. With *inflation* at almost 80 percent, people's wages could not keep up with the cost of goods.

Many Polish companies went out of business. They could not compete with high-quality foreign goods. More and more people lost their jobs. Poland's overall standard of living fell.

By 1999, inflation had dropped to around 7 percent. New Polish businesses were successful, so there were more jobs. By 2000, economic assistance from the United States was no longer needed.

Between 1995 and 2000, Poles bought half a million new cars each year. Today, Poland has two million successful small and medium-sized businesses. These are signs of a healthy economy.

3. What are some signs of economic improvement in Poland?

_____

_____

Poland's Culture (pages 402-403)
Do Polish artists have freedom of expression?

Poland was once a large and powerful kingdom. By 1795, however, it had been taken over by Russia, Prussia, and Austria and was no longer an independent country. Poland did not become a republic until 1918. In spite of these difficulties, Poland has kept its rich culture.

Czeslaw Milosz is one of Poland's best-known writers. He published his first book of poems in the 1930s. After World War II, he worked as a diplomat and later as a professor. Milosz won the Nobel Prize in Literature in 1980.

The Communist government in Poland controlled the media. It limited or stopped the flow of ideas and information, especially if they were critical of communism. Because of this **censorship,** many writers were unable to publish their works. Some of them became **dissidents,** openly disagreeing with the government's policies.

Today, the work of Polish writers published in Poland can be sold tax-free. Movie theaters are repaid their costs for showing Polish movies. This helps Polish actors, screenwriters, and directors. Free-market advertising and fees from television owners support public-sponsored television stations.

4. How did censorship affect culture in Poland?

_____

_____

Glossary/After You Read

assassinated murdered

assembly a body of lawmakers

civil rights rights of citizens, often guaranteed by a constitution

homogeneous the same or similar kind

imperial power a country that rules an empire

inflation an increase in prices

mixed economy an economy with a public and private sector

monarchy a government headed by a king or queen

nationalized taken over by the government

parliamentary republic a republic with a parliamentary system of government

prime minister head of the government in a parliamentary system

TERMS & NAMES

A. Insert the term or name that best completes each sentence.

1. _____ was a popular novelist in the nineteenth century.

   J.K. Rowling   Charles Dickens   Elton John

2. The _____ was made up of civilians who fought against the Nazis.

   French Resistance   European Community   ombudsmen

3. Sweden's governing body is called the _____.

   Riksdag   Parliament   Rilke

4. Limiting access to certain information is _____.

   civil rights   inflation   censorship

5. _____ is one of Germany's best-known composers.

   Ludwig van Beethoven Thomas Mann   Virginia Wolfe

B. Write the letter of the term or name next to the description that explains it best.

   a. hydroelectricity   **d.** socialism

   b. armed neutrality   **e.** reunification

   c. ombudsmen

   _____ 1. the rejoining of two things that have been separated

   _____ 2. when a country has an army but doesn't go to war

   _____ 3. a kind of government where some businesses are owned by the state

   _____ 4. energy generated from water power

   _____ 5. Swedish officials who protect citizens' rights

Sometimes kings conquered other city-states. Some of these kings allowed the conquered cities to continue worshiping their own special gods. They also allowed ruling families and temple priests to keep local control. Other kings built empires from conquered lands. An empire is a group of countries under one ruler's control. These emperors demanded that the conquered people honor them as gods. Local rulers could no longer turn to their own gods for advice. Now they had to take orders from the emperor.

Hammurabi, a famous emperor of ancient Mesopotamia, ruled from 1792 to 1750 B.C. During his reign, he unveiled a huge black stone containing 282 laws given to him by the god Shamash. These laws were called the Code of Hammurabi. According to this code of laws, the punishment must fit the crime. The basic idea was, "An eye for an eye, a tooth for a tooth."

1. What were three challenges that influenced the development of city-states?

_____

_____

The Class System (page 425)
What is a class system?

Mesopotamia had a **class system.** This meant society was divided into different social groups. Each social group, or class, had certain rights and was protected by law. The most favored classes had the most rights.

Kings, priests, and wealthy property owners were at the top of the class system. The middle class included skilled workers, merchants, and farmers. Skilled workers specialized in one craft, such as making pottery. Merchants often sold goods brought from other Mesopotamian cities or from other countries. Farmers worked fields that belonged to the temple or the palace.

Many workers in Mesopotamia were enslaved and were at the bottom of the class system. Some had been captured in war. Others sold themselves into slavery to pay off a debt. Once they paid the debt, their masters had to set them free.

2. Describe the people who were in Mesopotamia's middle class.

_____

_____

A Culture Based on Writing
(pages 426–427)
What is a scribe?

The Sumerians developed one of the first systems of writing, called **cuneiform.** With this wedge-shaped writing, they kept records and sent business letters. They recorded their history, their religious beliefs, and their knowledge of medicine, mathematics, and astronomy.

Few Sumerians learned to read and write. Schools, called tablet houses, trained **scribes** to be society's record keepers and meet the needs of the temple, the government, and the business world. Most students were the sons of wealthy merchants, government officials, and priests. A few girls also studied at the tablet houses. The school day lasted from sunrise to sunset, and students had to memorize about 600 characters.

Scribes did more than keep records and write business letters. Some wrote literary and scientific works of their own. Some lullabies and love songs were written by women scribes. Traveling scribes from Mesopotamia shared their writings with people from neighboring countries. Since few people in Mesopotamia could read, scribes read out loud to audiences, often reading hero tales from a book called *Gilgamesh.*

3. Who became scribes? What kind of work did scribes do?

_____

_____

Ancient Egypt

BEFORE YOU READ

In the last section, you read about ancient Mesopotamia. In this section, you will read about ancient Egypt.

AS YOU READ

Copy this chart to take notes about ancient Egyptian civilization.

Ancient Egypt	
Nile River	
Pyramids	
Religious Life	

TERMS & NAMES

papyrus a paperlike material made from a plant called papyrus

pyramids structures with four triangular sides that rise from a rectangular base to meet at a point on top

pharaohs kings of ancient Egypt

hieroglyphics a writing system that uses pictures or symbols to represent words or sounds

Re ancient Egyptian sun god

Horus ancient Egyptian sky god

Ancient Egypt and the Nile

(pages 429–430)

Why was ancient Egyptian civilization referred to as "the gift of the Nile"?

Many of the temples and other monuments of ancient Egypt still stand. Without the Nile River, however, they probably would never have been built. As the Greek historian Herodotus said about 2500 years ago, Egyptian civilization was "the gift of the Nile."

Desert covers most of Egypt. The sands spread for hundreds of miles to the west and the south, discouraging any invaders. The Nile River runs through the desert, and it is sometimes called "the river in the sand."

The Nile's annual floods deposited tons of *silt* in the river valley. These deposits made the soil black and fertile. Every year, around October, the floodwaters began to retreat. Then the farmers planted their seeds. They harvested their crops during the months the Nile was at its lowest levels. The Egyptians knew the Nile would flood each year. But they could not predict how high the water would rise. In years with very low floods, there might not be enough food. In

years with very high floods, the waters would destroy fields and homes.

The ancient Egyptians found ways to manage the unpredictable river. They built canals to carry water from the Nile to the parts of the land the floodwaters did not reach. They built up the riverbanks to keep the river from overflowing.

Egyptian towns and cities were spread along the Nile River valley. The river made it possible for Egyptians living far apart to come together. The Egyptians were expert boat builders. They built harbors and ports for large cargo boats. The Nile provided such good transportation that few roads were needed in ancient Egypt. Because goods moved easily along the Nile, trade was very profitable.

The ancient Egyptians used Nile mud to make pottery and bricks. They made a paperlike material called **papyrus** from the papyrus plant, which grew in marshes and swamps around the Nile. In fact, the English word *paper* comes from "papyrus." It was easier to write on papyrus than on the bulky clay tablets the Mesopotamians used.

1. How did the Nile help the ancient Egyptians?

_____

_____

The Great Builders (pages 431–432)

What is a pyramid?

The Egyptians noticed that bodies buried in the sand on the edge of the desert resisted decay. This discovery may have affected their beliefs in an afterlife. The concept of an afterlife played a central role in ancient Egyptian life and culture. It led the Egyptians to build huge **pyramids,** as well as many other monuments and temples.

Pyramids are easily recognized by their shape. Four triangular sides on a rectangular base meet at a single point. The pyramids were built for Egyptian kings, or **pharaohs.** Each pyramid is a palace where an Egyptian king planned to spend the afterlife.

The pyramids were built of large blocks of stone. A single pyramid might contain 92 million cubic feet of stone, enough to fill a large sports stadium. The tips of pyramids were often capped with gold.

Building a pyramid was complicated. The leader of the project and his staff used **hieroglyphics**—a writing system that uses pictographs to stand for words or sounds—to make lists of the workers and supplies needed.

The Egyptians had no cutting tools or machines to get the stone they needed. Removing the stone and shaping it into blocks was very difficult and dangerous work. Every Egyptian family had to help with the project. They either worked as laborers or provided food for the workers.

2. Why did the ancient Egyptians build pyramids?

_____

_____

The Pharaoh and the Gods
(pages 432–433)

What role did religion have in Egyptian life?

Egyptians believed that the ruling pharaoh was the son of the sun god, **Re.** The pharaoh was also linked with **Horus,** the sky god. Not only was the pharaoh ancient Egypt's chief judge and commander-in-chief, he was also the chief religious figure. His religious example guided the common people in their daily lives and in their preparations for the afterlife.

Temples were everywhere in ancient Egypt. Some were dedicated to major gods, like Re. Others were dedicated to local gods. Pharaohs had temples built in their honor so that people could worship them.

Ordinary citizens did not gather for prayer in the temples. Only priests carried out the temple rituals. Common people could pray or leave offerings to the gods in smaller buildings that stood outside the temple grounds. Many private homes also contained shrines where family members worshiped their gods and honored the spirits of dead family members.

Most Egyptians were not buried in pyramids. They made careful preparations for the afterlife, however. Family members were responsible for burying their dead relatives and tending their spirits. Egyptians believed they could help the dead person live comfortably in the afterlife. They prevented bodies from decaying by treating them with preservatives, or mummifying them. The Egyptians decorated tombs and filled them with things for the dead to use in the afterlife. They also made regular offerings to honor the dead.

3. Why did the ancient Egyptians mummify their dead relatives?

_____

_____

Birthplace of Three Religions

BEFORE YOU READ

In the last section, you read about ancient Egypt.

In this section, you will read about the origins of Judaism, Christianity, and Islam.

AS YOU READ

Copy this chart to take notes about the three religions.

	Leaders	Beliefs
Judaism		
Christianity		
Islam		

TERMS & NAMES

Abraham the first monotheist, whose descendants are known as Jews

Judaism the first monotheistic religion, founded by Abraham, and whose followers are called Jews

Jesus founder of a religion of love whose followers, called Christians, believe that he is the Messiah

Christianity a religion that developed out of Judaism and was based on the life and teachings of Jesus

Muhammad founder of Islam whom Muslims believe to be God's prophet

Islam a religion that teaches that there is one god and Muhammad is his follower

Muslim a follower of Islam

Qur'an the sacred text of Islam

Three Religions/Abraham and the Origin of Judaism (pages 435–436)

What do Judaism, Christianity, and Islam have in common?

Jews, Christians, and Muslims have been fighting over Jerusalem and other areas of Southwest Asia for centuries. Each of these religions got its start in this region. All three share common traits. Each was first led by a single person, and each reveres a set of sacred writings. Each believes there is only one god, a belief called monotheism. The Sumerians and Egyptians believed in many gods, a belief called polytheism.

The Hebrew people were the first monotheists. They called their god Yahweh. According to Hebrew scripture, Yahweh spoke to a man named **Abraham,** telling him to leave his native land, which was in southeastern Mesopotamia. Abraham obeyed and settled in Canaan, which

is in present-day Israel. Abraham's descendants are known as Jews, and their religion is **Judaism.**

The story of Judaism is partly a story of *exile*. In 586 B.C., the Babylonians from southern Mesopotamia destroyed the First Temple in Jerusalem. The Jews were exiled to Babylon. They continued to pray and read their holy texts.

About 50 years later, the Persians took control of Mesopotamia. The Jews were allowed to return to Jerusalem and rebuild their Temple. Much later, Israel was taken over by the Romans, who renamed it Palestine. The Jews revolted against Rome in A.D. 66. Jerusalem and the Second Temple were destroyed in the struggle.

Although the Temple was never rebuilt, Judaism survived. Religious leaders encouraged the Jews to replace worship in the Temple with prayer, study, and good deeds. For the next

1,800 years, most Jews lived outside Jerusalem. They hoped that Jerusalem might again become their home.

1. Why is Jerusalem important to the Jews?

_____

_____

Jesus and the Birth of Christianity (pages 436–437)

Who was Jesus, and why did people follow him?

Between the years 8 and 4 B.C., when the Romans ruled Palestine, a Jewish boy named **Jesus** was born in the city of Bethlehem. His life story is told in the four Gospels, which are part of the Bible.

According to the Gospels, Jesus grew up in Galilee in northern Palestine. His father trained him to be a carpenter. When he was about 30, his cousin John the Baptist baptized him. For the next three years, he traveled the countryside, preaching a religion of love and forgiveness and performing miracles. Many *disciples* gathered around him.

The Jewish people believed that a *Messiah* would some day come to lead them out of exile. Some people believed Jesus was the Messiah. He came to be called Christ, the Greek word for messiah. His followers were called Christians.

Some government leaders believed that their power was threatened by Jesus' teachings and by his large following. When Jesus came to Jerusalem to celebrate the Jewish feast of Passover, the Roman authorities arrested him. After a brief trial, he was crucified and died. According to his disciples, he was resurrected and went to heaven.

Jesus' disciples spread his teachings and their belief that he was the Messiah. A new religion called Christianity was born. It is based on the life and teachings of Jesus. Eventually, Christianity spread around the world. Today, only a few Christians live where Christianity began.

2. Why did the Roman authorities kill Jesus?

_____

_____

Muhammad, the Prophet of Islam (pages 437–438)

Who was Muhammad?

Less than 600 years after Christ's death, a third monotheistic religion arose in Southwest Asia. **Muhammad** was born in Mecca about A.D. 570. He is the founder of **Islam,** a religion whose followers believe there is one god and that Muhammad is his prophet. A believer in Islam is called a **Muslim.**

In about A.D. 610, according to Muslim beliefs, the angel Gabriel came to Muhammad and told him to praise only one god. The angel also told him how and when to pray. For the next 22 years, Gabriel continued to send revelations to Muhammad. Later, the revelations became the **Qur'an,** the sacred text of Islam. Muhammad told people about these divine messages. He criticized the wealthy people of Mecca for neglecting the poor and urged them to change their wicked ways.

The leaders of Mecca thought Muhammad's teachings threatened their traditions and businesses. Some plotted to kill him. In 622, Muhammad and some followers escaped to the city of Medina. Muslims date the beginning of their calendar from this year.

3. How did the Qur'an come to be written?

_____

_____

Muslim Empires

BEFORE YOU READ

In the last section, you read about the beginnings of Judaism, Christianity, and Islam.

In this section, you will read about the Muslim empires.

AS YOU READ

Copy this web to take notes about the Muslim Empires.

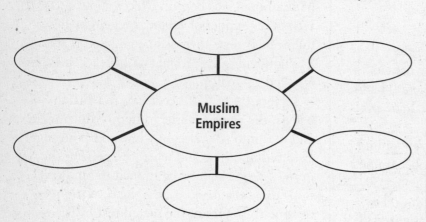

TERMS & NAMES

Five Pillars of Islam the most important teachings of Muhammad

caliph title used by rulers of the Muslim community from 632 to 1924

theocracy a government ruled by a religious leader

Ottoman Empire Muslim empire in Europe, early 1400s to the 1920s

Constantinople capital of Ottoman Empire; Istanbul in modern Turkey

Suleiman I ruler of Ottoman Empire from 1520 to 1566

Janissaries military group who grew powerful in the Ottoman Empire

Sultan Mehmed VI fought on the losing side in World War I, ending the Ottoman Empire

The Five Pillars of Islam
(pages 440–441)

What are the most important teachings of Muhammad?

The most important teachings of Muhammad are summed up in the **Five Pillars of Islam,** which are five religious duties that unite all Muslims:

   First Pillar: stating that there is only one God, and that Muhammad is God's prophet;

   Second Pillar: praying five times a day in the direction of *Mecca*, the holiest city in Islam;

   Third Pillar: giving to the poor and needy;

   Fourth Pillar: fasting during the month of *Ramadan;*

   Fifth Pillar: making a pilgrimage to Mecca.

1. What are the Five Pillars of Islam?

_____

_____

_____

Muslim Empires (page 441)

Who continued Muhammad's work after he died?

After Muhammad's death, his close associates selected a **caliph** to succeed him. Muslim rulers were called caliphs from 632 until 1924. The caliph's duty was to spread God's rule. In doing so, the caliphs founded a new empire, the *caliphate.* The caliphate was a **theocracy,** a government ruled by a religious leader.

   The caliphs created a vast trading system. Islamic ideas spread as books were exchanged along trade routes. Metalwork, pottery, and fabrics brought new and unique Muslim artwork to other peoples.

   In the early Middle Ages, Muslims collected and translated important books and papers. During the 1100s and 1200s, ancient texts were translated from Arabic into Hebrew and Latin. European scholars could now study the knowledge of the ancient world. They could see how

Islamic thinkers had preserved and developed learning.

The caliphs conquered Christian Spain and introduced Islamic culture there. They had hoped to spread their influence elsewhere in Europe. In 732, however, Muslim armies in what is now west-central France were defeated by Charles Martel, Charlemagne's grandfather. Yet by 1400, Muslims had conquered parts of Europe.

2. How did Islamic ideas spread?

_____

_____

The Ottoman Empire (page 442)
What parts of the world did the Ottoman Empire control?

The Muslim **Ottoman Empire** controlled what is now Turkey and parts of North Africa, Southwest Asia, and Southeast Europe. The Ottomans made **Constantinople,** called Istanbul in present-day Turkey, their capital. Rulers of the vast Ottoman Empire, called sultans, were tolerant of people of different backgrounds. Christians and Jews could pay a tax that allowed them to worship as they pleased. Some achieved prominence in banking and business.

From 1520 to 1566, **Suleiman I** ruled the Ottoman Empire. Christians called him "The Magnificent." Muslims called him "The Lawgiver." Suleiman published a code of laws that established a system of justice throughout his empire. His chief architect, Sinan, transformed Constantinople into an Islamic capital. Sinan designed famous mosques in the capital and elsewhere in the empire. As long as Suleiman ruled the Ottoman Empire, it was the richest and most powerful empire in Europe and Southwest Asia.

3. Why was Suleiman I a popular sultan?

_____

_____

Slaves and Soldiers (pages 442–443)
Who were the Janissaries?

Not everyone shared in the empire's wealth and glory. Many people were slaves, often prisoners from conquered nations. They served at court or in the homes of wealthy people. Many male slaves became soldiers.

A special group of soldiers loyal to the sultan, called **Janissaries,** developed in the late 1300s out of a small force of slaves. By the 1600s, they had become so powerful that even the sultans feared them. They refused to learn modern ways of fighting, however, and grew weak. In 1826, a group of Janissaries attacked the sultan. Forces loyal to the sultan fired on the attackers, killing 6,000. The sultan then disbanded the force.

4. Why did the sultans fear the Janissaries?

_____

_____

The Decline of the Ottoman Empire (page 443)
When did the Ottoman Empire begin to decline?

Over the centuries, the Ottoman Empire grew weak. It fought constant wars to maintain a hold on its empire. By the 1800s, the empire was nearly bankrupt. It had trouble competing in trade with industrialized Europe. **Sultan Mehmed V** fought on the losing side in World War I. After the war, the empire lost control of Arab lands. By 1924, the Ottoman Empire no longer existed. The modern country of Turkey had taken its place.

5. Why did the Ottoman Empire end?

_____

_____

Glossary/After You Read

oasis a fertile area in a desert

petroleum a thick, yellowish-black oil that is the source of gasoline, paraffin, and kerosene

Mesopotamia an ancient region of Southwest Asia located in modern-day Iraq

silt particles of earth and rock that build up in rivers or streams

exile forced removal from one's own country

disciple a follower of the teachings of another

Messiah a savior that Jews believe will come some day, and that Christians believe has already come through Jesus Christ

Mecca the holiest city in Islam

caliphate the Islamic empire ruled by a caliph

TERMS & NAMES

A. If the statement is true, write "true" on the line. If it is false, change the underlined word or words to make it true.

_____ **1.** <u>Fertile</u> soil provides nutrients that plants need to grow.

_____ **2.** <u>Hieroglyphics</u> were written on papyrus.

_____ **3.** <u>Horus</u> and <u>Re</u> were ancient gods.

_____ **4.** <u>Hunter-gatherers</u> farmed and raised animals.

_____ **5.** A class system is made up of <u>cuneiforms</u>.

_____ **6.** The process of bringing water to dry land is <u>irrigation</u>.

_____ **7.** <u>Hammurabi</u> was a famous emperor of ancient Mesopotamia.

_____ **8.** A Mesopotamian terraced <u>scribe</u> is a <u>ziggurat</u>.

_____ **9.** <u>Pharaohs</u> of ancient Egypt are called <u>pyramids</u>.

_____ **10.** The Sumerians were early inhabitants of the <u>Fertile Crescent</u>.

B. Fill in the blanks with the appropriate term or name.

Muhammad	Constantinople	Suleiman I
Jesus	Judaism	Islam
Abraham	Christianity	Qur'an
Five Pillars of Islam	caliph	Sultan Mehmed VI
theocracy	Ottoman	Muslim

1. Three major religions founded in the region are _____, _____, and _____.

2. The teachings of _____ and _____ still inspire people today.

3. The capital of the _____ Empire was _____.

4. The holy book of the _____ is the _____.

5. _____ and _____ were famous leaders of the Ottoman Empire.

6. The _____ are the main religious duties for Muslims.

7. Beginning in 632, Muslim leaders named _____ established a _____.

8. _____, the ancestor of the Jews, moved to present-day Israel from Mesopotamia.

MAIN IDEAS

1. How did some ancient people benefit from the rivers in North Africa and Southwest Asia?

_____

_____

2. What are some examples of ancient Mesopotamia's civilization?

_____

_____

3. Why did the ancient Egyptians build pyramids?

_____

_____

4. What are some similarities among Judaism, Christianity, and Islam?

_____

_____

5. Why was Suleiman I called "The Magnificent"?

_____

_____

THINKING CRITICALLY

Answer the following questions on a separate sheet of paper.

1. Do you think that Hammurabi's Code was too harsh? Explain your thinking.

2. The Five Pillars of Islam unite the world's Muslims. Name at least "Five Pillars" that unite the students and teachers of your school.

A Troubled Century

BEFORE YOU READ

In the last chapter, you read about the history of North Africa and Southwest Asia.

In this section, you will read about conflicts in this region that are rooted in history.

AS YOU READ

Copy this web to take notes about conflicts in North Africa and Southwest Asia.

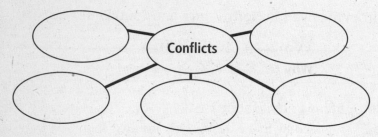

TERMS & NAMES

mandate a country placed under the control of another power by international agreement

Palestine an Arab region often called the Holy Land

Arab-Israeli Wars a series of wars between 1948 and 1973 that were fought between Israel and the Arab countries of Iraq, Syria, Egypt, Jordan, and Lebanon

Kurds a group of mountain people who live in Armenia, Iran, Iraq, Syria, and Turkey

Persian Gulf War a war in 1991 between the United States and Iraq

European Nations Take Over
(pages 449–450)

Who controlled Southwest Asia and North Africa after World War I?

During World War I, the Turkish Ottoman Empire had sided with Germany against Great Britain, France, and Russia. After the Ottoman Empire's defeat, most of its territory was divided between Great Britain and France, and conflicts began that still trouble the region today.

Europeans had been controlling the region since before the 19th century. After World War I, this control often took the form of mandates. A **mandate** is a country placed under the control of another power by international agreement. The European powers promised to give their mandates independence by a certain date. Countries that were not mandates often had to fight for independence.

1. What is a mandate?

_____

_____

Conflict Over Palestine (pages 450–451)

Why did the Jews want to live in Palestine?

After World War I, Great Britain controlled Palestine, an Arab region that was also home to the Jews 2,000 years earlier. Starting in the late 1800s, Jews fleeing persecution in Eastern Europe migrated there again. After World War II and the Holocaust, the number of Jews moving to Palestine increased.

Palestine, however, was already home to Arabs who did not want their land to be a Jewish state. In 1947, Great Britain asked the *United Nations* to solve the problem. The United Nations divided up Palestine. The Jews accepted the plan, but the Arabs did not. In May 1948, Jewish leaders declared their land an independent state called Israel. Iraq, Syria, Egypt, Jordan, and Lebanon immediately declared war on Israel. The Israelis won the first of the **Arab-Israeli Wars.**

After that war, about 700,000 Palestinians had to leave their homes and become refugees in Arab countries. In 1964, some Palestinians formed the *Palestine Liberation Organization*

(PLO). The PLO's goal is to have an independent Palestinian state.

In 1967 and 1973, Israel won the second and third of the Arab-Israeli Wars. Even in peacetime, conflict continued. Over the years, territory passed back and forth between Israel and Arab countries.

In 1977, Egypt became the first Arab country in the region to seek peace with Israel. Leaders of Egypt and Israel discussed the Palestinians' desire for their own state. Ten years later, Palestinian Arabs in the Israeli-controlled territories rebelled. In 1993, Israel and the PLO signed an agreement. The PLO recognized Israel's right to exist. Israel returned land to the Palestinians. The next year, Israel and Jordan signed a peace treaty. In 2000, however, another Palestinian uprising broke out.

2. Why were the Arab-Israeli Wars fought?

Sources of Conflict (pages 451–452)
What are some of the differences among people who live in North Africa and Southwest Asia?

Some conflicts in the region are the result of religious differences between Jews and Muslims. Religious conflicts between Christians and Muslims have erupted in Egypt, Lebanon, and Sudan. Conflicts also occur within religions.

Islam, for example, has two main sects, or groups—Sunnis and Shi'ites. Most Muslims in the region are Sunni. In Iran most people are Shi'ites. They are more willing than the Sunni to accept religious leaders as political leaders. This has caused conflict in the region.

Trouble also occurs when ethnic groups are in conflict. For example, Iraqis are descendants of Arabs. Most Iranians, however, are Persian people. Arabs and Persians have different histories and languages. These differences contribute to conflicts between Iran and Iraq.

Some ethnic groups want a country of their own. The **Kurds,** for example, live in Armenia,

Georgia, Iran, Iraq, Lebanon, Syria, and Turkey. Their independence movements have been defeated in Turkey, Iran, and Iraq.

Muslim *fundamentalists* believe Islam should be strictly observed. In 1979, fundamentalist leader *Ayatollah* Khomeini took over the government of Iran. Khomeini objected to the way the former ruler had been westernizing the country. Fundamentalist movements have arisen in other countries, often leading to conflict.

3. What is a fundamentalist government?

Wars in the Region (pages 452–453)
Why did the Iran-Iraq war take place?

Iran and Iraq had long disputed who owned the oil-rich territory between them. In 1980, Iraq, led by Saddam Hussein, invaded Iran. The Iran-Iraq War lasted eight years. As many as one million people died. Neither side won.

In 1990, Iraq invaded the small, oil-rich country of Kuwait. The United Nations imposed an *embargo* to prevent Iraq from importing goods or exporting oil. The embargo damaged Iraq's economy, but the war continued.

On January 16, 1991, the **Persian Gulf War** began when an international armed force launched missile attacks on Iraq, followed by a ground attack on February 24. One hundred hours later, Iraq surrendered. Iraq got out of Kuwait, but Saddam Hussein stayed in power.

In the early 2000s, President George W. Bush believed that Saddam Hussein had dangerous illegal weapons. On March 20, 2003, an alliance of the United States, Great Britain, and other countries invaded Iraq. On April 9, U.S. forces conquered Baghdad, and Hussein was overthrown.

4. Why was Kuwait the target of invasion by Iraq?

Resources and Religion

BEFORE YOU READ

In the last section, you read about conflicts in North Africa and Southwest Asia.

In this section, you will read about the resources and religions that influence the region's culture.

AS YOU READ

Copy this chart to take notes about the resources and religions of North Africa and Southwest Asia.

	Main Ideas
Oil	
Religion	
Westernization	
Islamic Women	

TERMS & NAMES

OPEC Organization of Petroleum Exporting Countries, which decides the price and amount of oil produced each year in Iraq, Iran, Saudi Arabia, Kuwait, and Venezuela

primary products raw materials used to manufacture other products

secondary products goods manufactured from raw materials

petrochemicals products made from petroleum or natural gas

hajj a pilgrimage to Mecca that most Muslims try to make at least once

Ramadan the ninth month of the Islamic year

The Importance of Oil (pages 455–457)

Why is oil such an important product in North Africa and Southwest Asia?

Oil was discovered in Iran in 1908. Soon afterward, it was discovered in other countries of Southwest Asia and North Africa. Great Britain, France, the United States, and other Western countries made agreements with the oil-rich nations to develop the oil fields. Today, half the world's oil is produced in Saudi Arabia, Iran, Kuwait, and Iraq. Saudi Arabia is the largest oil-producing country.

After World War II, many nations in the region chose to have their governments take over the oil industries. In 1960, Iran, Iraq, Saudi Arabia, and Kuwait joined with Venezuela, to form the Organization of Petroleum Exporting Countries, or **OPEC**. OPEC would decide the price and amount of oil produced in each country each year.

Since the early 1900s, oil has been the most important **primary product**, or raw material, in Southwest Asia and North Africa. Countries

in this region export mainly primary products. Many have also developed **secondary products**, or goods manufactured from primary products. In Iraq, for example, date palms are a primary product. From them, Iraq manufactures date syrup and paper.

The oil-rich countries also use oil to make secondary products, such as crude oil. They also make **petrochemicals** from crude oil and natural gas. Petrochemicals are used in cosmetics, plastics, and other products.

1. What is the difference between a primary product and a secondary product?

_____

_____

Religion in the Region (page 457)

What religions are practiced in the region?

Islam is the region's dominant religion. Jews and Christians have also lived there for thousands of years. Most Jews in the region moved to Israel after it was created, but some Jews remain in Turkey, Egypt, and Iran. Many Christians left at the end of the Ottoman Empire. Egypt and Lebanon now have two large Christian communities.

Islamic culture is apparent in everyday life. Muslim people pray five times a day. Radio stations air readings from the Qur'an. Muslims try to go on a *hajj,* or pilgrimage to Mecca, once in a lifetime.

During the ninth month of the Islamic year, called **Ramadan,** Muslims fast from sunrise to sunset. There is a joyous feast at month's end.

2. How does Islam influence the culture of the region?

_____

_____

Westernization vs. Traditional Culture (page 458)
What is westernization?

Many people in the region are opposed to Western influence. Others are open to *westernization,* adopting ways of life common in Europe and the United States. Eating at fast-food restaurants is a form of westernization. So are advances in business and science. Some people believe westernization will give them a higher standard of living. Others embrace their traditional culture

3. Why is westernization appealing to some people in the region?

_____

_____

The Roles of Women/Clothing and Culture (pages 458–459)
What is the role of women in the region?

Women in the region have different roles. In Israel, Jordan, and Egypt, many women are educated and work in business and government.

In some countries, religion limits women's roles. Saudi Arabian women cannot attend gatherings with men, or drive cars. A Saudi woman can have one husband, but a Saudi man is allowed four wives. Few Saudi women work outside the home.

Clothing reveals much about the region's cultures. In Israel, some women and men dress in Western clothing. Orthodox Jewish women dress modestly as their religion dictates. Some Orthodox men wear black suits and hats and grow ringlets of hair in front of their ears. In some Islamic countries women are forced by law to wear *chadors,* long cloaks that cover everything but their eyes. Men dress and grow facial hair as Islamic law demands.

4. What are some examples of the inequality of women in Islamic countries

_____

_____

A Disappearing Nomadic Culture (page 459)
What is a nomadic culture?

Once *nomads* lived in the deserts of the region. Most herded sheep in search of grazing lands. Others escorted camel caravans of traders across the desert. Today, only one percent of the population is nomadic. Trucks, not camels, cross the desert on roads. Grazing lands have been lost to droughts. Governments encourage nomads to settle, and they make it difficult for nomads from other countries to cross borders.

5. Why is the nomadic culture in the region almost gone?

_____

_____

Egypt Today

BEFORE YOU READ

In the last section, you read about the resources and religion of North Africa and Southwest Asia.

In this section, you will read about modern-day Egypt.

AS YOU READ

Copy this web to take notes about Egypt today.

TERMS & NAMES

King Farouk monarch of Egypt from 1936 until 1952

Gamal Abdel Nasser an army officer who overthrew King Farouk in 1952 and established Egypt as a republic

Aswan High Dam a dam built in 1956 by Egyptian leader Gamal Abdel Nasser to control the flooding of the Nile River

tradeoff an exchange of one benefit for another

Anwar Sadat President of Egypt who was assassinated in 1979 after he signed a peace treaty with Israel

Muslim Brotherhood an extremist Muslim group that insists that Egypt be governed solely by Islamic law

fellahin peasant farmers in Egypt

The Suez Canal (page 462)

Why was the Suez Canal built?

The Suez Canal was completed in 1869. It allowed ships to travel easily between the Mediterranean and Red seas. It was the grand project of Egyptian ruler Ismail Pasha. But the cost of the canal and other projects drove Egypt into bankruptcy. Ismail had to sell Egypt's shares in the canal company to the British. From then until 1956, Great Britain had some control over Egypt.

1. Why did Ismail sell Egypt's shares of the canal company to Great Britain?

_____

_____

From Ancient to Modern Times

(pages 463–464)

How has Egypt changed and developed since ancient times?

Great Britain was not the first foreign power to rule Egypt after the pharaohs. For 2,500 years, Egypt was under foreign influence. Many nations ruled Egypt until the Ottoman's took over in 1517. From the late 1700s to the early 1900s, France and then Britain ruled over Egypt. Britain gave up some control in 1922. Egypt then became a monarchy, ruled by King Fuad and then by his son **King Farouk.** Foreign policy, defense, and communications remained under British control.

An Egyptian Army officer, **Gamal Abdel Nasser,** resented the British influence over his country. In 1952, he and other officers overthrew King Farouk. Egypt became a republic in 1953 and was led by Nasser from 1954 to 1970.

Nasser's most significant accomplishment was building the **Aswan High Dam.** Construction began in 1956 to control the flooding of the Nile and give Egypt more electrical power. Because of the dam, however, the river no longer has yearly deposits of rich soil. Farmers now use artificial fertilizers, which pollute the water. The Aswan High Dam is an example of a **tradeoff,** an exchange of one benefit for another.

Many people in Egypt are interested in freedom and compromise. From 1919 to 1922, women were active in Egypt's independence movement yet couldn't vote and had few marital rights. In 1956, women gained voting rights and were permitted to run for office. In 2000, a new law made it easier for women to divorce.

In 1979, led by President **Anwar Sadat,** Egypt became the first Arab state to sign a peace treaty with Israel. In 2000, President Hosni Mubarak met with leaders to talk about how to end Israeli-Palestinian violence.

Not every Egyptian values freedom. **The Muslim Brotherhood,** an extremist Muslim group, insists Egypt should be governed by Islamic law.

2. When, and how did Egypt become a republic?

_____

_____

The Land and the People (page 465)
Where do Egyptians live today, and how do they earn a living?

Most of Egypt is uninhabitable desert land. Almost all of its 70 million people live along the Nile or in desert oases. Some live in cities. Others farm fields made fertile by the Nile.

Egypt produces some of the world's finest cotton, a major primary product and export. Cotton-growing developed in Egypt during the 1860s.

More than half the population of Egypt lives in villages. Most villagers are **fellahin,** or very poor peasant farmers who are illiterate and malnourished. Most rent land or work their own fields. Many of their children do not go to school.

3. Who are the fellahin?

_____

_____

Africa's Largest City (page 466)
Why is Cairo's population so large, and what are people's lives like there?

Cairo is the capital of Egypt. It is polluted and overpopulated. Thousands leave Egypt's villages each year to look for work in Cairo, with little success. In 2000, the population of Cairo exceeded 12 million. It is now the most populated African city.

Cairo has historic and modern sections. Many poor, unskilled people live in the older sections and are unemployed. Most well-educated *Cairenes* live in the modern sections near the universities and foreign embassies.

4. What is Egypt's capital city, and how would you describe it?

_____

_____

The Region's Cultural Leader
(page 467)
Why is Egypt considered the region's cultural leader?

Egypt is the Arab world's cultural leader. In the 1950s, it became the first Arab country to require children to attend elementary school. It also has a strong *feminist* movement. The media entertains and informs Arabs throughout the region.

5. What are some ways that Egypt is a cultural leader in the region?

_____

_____

Israel Today

BEFORE YOU READ

In the last section, you read about Egypt today.

In this section, you will read about Israel today.

AS YOU READ

Copy this chart to take notes about why people have immigrated to Israel.

Immigrant Groups	Why They Came to Israel
Europeans	
Russians	
Ethiopians	

TERMS & NAMES

Zionism a movement that encouraged Jews to return to Palestine, the Jewish homeland, which many Jews call Zion

kibbutz a Jewish farming village in Palestine (modern-day Israel) whose members own everything in common, sharing labor, income, and expenses

Law of Return a law enacted in 1950 in Israel granting permission to Jews anywhere in the world to immigrate to Israel and become citizens

Orthodox Jews Jews who strictly follow Jewish law

Rosh Hashanah the Jewish New Year

Yom Kippur in Judaism, the Day of Atonement

secular not specifically relating to religion

From Zionism to a Modern State
(pages 470–471)

Why did the Jews leave Jerusalem, and why did they return there?

After A.D. 70, when the Romans destroyed the Temple in Jerusalem, the Jews no longer had their own country. They lived scattered around the world but still considered Palestine their home. **Zionism** was a Jewish movement that encouraged Jews to return to the homeland, which many called Zion. In the late 1800s, Jews began immigrating there.

The new arrivals came mostly from Eastern Europe, where the rights of Jews were severely limited. Some of the newcomers formed communities called kibbutzim. A **kibbutz** (*kibbutzim* is the plural) is a farming village whose members own everything in common, sharing labor, income, and expenses. The people of the kibbutzim saw themselves as brave, hard-working pioneers.

After the *Holocaust*, hundreds of thousands of Jews were left homeless and many of them sought refuge in Palestine. Some settled in cities like Jerusalem and Haifa, and others joined kibbutzim. About 270 kibbutzim still exist in Israel today. They raise crops, manufacture products, and welcome tourists.

Israel produces nearly all of its own food. To improve the dry soil, Israelis practice drip irrigation. Tubes in the ground deliver the exact amount of water each plant needs.

1. What is a kibbutz?

_____

_____

The People of Israel (pages 471–472)
How are Arab Israelis represented in the Israeli government?

Israel was established in 1948 as a Jewish state. Judaism is the state religion, and Hebrew is the official language. Of its six million inhabitants, over 80 percent are Jews. The *Declaration of the Establishment* promised that Israel would treat all its inhabitants equally.

About 20 percent of the people in Israel are Arabs. They carry Israeli passports and vote. Arab politicians serve in Israel's government. However, most do not have equal rights and opportunities in jobs, job training, higher education, and housing. In 2003, Arabs were elected to 8 of the 120 seats in the Knesset, the Israeli parliament. In 2000, the Israeli government announced that it planned to spend a billion dollars on schools, housing, and new jobs for Arab Israelis.

Some Palestinians are refugees from Israel who fled to the Gaza Strip and the West Bank after the 1948 Arab-Israeli War. Israel now occupies these territories. Constant tension between Arabs and Israelis often leads to violence.

Even before Israel was a state, its women were encouraged to work outside the home. Children on kibbutzim lived and slept in separate children's houses and visited their parents evenings and weekends. Both men and women serve in the military. An American-educated woman, Golda Meir, was the prime minister of Israel from 1969 to 1974.

2. What groups make up most of Israeli society now?

_____

_____

The Law of Return (pages 472–473)
What groups of immigrants have most recently emigrated to Israel?

Since 1948, Israel has taken in nearly 3 million Jewish immigrants. The 1950 **Law of Return** states that Jews anywhere in the world can immigrate to Israel and become citizens.

In 1987, the Soviet Union finally allowed Jews within its borders to emigrate. By 2000, one million arrived in Israel. Many were skilled engineers and technicians. Because of their numbers, however, they had a hard time finding jobs and good housing.

Since the 1980s, groups of Jews from Ethiopia, Eastern Europe, and North Africa arrived in Israel.

3. How has Israel put the Law of Return into effect?

_____

_____

Religion in Israel Today (page 473)
What do Orthodox Jews believe?

Only about one in four of Israel's Jews strictly follow Jewish law. They are called **Orthodox Jews.** These Jews believe that Jewish law should help form government policy. Orthodox rabbis have official control over marriage, divorce, and burial. **Rosh Hashanah** is the Jewish New Year. **Yom Kippur** is the Day of Atonement, a day for fasting and reflecting on one's sins. It is the holiest day in the Jewish year. Most of Israel's Jews are **secular,** and religious practices play a less important role in their lives. They are more interested in living a modern way of life. Many resent Orthodox control of daily life.

4. What role does Orthodox Judaism play in Israeli society?

_____

_____

CHAPTER 16

Section 5 (pages 476–479)

Turkey Today

BEFORE YOU READ

In the last section, you read about Israel today.
In this section, you will read about Turkey today.

AS YOU READ

Copy this web to take notes about Mustafa Kemal's influence on Turkey.

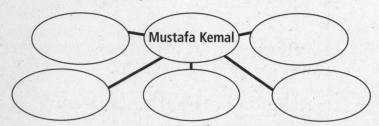

TERMS & NAMES

Mustafa Kemal the founder and president of the republic of Turkey

Grand National Assembly Turkey's legislature

Atatürk, or "Father of Turks," the name given to Kemal

Tansu Ciller a Turkish woman who was prime minister of Turkey during the 1990s

Between Two Worlds (page 476)

Who was determined to westernize Turkey after World War I?

If you look at a map of Turkey, you will see that it is joined to Southwest Asia on the east and Europe on the west. The question after World War I was: Would Turkey be like its Islamic neighbors and hold on to its traditions, or would it become more like the West? Its powerful new ruler, **Mustafa Kemal,** believed in westernization, by force if necessary.

1. In what way was Turkey "between two worlds" after World War I?

_____

_____

A Powerful Ruler (page 477)

Why is Mustafa Kemal considered the "Father of Turks?"

Mustafa Kemal was the founder of modern Turkey. He had been a Turkish officer and war hero for the Ottoman forces during World War I. The Ottomans had continued to rule Turkey even after the empire became weak. Turkey fought on the losing side during the war,

which weakened it even more. In 1920, Great Britain occupied Turkey.

Kemal opposed Britain's action. He organized Turkey's first **Grand National Assembly,** or legislature, which then elected him president. At his suggestion, the assembly officially adopted the name Turkey, the land of the Turkish people. In 1923, Kemal declared Turkey a republic and got rid of the old Islamic government the following year.

While Kemal was in the Ottoman army, he spent time in European cities. He admired what he saw there. He believed that adopting modern, "western" ways and ideas would benefit Turkey. Over the next nine years, Kemal introduced his changes. The Western alphabet replaced the Arabic alphabet. The Western calendar replaced the Islamic calendar.

Many Turks had used only first names. In 1934, a new law required the use of last names. The National Assembly gave Kemal the name **Atatürk,** which means "Father of Turks."

2. What are some examples of Western ways that were adopted by the Turks?

_____

_____

Changes Brought by Modernization (page 477)

What role did Islamic law have in the new Turkish government?

For nearly 1,000 years, Islamic law had shaped Turkish life. Atatürk, however, believed in secular government. He closed all institutions that had been founded on Islamic law. He replaced religious schools with secular schools. Since people were used to having Islam play a major role in all aspects of their lives, many protested Atatürk's reforms.

Turkish women benefited from Atatürk's reforms. He made it easier for women to divorce their husbands. Marriages could no longer be arranged by a woman's parents unless she agreed. Men could no longer have more than one wife. Women could now also vote and run for office. In the mid-1930s, women were elected to the national parliament. The world's first woman supreme court justice was a Turk. For several years during the 1990s, a woman named **Tansu Ciller** was Turkey's prime minister.

3. How did women benefit from Atatürk's reforms?

_____

_____

Rights and Freedoms Today (page 478)

What are the limits to rights and freedoms in Turkey?

Turkey adopted its most recent constitution in 1982. The Turkish Constitution promises freedom of religion, freedom of speech, freedom of the press, and other rights. The government, however, does not always live up to these promises. It sometimes limits freedoms. Turkish journalists can be arrested for writing articles against the government. Some publications are banned.

The *Kurds* are a group of people who live in the mountainous regions of southeastern Turkey, Iraq, Iran, and Syria. They have been fighting for their own state since 1984. The Turkish government has made suspected Kurd fighters leave their homes. It limits the right to teach the Kurdish language in schools. It also limits the use of Kurdish in television and radio programs.

4. How does the Turkish government limit its citizens' rights?

_____

_____

International Alliances (pages 478–479)

Why did Turkey join NATO?

Turkey and the United States are both members of the North Atlantic Treaty Organization (NATO). This alliance was formed in 1949 to keep the Soviet Union and its allies from attacking non-Communist countries in Western Europe. Turkey joined the alliance in 1952. When the Soviet Union fell apart in 1991, some NATO members felt the alliance was no longer necessary. Turkey disagreed because NATO membership helps protect its borders. Membership also gives Turkey a say in major decisions other members make.

Most of Turkey's trade is with Western Europe. In 1987, Turkey applied to join the European Union. The EU was reluctant to accept Turkey, partly because of the size of its population. There are not enough jobs in Turkey for all the people who want them. Two million Turks have gone to Germany to work. Millions more work in other European countries. Workers from EU countries are allowed to move freely within the region. European countries worried that membership in the EU would let more Turkish workers into their countries than they could handle.

5. Why have so many Turks moved to Europe?

_____

_____

Glossary/After You Read

United Nations an international organization formed after World War II to settle disputes around the world

Palestine Liberation Organization (PLO) a group founded in 1964, whose goal is the establishment of a Palestinian state

fundamentalists people who believe their religion should be strictly observed

trade embargo a policy that prevents a country from importing or exporting goods

chador a cloak that covers the entire body and most of the face, worn by some women in Islamic countries

TERMS & NAMES

A. Write the name or term next to the statement that describes it best. Not all of the names or terms will be used.

mandate	petrochemicals	Kurds	King Farouk
Arab-Israeli Wars	Ramadan	OPEC	Aswan High Dam
Persian Gulf War	Gamal Abdel Nasser	Palestine	tradeoff
primary products	secondary products	*hajj*	Anwar Sadat

_____ **1.** Under his leadership, Egypt signed a peace treaty with Israel

_____ **2.** raw materials used to manufacture other products

_____ **3.** a pilgrimage to Mecca

_____ **4.** the ninth month of the Islamic year when Muslims fast

_____ **5.** where many Jews migrated after the Holocaust

_____ **6.** a country placed under the control of another power

_____ **7.** began on January 16, 1991

_____ **8.** fought because of unrest over the division of Palestine

_____ **9.** helped Egypt become a republic in 1952

_____ **10.** built in 1956 to control the flooding of the Nile River

B. Fill in each blank with the appropriate term or name.

Muslim Brotherhood	Rosh Hashanah	Yom Kippur	kibbutz
Grand National Assembly	Law of Return	fellahin	
Mustafa Kemal	Zionism	Tansu Ciller	
secular	Atatürk	Orthodox Jews	

1. The _____ thinks that Egypt should be governed solely by Islamic law.

2. More than half of Egypt's population are _____.

3. _____ was the founder of modern, westernized Turkey.

4. _____ was the name given to Kemal by Turkey's National Assembly.

5. Turkey's prime minister during the 1990s was _____.

6. _____ is the idea that Jews should return to their homeland.

7. A _____ is a farming village whose members share everything.

8. Jewish people can always emigrate to Israel because of the _____.

9. _____ and _____ Jews have very different ideas about the role of Judaism.

10. Two important days in the Jewish calendar are _____ and _____.

11. The _____ is Turkey's legislature.

MAIN IDEAS

1. How did the United Nations attempt to resolve the conflict between Jews and Arabs in 1947?

_____

_____

2. What is life like for women in the region?

_____

_____

3. What role has Egypt played in creating peace in the region?

_____

_____

4. How did Atatürk's reforms change Turkey?

_____

_____

THINKING CRITICALLY

Answer the following questions on a separate sheet of paper.

1. Imagine that you are meeting with the leaders of Israel and the PLO. What advice would you give them?

2. Why do you think that fundamentalist Islamic groups are critical of Western culture?

The Geography of Africa South of the Sahara

BEFORE YOU READ

In the last chapter, you read about North Africa and Southwest Asia.

In this section, you will read about Africa's geography south of the Sahara.

AS YOU READ

Copy this chart to take notes about the geography of Africa south of the Sahara.

	Africa South of the Sahara
Landforms	
Waterways	
Climatic Regions	
Resources	

TERMS & NAMES

plateau a raised area of relatively level land

Great Rift Valley a series of broad, steep-walled valleys that stretch from the Red Sea to Mozambique

Sahel a semiarid region south of the Sahara

desertification the process by which land that could be farmed or lived on turns into desert

drought a long period of time without rain

savannas flat grasslands with scattered trees and shrubs

nonrenewable resources resources that cannot be replaced or that can be replaced only over millions of years

renewable resources resources that can be used and replaced over a relatively short time period

The African Continent (page 497)

How was Africa formed?

About 225 million years ago, Africa was the center of Pangaea, Earth's only continent. Pangaea broke up into separate continents that drifted apart over millions of years. The piece that became Africa stayed where it was.

1. What was Pangaea?

_____

_____

Landforms of Africa South of the Sahara (pages 498–499)

What is the highest peak in the highlands?

Africa has two major land types: lowlands in the north and west, and highlands in the south and east. Several peaks rise out of the highlands of Kenya and Tanzania. The highest is *Mount*

Kilimanjaro. It is snowcapped all year even though Kilimanjaro sits almost on the Equator.

Most of Africa south of the Sahara lies on a **plateau**, a raised area of relatively level land. The plateau rises from coastal plains.

The tectonic plates on which Africa sits have been slowly pulling apart for 50 million years. The separation of the plates has been forming broad valleys called *rifts*. The rifts make up the **Great Rift Valley,** which stretches from the Red Sea to Mozambique. The Great Rift Valley will become larger as East Africa pulls away from the rest of the continent. Eventually, East Africa may become an island. The island of Madagascar was formed in this way.

2. How will the Great Rift Valley change over time?

_____

_____

Copyright © McDougal Littell Inc.

Waterways of Africa South of the Sahara (page 499)

What are the major lakes and rivers in the region?

Parts of the Great Rift Valley have filled with water to form huge lakes such as Lake Tanganyika. Africa's largest lake is Lake Victoria. It lies in a shallow basin between two rift valleys on the borders of Uganda, Kenya, and Tanzania.

Many of Africa's rivers have exceptional features. The Nile, the world's longest river, flows north from central Africa. The Okavango crosses Angola, Namibia, and Botswana before emptying into marshes north of the Kalahari Desert. The Zambezi has many powerful waterfalls like Victoria Falls.

3. What is Africa's largest lake?

_____

_____

Many Climates (pages 500–501)

How does climate influence where animals and plants live?

Four major climatic regions of Africa south of the Sahara are desert (arid), semiarid, tropical, and equatorial. The different temperatures and amounts of rainfall influence which plants and animals live in each region.

Desert climates are found in the Sahara to the north, and the Namib and Kalahari to the south. These areas have little rain, high temperatures, and few plants and animals. Semiarid regions around the desert areas also have high temperatures, but more rainfall than the deserts.

The **Sahel** is a semiarid region south of the Sahara. This area is experiencing **desertification**—a process by which a desert spreads. **Drought,** or the lack of rain, is one cause. Fewer plants grow and soil blows away, leaving a dry, barren landscape. Other causes are overgrazing and overuse of the land for farming. This process contributes to widespread hunger in many African countries.

The tropical climate extends from the semiarid areas toward the Equator. It has a rainy season of up to six months.

Savannas, found in both semiarid and tropical areas, are flat grasslands with scattered trees and shrubs. More than 4.5 million square miles of Africa are savannas—and home to lions, elephants, giraffes, zebras, and other animals.

The equatorial region has two rainy seasons and two brief dry seasons each year. Located at the Equator, this climate has high temperatures year-round and annual rainfall of 50 to 60 inches. Rain forests with trees as tall as 195 feet grow here. Many animals including the chimpanzee, gorilla, hippopotamus, and African gray parrot live in the rain forest.

4. What is currently happening in the Sahel region?

_____

_____

Resources of Africa South of the Sahara (page 501)

What are some of the region's natural resources?

Africa is rich in resources. Minerals include gold, diamonds, copper, tin, chrome, nickel, and iron ore. **Nonrenewable resources,** such as copper and diamonds, cannot be replaced or can be replaced only over millions of years.

Renewable resources can be used and replaced over a relatively short time period. The renewable resources of this region include trees used to make wood products, cocoa beans, cashew nuts, peanuts, vanilla beans, coffee, bananas, rubber, sugar, and tea. Africa's wildlife and historic sites are resources that draw tourists from all over the world.

5. What is the difference between a nonrenewable resource and a renewable resource?

_____

_____

African Cultures and Empires

BEFORE YOU READ

In the last section, you read about Africa's geography south of the Sahara.

In this section, you will read about the cultures and empires of Africa south of the Sahara.

AS YOU READ

Copy this chart to take notes about the history and early development of Africa south of the Sahara

	Notes
Early Farmers	
Trade Networks	
Ancient Ghana	
The Mali Empire	
The Songhai Empire	

TERMS & NAMES

paleontologists scientists who study fossils

Bantu migration the gradual spreading of the Bantu across Africa over 2,000 years

Mansa Musa ruler of Mali during its golden age, from about 1312 to 1332

The First Humans (page 502)

How long ago did humans first inhabit Africa?

Fossil evidence shows that the first known humans lived in Africa several million years ago. **Paleontologists,** or scientists who study fossils, have discovered human remains in Kenya, South Africa, and other African nations. Fossilized human footprints, 3.6 million years old, have been found in Tanzania. It is now known that humans in Africa were the first to develop languages, tools, and culture. Then, over tens of thousands of years, they migrated to other continents.

1. What do paleontologists study?

_____

_____

Early African Farmers (page 503)

Who were the Bantus?

The first humans lived in small groups. For food, they collected berries, plants, and nuts and hunted wild animals. As plants and animals

became scarce, the people moved on. During this time, a group known as *Bantu* lived in what is now Cameroon. Around 5,000 years ago, the Bantu became farmers instead of hunter-gatherers. They learned to grow grain and herd cattle, sheep, and other animals. Later, they learned how to work with iron to make tools and weapons.

The Bantu began to move to other parts of Africa around 1000 B.C. and gradually spread across the continent over 2,000 years. Their great movement is called the **Bantu migration.** In their new homes, they grew and used different plants. Sometimes they lived apart from the local people, as did the Sans, or Bushmen. The Pygmies intermarried with the Bantu and lived amongst them. Over time, Bantu culture spread throughout Africa. Today, many Africans speak Swahili, Zulu, and other Bantu languages.

2. How did the Bantu migration affect Africa south of the Sahara?

_____

_____

Trade Networks (page 504)

Why was salt so precious that people were willing to trade gold and diamonds for it?

Eventually, the Bantu built permanent villages. Trade routes began to develop between these communities across Africa.

Salt was as precious to ancient Africans as gold and diamonds. People needed salt each day to stay alive and to preserve food. However, most of Africa south of the Sahara had no salt deposits. The closest source was in the Sahara. A vast trade network developed between the salt mines and the area south of the Sahara. To get salt, people in Southern Africa traded gold, slaves, ivory, and cola nuts.

African trade expanded even further when the Arabian camel was introduced to Africa in the A.D. 600s. Camels are well adapted for long treks across the desert. Using camels, salt traders could carry goods across the desert to Northern Africa. There they traded for goods from Europe and Asia. The desert trade was profitable, but risky. Robbers lived in the desert. For protection, traders traveled together in *caravans*.

3. How did camels help salt traders?

_____

_____

An Empire Built by Trade (page 505)

How did Ghana become an empire?

In the 4th century, a kingdom called Ghana arose in the Niger River valley. Ancient Ghana's location allowed it to control trade between Northern and Southern Africa. Traders had to pay a tax in gold nuggets to pass through the kingdom. Ghana also had many gold mines. The kingdom was called the Land of Gold.

People eagerly traded gold for other precious items, such as salt. Ghana's merchants also traded gold and slaves for cooking utensils, cloth, jewelry, copper, and weapons.

4. Why was Ghana called the Land of Gold?

_____

_____

The Mali Empire (pages 505–506)

How did the Mali Empire come to power?

Muslim armies began a war with Ghana in 1054. The fighting continued for many years and weakened the empire. By the 1200s, the people under Ghana's rule began to break away.

Around 1235, a Muslim leader named Sundiata united warring tribes. He then brought neighboring states under his rule and took control of what was left of the Ghana Empire along with lands to the east. Mali controlled important trade routes. Many people of the Mali Empire became Muslims.

Mansa Musa ruled Mali from about 1312 to 1332. Under his rule, Mali flourished. In 1324, he made a religious pilgrimage to Mecca. During his journey, he persuaded Muslim scholars and artisans to return to Mali with him. Timbuktu, Mali's major city, became a cultural center. Architects built beautiful mosques there. Scholars brought their knowledge of Islamic law, astronomy, medicine, and mathematics. Universities in several West African cities became centers of Islamic education.

5. How did Timbuktu become an Islamic center?

_____

_____

The Songhai Empire (page 506)

Why did Mali lose control of its empire?

Mali's power declined after Mansa Musa's death in 1337. Eventually, Mali was conquered by nearby Songhai, which now controlled trade across the Sahara. By the early 1500s, it was larger than Mali had been. Timbuktu again became a center of Muslim culture. A Moroccan army defeated the Songhai Empire in the 1590s.

6. How was the Songhai Empire similar to the Mali and Ghana empires?

_____

_____

The Impact of Colonialism on African Life

BEFORE YOU READ

In the last section, you read about the cultures and empires of Africa south of the Sahara.

In this section, you will read about how the slave trade and colonialism affected African life.

AS YOU READ

Copy this chart to take notes about the impact of the slave trade and colonialism on African life.

	Impact on African Life
Slave Trade	
Colonialism	

TERMS & NAMES

missionary a person who goes to another country to do religious and social work

Hutu the ethnic majority of Rwanda-Burundi

Tutsi the ethnic minority of Rwanda-Burundi

Africa Before the Europeans
(page 507)

What was life like for Africans before the Europeans came?

Before Europeans came, Africans had varied ways of life under different governments. Kings ruled great empires like Mali and Songhai. Some states had democratic rule. Some groups had no central government. Some Africans lived in great cities like Timbuktu, while others lived in small villages deep in the forests. Some were nomadic hunters, and others were skilled artists who sculpted masks and statues of wood, gold, or bronze.

1. What kinds of government did Africans have?

_____

_____

The Slave Trade (page 508)

When did European traders begin to capture and sell African slaves?

Slavery existed in Africa long before Europeans arrived. Rulers in Mali and Songhai had

thousands of slaves who worked as servants, soldiers, and farm workers. Villages raided one another to take captives and sell them. Often, a slave could work to earn his or her freedom. In the 1400s, however, Europeans introduced a form of slavery that devastated African life and society.

In the early 15th century, European traders began to sell slaves. They raided towns to capture unwilling Africans. Some Africans captured in wars were sold to European traders by other Africans. One estimate is that 10 to 12 million Africans were forced into slavery and sent to European colonies in North and South America from 1520 to 1860. Many more were captured but died of disease or starvation before arriving. By about 1750, movements to stop the slave trade had begun. By 1808, the United States, the United Kingdom, and Denmark had made it illegal to bring slaves from Africa. However, it would take longer for countries to make owning a slave illegal.

In addition to the Africans captured and sold, many were killed during raids. About two-thirds of those taken were men between the ages of

18 and 30. Slave traders chose young, strong, healthy people, leaving fewer people to lead families and villages. African cities and towns did not have enough workers. Family structures were destroyed.

2. From 1520 to 1860, about how many African slaves were sent to European colonies in North and South America?

_____

_____

European Colonialism (page 509)

Why were Europeans still interested in Africa after the slave trade had ended?

When Europeans ended the slave trade, they did not lose interest in Africa. The Industrial Revolution had changed economies in Europe and the United States. Africa could supply both raw materials, such as minerals, and new markets for goods.

Europeans knew little about the interior of Africa, but many were curious. Scientists and explorers were interested in African wildlife and natural resources. European **missionaries** also traveled to Africa. A missionary is a person who goes to another country to do religious and social work. Missionaries wanted to convert Africans to Christianity and bring education and health care to Africa. Many also taught European ways of thinking, which often conflicted with, and destroyed, African traditions.

In the 19th century, European nations began to compete for control of Africa. Each wanted the biggest or richest colonies and control of trade. To avoid wars over territory, European and U.S. leaders met in Berlin in 1884. There, and in later meetings, they discussed how to divide Africa. No Africans were consulted. Over the next 20 years, Belgium, France, the United Kingdom, Germany, Italy, Spain, Portugal, and the Ottoman Empire all established colonies in Africa. By 1912, only Ethiopia and Liberia remained independent.

3. Why did European countries want to establish colonies in Africa?

_____

_____

Impact of Colonial Rule (page 511)

How did Europeans create conflicts between ethnic groups in Africa?

When Europeans divided Africa, most colonizers cared mainly about gold, diamonds, and other resources. The Europeans knew little about Africa's political and social systems. Many Europeans looked down on Africa's rich cultures and tried to make Africans more like Europeans.

Europeans also created conflicts that had not existed before among ethnic groups. For example, the Belgian rulers of Rwanda-Burundi insisted that everyone carry identity cards saying whether they were **Hutu,** the ethnic majority, or **Tutsi,** the minority that had ruled the Hutu. Many people did not know which of these they were. The Belgians decided that anyone who owned more than ten cows was Tutsi. The Tutsi got the best education and jobs. Soon the Hutu were resentful, and a violent conflict began. In 1994, the conflict between the Hutu and the Tutsi escalated into a brutal civil war. The Tutsi were victorious and formed a new government in Rwanda.

4. Why was there a war between the Hutu and the Tutsi?

_____

_____

The Road to Independence

BEFORE YOU READ

In the last section, you read about how the slave trade and colonialism affected African life.

In this section, you will read about how African nations gained independence during the 20th century.

AS YOU READ

Copy this chart to take notes about how Nigeria and South Africa gained independence.

	Problems	Solutions
Nigeria		
South Africa		

TERMS & NAMES

racism the belief that one race is inferior to another

diversity a variety of cultures and viewpoints

apartheid an official policy of racial segregation formerly practiced in South Africa

Moving Toward Independence
(page 513)

***How* did Africa start moving toward independence in the 1920s and 1930s?**

Colonial rule in Africa disrupted social systems and governments, and robbed Africa of resources. Many Africans objected, but they did not have enough power to act. During the 1920s and 1930s, colonial rulers sent a few Africans to attend universities in Europe and the United States. These educated young people started to dream of independence. *Nationalism* grew strong.

1. Why were some of the young people of Africa thinking about independence in the 20s and 30s?

_____

_____

Journey to Freedom (page 514)

***Why* did many Europeans feel that Africans were unable to govern themselves?**

European nations wanted to keep their colonies for their valuable resources, even though they were expensive to maintain. Many Europeans believed that Africans were unable to govern themselves. This attitude is an example of **racism,** the unfounded belief that one race is inferior to another race.

Educated Africans believed they could govern themselves. African men had fought for the European Allies during World War I, and thousands had died. Ex-soldiers wanted self-rule. *Pan-Africanism*, an idea that people of African descent around the world should work together for their freedom, attracted more supporters. In 1919, the first Pan-African Congress was organized. Africans again fought in World War II. After this war, many felt that they now deserved independence.

At the fifth Pan-African Congress in 1945, there were 90 delegates; 26 were from all over Africa. Several of these men would become the political leaders of their countries, including Kwame Nkrumah of Ghana, and Jomo Kenyatta of Kenya.

2. How did Pan-Africanism help bring about change in Africa?

_____

_____

New African Countries/Nigeria: Diversity Brings Division (page 515)

Why was it difficult for Nigeria to organize the nation after independence?

Between 1951 and 1980, most of the colonies in Africa south of the Sahara gained independence. For some countries, the path to nationhood was smooth. For others, it was not. Nigeria and South Africa had different experiences in achieving independence.

Before Nigeria gained independence from the United Kingdom in 1960, it had experienced a well-organized government, rich resources, and a strong economy under British rule. It was hoped that Nigeria's **diversity**—its many different cultures and viewpoints—would be a source of strength. Many Nigerians are Muslim, while others are Christian or follow traditional African religions. Nigerians speak more than 400 languages. However, instead of being a source of strength, this diversity caused problems.

The slave trade and colonial rule had created hostility between the ethnic groups in Nigeria. Many Nigerian politicians focused on their ethnic group and not the whole country. Some leaders stole money and gave or took bribes.

In 1966, deadly riots broke out, and many were killed. The next year, people in the eastern part of Nigeria announced the formation of a separate country, Biafra. After three years of civil war between Biafran Nigerians and the Nigerian army, Biafra was defeated and rejoined Nigeria. Since then, military leaders have primarily ruled Nigeria.

3. How did diversity cause problems for Nigerians after they gained independence?

_____

_____

Independence of South Africa
(page 516)

What is apartheid?

The United Kingdom gave South Africa independence in 1910. This action did not bring freedom to most South Africans. Only white South Africans could vote, and many laws were passed to restrict nonwhites.

In 1948, an official policy of racial segregation known as **apartheid** was adopted. Apartheid strictly separated people by color. Many people resisted apartheid. Protesters held marches, went on strike, and sometimes became violent. Although many protesters were jailed or killed, they did make progress. In 1991, apartheid ended. In 1994, for the first time, all South African adults could vote.

4. Why did apartheid in South Africa end?

_____

_____

Glossary/After You Read

Pangaea 225 million years ago, Earth's only continent

Mount Kilimanjaro the highest peak in the highlands of Africa south of the Sahara

rift a deep crack formed when plates of Earth separate

fossil the remains of an animal or plant from an earlier age, hardened and preserved in earth or rock

Bantu early farmers whose culture spread throughout Africa

pilgrimage a journey to a place that is held in reverence or honor

nationalism patriotic feelings for one's own nation

Pan-Africanism a movement to unite African nations politically

TERMS & NAMES

A. Fill in the blank with the name or term that best completes the sentence.

1. Nigeria's _____ caused problems after independence.

   drought   racism   diversity

2. The _____ are the ethnic majority of Rwanda-Burundi.

   Sahel   Tutsi   Hutu

3. A tree used to make wood products is an example of a _____.

   renewable resource   nonrenewable resource   savanna

4. One cause of desertification is _____.

   apartheid   diversity   drought

5. In South Africa, the major cause of apartheid was _____.

   racism   savanna   diversity

B. In the space provided, write the letter of the term or name that matches the description.

a. Bantu migration   _____   **1.** a scientist who studies fossils

b. Sahel   _____   **2.** This stretches from the Red Sea to Mozambique.

c. paleontologist   _____   **3.** someone who goes to another country to do religious and social work

d. Great Rift Valley

e. plateau   _____   **4.** the ruler of Mali during its golden age

                            _____   **5.** a raised area of level land

f. Mansa Musa   _____   **6.** the gradual spreading of the Bantu across Africa

g. missionary   _____   **7.** a semi-arid region south of the Sahara

MAIN IDEAS

1. How would you describe the landforms of Africa south of the Sahara?

_____

_____

_____

2. Why did the Bantu culture spread?

_____

_____

_____

3. How did the slave trade affect life in the region?

_____

_____

_____

4. Why were the Europeans still interested in the region after the slave trade ended?

_____

_____

_____

5. What is racism, and how did Africans try to overcome it after they gained independence?

_____

_____

_____

THINKING CRITICALLY

Answer the following questions on a separate sheet of paper.

1. Why do you think that countries with great diversity sometimes have internal conflicts?

2. Do you think that missionaries had a positive or negative impact on Africans after the slave trade? Explain.

Name _____ Date _____

Section 1 (pages 523–527)

History and Political Change

BEFORE YOU READ

In the last chapter, you read about Africa south of the Sahara.

In this section, you will read about the difficulties faced by some countries in Western and Central Africa in creating stable governments.

AS YOU READ

Copy this web to take notes about the challenges faced by countries in Western and Central Africa in creating stable governments.

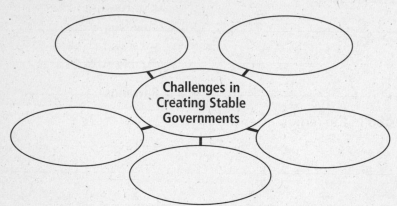

TERMS & NAMES

coup d'état an overthrow of a government by force

OAU the Organization of African Unity, an organization formed in 1963 to promote unity among all Africans

mediate to help find a peaceful solution.

ECOWAS the Economic Community of West African States, formed in 1975 to improve trade within Western Africa and with countries outside the region

Dividing Western and Central Africa/New Maps of West Africa
(pages 523–524)

How did the European powers avoid war in Africa?

European nations divided the African continent in the late 1800s. They were not thinking about creating new nations. Their goal was to control Africa's resources.

When Europeans divided Africa, they ignored traditional borders between Africa's ethnic groups. They drew new maps based on the location of rivers or lakes. For example, Belgium, France, and Portugal all wanted the *Congo River* and the lands around it. In 1885, the three nations agreed to divide the Congo Basin. King Leopold of Belgium took what is now the Democratic Republic of the Congo as

his personal property. France took what is now the Republic of the Congo. Portugal controlled present-day Angola.

1. How did European nations' interest in African rivers affect the way they divided up the continent?

Governments in Western and Central Africa (pages 524–525)

Why have many African governments been unstable?

When African nations became independent, many colonial borders stayed the same. These borders split ethnic groups, making it difficult for nations to establish stable governments.

Since 1963, about 200 African governments have been ousted by coups d'état. A **coup d'état** is an overthrow of a government by force. Two of the countries that have struggled to create stable democratic governments are the Democratic Republic of the Congo and Ghana.

2. Why have there been so many coups d'état since 1963?

_____

_____

Government in the Democratic Republic of the Congo (page 525)

How was the Democratic Republic of the Congo established?

In 1960, the former Belgian Congo gained independence, but a series of coups d'état toppled each established government. Five years later, an army general, Joseph Désiré Mobutu, took power. Mobutu tried to wipe out all traces of colonialism and changed the name of the country to Zaire. He made people wear African-style clothing and take names that were African instead of Belgian.

Mobutu ruled as a *dictator,* allowing no criticism of his rule. He became rich by stealing government money.

A brutal civil war began in Zaire in 1994. It resulted in Laurent Désiré Kabila overthrowing Mobutu's government. Kabila changed Zaire's name to the Democratic Republic of the Congo. Civil war started again, and Kabila was assassinated in 2001. His son, Joseph Kabila, replaced him.

3. What happened between 1994 and 2001?

_____

_____

Government in Ghana (pages 525–526)

How did the government of Ghana become modernized?

In 1957, the British colony of Gold Coast became the first independent country in the

region. Kwame Nkrumah was the country's first leader. Nkrumah wanted to make Ghana modern. He built a new seaport, roads, and railroads. Foreign trade improved. Ghana became the first country in the region to have compulsory primary education.

Nkrumah was a dictator. In 1966, a coup d'état was staged. The new leaders freed political prisoners and tried to help businesses. Still, conditions in Ghana grew worse. People lost jobs and did not have food. More coups d'état followed. In 1979, Jerry John Rawlings, a soldier, took power.

In 1992, Rawlings allowed an election to take place. Soon, a constitution and parliament put limits on his power. In 2000, Rawlings became the first African military ruler to give up power. Elections brought a new president. Today, Ghana is one of the most stable African nations.

4. How did Nkrumah and Rawlings change Ghana?

_____

_____

Nations Helping Nations (page 527)

How have African nations supported each other?

In 1963, the **OAU,** or the Organization of African Unity, was formed. This organization promotes unity. It would like a single currency for Africa. It also mediates disputes between nations. To **mediate** means to help find a peaceful solution.

ECOWAS, or the Economic Community of West African States, was formed in 1975. It works to improve trade, mediate disputes, and end government corruption in Western Africa and in other countries.

5. What is the OAU?

_____

_____

Economies and Cultures

BEFORE YOU READ

In the last section, you read about history and political change in Western and Central Africa.

In this section, you will read about the economies and culture of the region.

AS YOU READ

Copy this web to take notes about the economies and culture of Western and Central Africa.

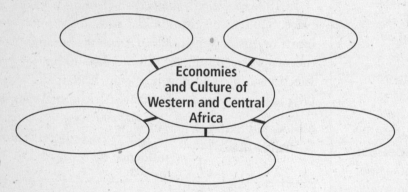

Economies and Culture of Western and Central Africa

Economies of Western and Central Africa (page 530)

What is the economic history of Western and Central Africa?

Most African countries once had *traditional economies*. This means that they followed customs of trading goods. Then colonial governments introduced the market economy, in which goods were bought and sold. Command economies were common after independence. Today, most African countries are moving back to market economies.

1. Who introduced the market economy to Africa?

_____

_____

Agriculture in Western and Central Africa (page 531)

What is the difference between subsistence and cash crops?

Most people in Western and Central Africa practice **subsistence farming**. That is, they grow food mainly to feed their own households. During the colonial era, European and African business owners started large plantations. They grew tropical crops—sugar cane, coffee, and cacao—for export. A crop grown only for sale is called a **cash crop**.

Coastal West African countries export cacao beans, coffee, bananas, pineapples, palm oil, peanuts, and kola nuts. Central African countries produce coffee, rubber, and cotton. These exports bring income for development, such as building roads and schools.

2. Which crops are mainly cultivated for export?

_____

_____

Copyright © McDougal Littell Inc.

African Artisans (page 531)
What jobs do people in western and central Africa have?

Most people in western and central Africa are farmers, but some have other jobs. Some people work with metal, leather, or wood. They make iron hoes, leather shoes, and artworks. Other people are entertainers and musicians. Musicians act as the historians in some traditional African societies. Their stories are passed down from generation to generation.

3. How do the region's musicians act as historians?

_____

_____

African Minerals (pages 531–532)
What valuable minerals are found in this part of Africa?

Almost every type of mineral can be found in Africa. Valuable minerals exported from Western and Central Africa include diamonds, gold, petroleum, manganese, and uranium. Many Africans earn their living by working in mines.

Africa's mineral wealth is sometimes used to help fund wars. During Angola's civil war, the government used income from oil exports to buy weapons, while rebel forces traded diamonds for guns. Diamonds have also been exported illegally to support brutal wars in Sierra Leone and the Democratic Republic of the Congo. In Sierra Leone, diamonds were sold to buy weapons for rebel forces.

4. How has Africa's mineral wealth been misused?

_____

_____

Ways of Life in Western and Central Africa (page 532)
How is life changing in Western and Central Africa?

In Western and Central Africa, hundreds of different ethnic groups speak more than 1,000 languages. People practice many different religions, including Islam and Christianity. Most Africans live in villages, but many are moving to large cities. City living has strained traditional family life and culture.

Society in Western and Central Africa is based on *extended families* that include children, parents, grandparents, and other close relatives. Some ethnic groups trace ancestry through the mother's family; others through the father's family. People share both work and free time with their family.

5. How do extended families affect society in Western and Central Africa?

_____

_____

Social Status (pages 533–534)
What role does age play in African societies?

In many African societies, older people have higher status and more influence than younger ones. For example, when the Igbo of Nigeria gather, the men sit in order of age. The eldest men are served food and drink first. In some communities, each age group has different responsibilities. Men of the most senior rank settle legal disputes and police the village. Female elders punish behavior that harms women, such as unfair treatment by husbands.

Because age is so important, a special ceremony called a **rite of passage** marks the transition from one stage of life to another. A major rite of passage occurs when young men and women are recognized as adults. However, this tradition is dying out in parts of Africa. Some younger people are gaining higher status because of their skills. For example, educated youths who know a European language are highly valued.

6. What tradition is dying out in parts of Africa?

_____

_____

Nigeria Today

BEFORE YOU READ

In the last section, you read about the economies and culture of Western and Central Africa.

In this section, you will read about Nigeria today.

AS YOU READ

Copy this web to take notes about modern-day Nigeria.

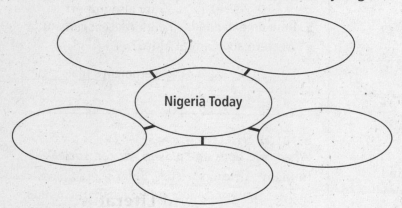

Nigeria Today

TERMS & NAMES

Yoruba an ethnic group in southwestern Nigeria

Igbo an ethnic group in southeastern Nigeria

Hausa the largest ethnic group in Nigeria

Wole Soyinka a Yoruba man who was the first African to receive the Nobel Prize in literature

A Look at Nigeria (page 536)

How would you describe Nigeria?

Nigeria is a diverse nation. Its land includes several types of environments, such as tropical rain forests, mangrove swamps, and savannas. Its people and cultures come from more than 250 ethnic groups. Nigeria has a long history and a rich artistic heritage. However, like other African countries, Nigeria faced violence as it became a modern democracy.

1. How is modern-day Nigeria a diverse nation?

_____

_____

History of Nigeria's People

(page 537)

What are Nigeria's three main ethnic groups?

The Nok people were one of the earliest known cultures in the land that is now Nigeria. By about 500 B.C., they occupied the central plateau.

Today, about 60 percent of Nigerians belong to one of three major ethnic groups: the **Yoruba**, the **Igbo**, and the **Hausa**. The first Yoruba established their kingdom on the western bank of the Niger River. The Igbo were part of the Nri kingdom in the southeast and the Hausa built cities in the northern savannas.

Most of the **Yoruba** today live in southwestern Nigeria. Before colonial rule, Yoruba society was organized around powerful *city-states*. Yoruba men grew yams, peanuts, millet, beans, and other crops. Artists and poets had great prestige. Yoruba women specialized in marketing and trade. Their businesses made some women wealthy and independent.

For thousands of years, the **Igbo** have lived in the southeast region of Nigeria. Igbo villages are democratic, with leaders chosen rather than inheriting their position. They are known for their metalworking, weaving, and woodcarving. In colonial times, many Igbo held jobs in business and government.

The **Hausa** are the largest ethnic group in Nigeria. Almost all Hausa are Muslims. Most live in farming villages in northern Nigeria. Crafts such as leatherworking, weaving, and blacksmithing have been passed down through generations.

2. What crafts are the Igbo and Hausa known for?

_____

_____

Becoming a Democracy (page 538)
How did Nigeria become a democracy?

In the 1800s, the United Kingdom *colonized* the northern and southern areas of what is now Nigeria. English became the common language. The two regions were united in 1914. In the 1920s, Nigerians began working toward separating from Great Britain.

When oil was found in eastern Nigeria, the Igbo people finally declared their independence in 1960. They set up the Republic of Biafra. Civil war raged from 1966 to 1970, causing a million deaths. After the war, military rulers took over. People had little freedom. Sometimes elections were held, but leaders often ignored the results. Finally, in May 1999, Nigeria had a free election. Former military ruler Olusegon Obasanjo was elected president.

3. How was life for Nigerians after they declared independence from Great Britain in 1960?

_____

_____

Nigeria's Economy (page 538)
What resources are important to Nigeria's economy?

Nigeria has more than 123 million people—the largest population in Africa. More than half of Nigerians are farmers. Huge areas of the country have rubber, cacao, peanut, and palm oil plantations. The country has rich deposits of oil and natural gas. Oil is Nigeria's main export, supplying more than 90 percent of government income. Minerals, such as coal, iron ore, tin, lead, limestone, and zinc, are also important to the economy. Factories produce cars, cement, chemicals, clothing, and processed foods.

4. What is the Nigerian government's main source of income?

_____

_____

Nigerian Art and Literature
(page 539)
What are some examples of Nigerian art?

Nigeria's many cultures and ethnic groups have produced a mix of artistic styles. Yoruban artists have been making metal sculptures for about a thousand years. Yoruba also carve wooden masks and figures, and make calabashes, or gourds. Dried, hollow gourds are used as food containers or musical instruments. Baskets are made from local plants.

Nigerians are also famous for their literature. Nigerian writers such as Amos Tutuola, Ben Okri, and Wole Soyinka have used folktale themes. Their novels and plays combine these themes with modern-day concerns such as human rights.

5. Who are some of Nigeria's famous writers?

_____

_____

Glossary/After You Read

city-state an independent state that consists of a central city and its surrounding villages

colonize to settle in a territory that is governed by a distant country

Congo River the second longest river in Africa

dictator a person who rules over a country with absolute power

extended family a group of relatives who live together, including others besides parents and children

status position or rank

status quo the existing state of affairs

traditional economy an economy based on trading goods

TERMS & NAMES

A. If the statement is true, write "true" on the line. If it is false, change the underlined word or words to make it true.

_____ **1.** A <u>rite of passage</u> is the overthrow of a government by force.

_____ **2.** To <u>mediate</u> means to settle disputes.

_____ **3.** The <u>Yoruba</u> is the largest ethnic group in Nigeria.

_____ **4.** Most of the <u>Hausa</u> live in farming villages in northern Nigeria.

_____ **5.** A <u>cash crop</u> is a crop grown for sale.

B. Write the letter of the term or name next to the description that matches it.

_____ **1.** a special ceremony that marks the transition from one stage of life to another

_____ **2.** formed in 1975 to improve trade within Western Africa and with countries outside the region

_____ **3.** an organization formed in 1963 to promote unity among all Africans

_____ **4.** the growing of food to feed farmers' own households

_____ **5.** an ethnic group in southeastern Nigeria

_____ **6.** the first African to receive the Nobel Prize in literature

a. subsistence farming

b. ECOWAS

c. OAU

d. rite of passage

e. Igbo

f. Wole Soyinka

MAIN IDEAS

1. How did colonization affect the governments of modern African nations?

_____

_____

_____

2. How do people in Western and Central Africa earn a living?

_____

_____

_____

3. How does social status affect life in many African societies?

_____

_____

_____

4. Describe the three ethnic groups to which most Nigerians belong.

_____

_____

_____

5. How do modern-day artists keep African heritage alive?

_____

_____

_____

THINKING CRITICALLY

Answer the following questions on a separate sheet of paper.

1. Do you think that Mobutu was a popular leader? What qualities do you think make a great leader?

2. How do you think that a rite of passage could influence a young person?

History and Governments

BEFORE YOU READ

In the last chapter, you read about Western and Central Africa.

In this section, you will read about the history and governments of Eastern and Southern Africa.

AS YOU READ

Copy this chart to take notes about Eastern and Southern Africa's history and its governments.

	The History and Governments of Eastern and South Africa
History	
Governments	

TERMS & NAMES

Great Zimbabwe a stone city built by the Shona empire beginning in the A.D. 900s in the area that is today Zimbabwe

Masai an ethnic group in Africa

Zulu an ethnic group in Africa

Early Humans in Eastern and Southern Africa/Early Eastern and Southern African Kingdoms
(pages 545–547)

Why did empires develop in Eastern and Southern Africa?

The oldest fossils of humans have been found in sites from Ethiopia to South Africa dating back 3.5 million years. Tools of stone made 2.5 million years ago have also been found in Eastern Africa. Early humans spread slowly across Africa before migrating to other continents. Those that remained became farmers and herders.

As the population grew, societies became complex, and trade developed. Income from trade helped to build kingdoms.

About 2,000 years ago, a trading empire called Aksum developed in what is now Ethiopia. Ships carried goods to Aksum from Southern Africa, Arabia, Europe, and India. About A.D. 350, Christianity spread throughout Ethiopia. When Islam came to Arabia, Aksum lost much of its trade because the Muslim nations preferred to trade with each other.

Around A.D. 700, trading empires arose in Southern Africa. The Africans traded their precious metals for textiles and spices from India, and silk and porcelain from China.

The Shona was one of the great trading empires of the lower Zambezi River from about 1100 to 1500. Its people created walled stone structures called *zimbabwes*. **The Great Zimbabwe** is a spectacular stone ruin of a city made up of three parts. The Great Enclosure is the largest single ancient structure in Africa south of the Sahara. The Hill Complex is the oldest section. The Valley Ruins include remnants of brick buildings.

1. What is the Great Zimbabwe?

_____

_____

Other Eastern and Southern African Societies (pages 547–548)
How did the Masai and Zulu societies develop?

Eastern and Southern Africa had other societies besides the great trade kingdoms. Two of these societies were the Masai and the Zulu.

The **Masai** once lived in nearly all of Kenya and about half of what is now Tanzania. They were nomads who moved from place to place so their animals would have fresh land to graze. Land belonged to the group, not to individuals. In the 1800s, the Masai fought each other over water and grazing rights, and many died. The Masai also suffered during long droughts when many cattle died.

The **Zulu** migrated to Southern Africa about 1,800 years ago. They lived in villages, farmed, and raised cattle. *Shaka Zulu* became chief of the Zulu in 1815. He led wars to expand Zulu territory. Shaka Zulu abused his unlimited power; his half-brother assassinated him in 1828.

Soon after the death of Shaka Zulu, the British and Germans invaded Masai territory. Weakened by war and drought, the Masai were no longer powerful. The Europeans then took the lands they wanted. The Masai had to live on *reserves*—small territories set aside for them. By the late 1800s, the United Kingdom, Germany, and France had claimed most of Eastern and Southern Africa.

2. Why did the Masai and the Zulu lose most of their territory?

_____

_____

African Independence (page 548)
Why were the nations of Eastern and Southern Africa able to achieve independence?

World Wars I and II weakened Europe. After the wars, European nations began to lose control of African colonies. This paved the way for independence. Most of the countries of Eastern Africa, such as Djibouti, Kenya, Tanzania, Rwanda, and Burundi, became independent between 1960 and 1964. Most of the countries of Southern Africa achieved independence later. Almost all of the new African governments were democracies, but many were later overthrown and became dictatorships. Today, many African nations are again turning toward democracy.

3. What kind of government did most nations in Eastern and Southern Africa chose after independence?

_____

_____

Government in Somalia (pages 548–549)
How was Somalia governed from 1969 until 1991?

From 1969 to 1991, Somalia was ruled by the dictator Siad Barre. In the 1980s, about 100 citizens published an open letter criticizing his government. In the United States, it is legal to publish letters criticizing leaders. In Somalia, it was not. Forty-five of those who signed the letter were arrested.

The arrests led to more protests. By 1990, Barre was forced to *reform* his government. In 1991, he was driven from office. Since then, twelve clans have been fighting for control.

4. Why were forty-five Somalians sent to jail for writing an open letter?

_____

_____

Government in Rwanda (page 549)
How did a new constitution help Rwandan women in 1991?

Through much of the 1900s, Rwandan women could not own land, hold jobs, or participate in government. In 1991, a new constitution was passed. It gave women the right to own property and hold jobs. But the new laws were not enforced. Then, in 1994, a civil war began in Rwanda. So many men were killed that women began taking over as heads of households. As a result of the wars, women were able to claim their constitutional rights. Since the conflict, more laws benefiting women have been passed. Today, Rwandan women can both own and inherit property.

5. How did women gain their constitutional rights?

_____

_____

Economies and Cultures

BEFORE YOU READ
In the last section, you read about the history and governments of Eastern and Southern Africa.

In this section, you will read about the economies and cultures of Eastern and Southern Africa.

AS YOU READ
Copy this chart to take notes about the economies, the culture, and the religions of Eastern and Southern Africa.

	Eastern and Southern Africa
Economics	
Culture	
Religions	

TERMS & NAMES

pastoralism a way of life in which people survive by raising cattle, sheep, or goats

overgrazing the process in which animals graze grass faster than it can grow back

kinship family relationships

Agriculture in Eastern and Southern Africa (pages 552–553)

What industries make up the economy of Eastern and Southern Africa?

Agriculture is the primary industry in Eastern and Southern Africa, even though drought is a serious problem. An exception is the area around Lake Victoria that tends to get enough rain to support the growth of crops. People in this area grow bananas, strawberries, sweet potatoes, and yams. Cash crops such as coffee and cotton are grown in parts of Kenya, Rwanda, Burundi, and Uganda.

In some areas of Africa, there is not enough rain to grow any crops. Somalia and most of Kenya receive less than 20 inches of rain each year. People survive by raising grazing animals, such as cattle, sheep, or goats. This way of life is called **pastoralism.** Many pastoralists are nomads. Today, because of Africa's increasing population, there are fewer places for nomads to graze their animals. As a result, the land is suffering from **overgrazing,** or the process in which animals graze grass faster than it

can grow back. Overgrazing is a cause of desertification in Africa.

Africa's large lakes support *commercial* fishing. Lake Victoria was once home to almost 500 native species of fish. Most of these fish were too small to support a large fishing industry. The large Nile perch was then introduced into Lake Victoria. Since then, nearly all the native fish have disappeared. Today, commercial fishing of the Nile perch has brought many jobs to the area and provided an important export.

1. How has pastoralism affected the land in parts of Africa?

_____

_____

Africa's Economic Strength
(pages 554–555)

Why is Southern Africa's economy so strong?

Eastern Africa is the poorest region on the continent. Countries in Southern Africa have more diverse economies than do those in Eastern Africa. This means people have more ways to earn a living. For example, several countries in Southern Africa are rich in mineral resources, so there are jobs in mining. South Africa and Zimbabwe also have many manufacturing jobs. South Africa has by far the strongest economy in the region. In 2000, it had a Gross Domestic Product, or GDP, of approximately $369 billion.

The countries of Southern Africa work together to improve the economy of the region. This includes improving transportation and communication among countries. For example, the railway lines of Botswana, Namibia, Lesotho, South Africa, and Swaziland are linked. These lines carry goods from all areas of Southern Africa to major ports along the Atlantic and Indian coasts.

2. What are some industries that contribute to Southern Africa's economic strength?

_____

_____

Cultures of Eastern and Southern Africa (pages 555–556)

How are family relationships changing in Eastern and Southern Africa?

Marriage and kinship are changing in Eastern and Southern Africa as people move to cities. **Kinship** means family relationships. Economic activity brings people together; as they trade goods, they trade ideas. Their behavior and attitudes change as well.

In Eastern and Southern Africa, musical traditions of different cultural groups come together. One characteristic of Southern African music is repetition. The Shona people of Zimbabwe make mbira music. Mbira music forms patterns of repetition using different voices or instruments. In Zulu choral music, voices singing different parts enter a song at various points. This creates a rich sound pattern. Another kind of traditional music is called

hocketing. Groups of musicians play flutes or trumpets. Each musician plays one note. Then they rotate playing to create a continuous song.

African musical traditions moved across North America, South America, and Europe because of the slave trade and European colonization. African musicians have added elements of European, West Asian, and American music to their musical styles to create new types of music. Jiti, for example, is a type of Shona mbira music that follows the traditional mbira rhythms using an electric guitar.

3. How did African music reach different parts of the world?

_____

_____

Religion in Eastern and Southern Africa (page 556)

What religions do most people in Southern and Eastern Africa practice?

Today, about 85 percent of Southern and Eastern Africans practice Islam or Christianity. Only 15 percent practice a traditional African religion. Many traditional African religions focus on the worship of sky gods, ancestors, or spirits of rivers and of Earth. However, like Islam and Christianity, African religions recognize one supreme creator. Many Africans practice a traditional African religion that is combined with another religion.

4. What do most of the religions practiced in Southern and Eastern Africa have in common?

_____

_____

South Africa Today

BEFORE YOU READ

In the last section, you read about the economies and cultures of Eastern and Southern Africa.

In this section, you will read about historical events that have influenced South Africa.

AS YOU READ

Copy this time line to take notes about events that influenced modern-day South Africa.

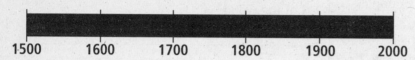

1500 1600 1700 1800 1900 2000

TERMS & NAMES

veldt the flat grassland of Southern Africa

Afrikaners descendants of the Dutch settlers of South Africa

Boers a group of Dutch pastoral farmers in South Africa

African National Congress a group of black South Africans opposed to apartheid

Nelson Mandela an African man who led the fight against apartheid, was jailed for 26 years, and later became South Africa's president

sanction a measure taken by a nation or nations against a country that is violating international law

Willem de Klerk a white South African who opposed apartheid and became the country's president in 1989

Geography of South Africa (page 560)

How would you describe the geography of South Africa?

South Africa is located at the southern tip of Africa. The world's largest and richest gold field is located in the South African city of Johannesburg. It is called Witwatersrand, or the Rand, and contains diamonds, uranium, and platinum. Since South Africa is south of the Equator, winter is in July and summer is in January. Most of South Africa is on a plateau. Farmers raise cattle, corn, fruit, potatoes, and wheat on a flat grassland called the **veldt.**

1. What is the veldt?

_____

_____

History of South Africa (page 561)

Which groups have ruled over South Africa?

South Africa was home to Khoisan and Bantu peoples for more than 1500 years. The Khoisan were herders and hunters and the Bantu were farmers.

In 1652, the Dutch founded the Cape Town colony. Their descendents, called **Afrikaners,** make up more than half of modern South Africa's white population. Over time, Dutch settlers left Cape Town to become pastoral farmers. Known as **Boers,** they developed their own culture and fought with Africans over land.

German, French, and British settlers followed the Dutch. The Cape Town colony came under British control in the early 1800s. Africans resisted British efforts to force them out of the region. Thousands of Boers established two independent states in the 1850s and followed a policy of apartheid.

The discovery of diamonds and gold in the second half of the 19th century renewed European interest in the area. Between 1899 and 1902, the British and the Boers fought each other in the South African War. Africans supported the British in hopes of gaining equal rights. The British won and the Boer states came under British rule. Black protest organizations were formed when their situation did not improve.

2. Why did Africans support the British during the South African War?

_____

_____

A Nation of Apartheid (pages 562–563)
Why was the African National Congress created?

In 1910, the British colony became the Union of South Africa. Afrikaners had a political voice in the new nation. *Racial segregation* or separation continued under several new laws. Nonwhites were *discriminated* against in terms of housing, travel, employment, and education. Many were forced to leave their homes. Apartheid became the official policy of South Africa in 1948 under the rule of the Afrikaner Nationalist Party.

The ANC, or **African National Congress,** was a group of black South Africans that opposed apartheid. **Nelson Mandela** led the anti-apartheid movement in the 1950s and encouraged people to use non-violent methods to show their feelings, rather than using violence. When the government responded with arrests and violence, the ANC became more aggressive. The fight continued for decades. Hundreds of demonstrators were killed, and thousands more were arrested. Mandela was one of the people arrested and jailed. He remained in a small cell for 26 years.

In the 1970s and 1980s, strikes by Africans had a negative impact on the economy and forced the government to change some apartheid laws. In 1985, the United States and Great Britain agreed to impose economic

sanctions against South Africa. A **sanction** is a measure taken by nations against a country violating international law. **Willem de Klerk,** a white South African who opposed apartheid, became president in 1989. He helped to *repeal* apartheid laws and to release Nelson Mandela from jail. After Mandela's release in 1990, he and de Klerk worked to end apartheid.

In 1993, a new constitution gave all adults the right to vote and Mandela and de Klerk shared the Nobel Peace Prize for their efforts. In 1994, Nelson Mandela was elected president, served one five-year term, and retired in 1999. Thabo Mbeki became president.

3. Who is Nelson Mandela, and why was he in jail for 26 years?

_____

_____

A New Era for South Africa
(page 563)
How has the constitution of South Africa changed?

Today, the constitution of South Africa guarantees the same rights to everyone in South Africa. However, most black South Africans remain very poor. The government is working to provide better housing and to bring electricity and water to communities without them. South Africa continues to have the strongest economy in Southern Africa.

Like its people, the cultures of South Africa are diverse. For example, South Africa has 11 official languages. However, English is understood by almost every South African because it is used in schools and universities. South African art and music are other examples of the country's diverse culture. Jazz and jive have combined with Zulu and Sotho rhythms to make a new, vibrant musical style.

4. What is the government doing to help poor South Africans?

_____

_____

Kenya Today

BEFORE YOU READ
In the last section, you read about South Africa today. In this section, you will read about Kenya today.

AS YOU READ
Copy this web to take notes about life in Kenya.

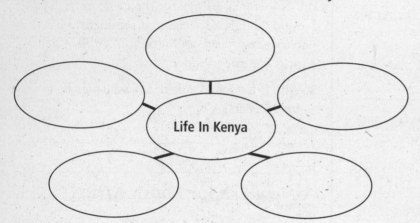

TERMS & NAMES

multiparty system a political system in which two or more parties exist

Swahili a Bantu language in Africa

harambee a Swahili term that means "pulling together" and that is used in reference to Kenyan schools built by Kenyan people rather than the government

Geography of Kenya (page 564)
How would you describe Kenya's geography?

Kenya, on Africa's east coast, lies directly on the Equator. Its national park system is home to many threatened species, including rhinoceros, elephants, and cheetahs. Most of Kenya's human population lives in the highlands in the southwest where there is rich soil and plenty of rain. Nairobi, the capital and largest city, and Mount Kenya are found here. Kenya's coast has tropical beaches and rain forests. The remaining three-quarters of Kenya are covered by a plain that is too dry for farming. Kenyans who live here are herders.

1. Why do most Kenyans live in the highlands?

_____

_____

Early History of Kenya (page 565)
Where did early Kenyans come from?

About 3,000 years ago, farmers, herders, and hunters from other parts of Africa began arriving in Kenya. Some were part of the Bantu migration. Others came from the northeast. Greek, Roman, and Arabian traders and sailors often visited Kenya's coast along the Indian Ocean. Arabs set up trading posts there about 1,200 years ago. Portuguese sailors arrived in the early 1500s and took control of these trading posts. In the late 1800s, Kenya became a British colony. It gained independence in 1963.

2. When did Kenya gain Independence from Great Britain?

_____

_____

Government of Kenya (page 565)

Why were many Kenyans dissatisfied with Prime Minister Moi's political system in the early 1990s?

Kenya's first prime minister, Jomo Kenyatta, ruled from 1963 until 1978, when he died in office. Vice President Daniel arap Moi then became prime minister. Moi's party was the only political party. By the early 1990s, however, many Kenyans became dissatisfied with this political system. One problem was that Moi gave special favors to people of his own ethnic group, the Kalenjin. After Kenyans held violent demonstrations in 1991, Moi agreed to allow a **multiparty system.** This meant other parties could offer ideas for new laws and policies that might be different from Moi's ideas. Despite the change, Moi remained in power. Some people believe that Moi won the 1992 and 1997 elections through fraud.

3. How did Moi attempt to change Kenya's political system in 1991?

_____

_____

The People of Kenya (page 566)

Who are the people who live in Kenya today?

Thirty to forty different ethnic groups live in Kenya today. The Kikuyu are the largest group, making up approximately 20 percent of the population. Other large ethnic groups include the Kalenjin, Kamba, Luhya, and Luo. Most groups have their own language. Many people also know Swahili and use it to communicate with other groups. **Swahili** is a Bantu language that includes many Arabic words. Swahili and English are the official languages of Kenya.

Education is very important to Kenyans. About 80 percent of Kenya's children go to elementary school. Government-run elementary schools are free, but students must pay tuition to attend their high schools. Most parts of Kenya have government-run schools. However, in some places where the government has not built schools yet, Kenyans build them themselves. These schools are called **harambee** schools. Harambee means "pulling together" in Swahili.

About 80 percent of Kenyans work in agriculture. The most profitable cash crops are coffee and tea. Farmers also grow bananas, corn, pineapples, and sugar cane. Tourism brings the most money into Kenya's economy. More than 500,000 tourists visit Kenya each year. Tourists visit the national parks to see the antelope, buffalo, elephants, giraffes, lions, and other native animals. Kenya protects these animals as an important natural resource.

4. What industry makes the most money for Kenya's economy, and why?

_____

_____

Nairobi (page 567)

What is Nairobi like?

Nairobi is Kenya's capital. The city's name comes from a Masai word meaning "place of cool waters." With 2 million people, Nairobi is the biggest city in Eastern Africa. It has restaurants, bookstores, museums, and skyscrapers. Many foreign companies have offices in Nairobi. Every year, many Kenyans leave their rural homes to move to Nairobi. Not all of them find life in the city as easy as they had hoped. They are often unable to find work. Also, Nairobi suffers from water shortages and power outages. Despite these problems, many residents enjoy the big-city lifestyle that can be found in Nairobi.

5. Why do many Kenyans move to Nairobi each year, and what challenges do they face there?

_____

_____

Glossary/After You Read

commercial created or made to be sold, with profit as the object

discriminate to treat people differently based on prejudice

hocketing a musical style performed by the Zulu

racial segregation the process of separating groups and people based on their race

reform correcting wrongs or abuses

repeal to take back or cancel

reserve small territories set aside for the Masai and the Zulu after their land was seized by other countries

Shaka Zulu chief of the Zulu in 1815, he led a series of wars to expand Zulu territory

zimbabwes walled stone enclosures created by the Shona

TERMS & NAMES

A. Circle the name or term that best completes the sentence.

1. The _____ was a walled stone structure built by the Shona.

   veldt   **Great Zimbabwe**   **Zulu**

2. Unlike the Zulu, members of the _____ society were nomadic.

   Masai   **harambee**   **Swahili**

3. The Boers and the _____ fought each other in South Africa.

   Masai   **Zulu**   **Afrikaners**

4. In some cases, the lifestyle of pastoralism in Africa can lead to _____.

   overgrazing   **veldt**   **kinship**

5. As people move to cities, _____ is changing in Eastern and Southern Africa.

   Masai   **overgrazing**   **kinship**

B. Write the term next to the description that matches it.

   African National Congress   **multiparty system**   **Willem de Klerk**

   veldt   **Swahili**   **Nelson Mandela**

   sanctions   **harambee**

_____ 1. A Bantu language spoken in Africa.

_____ 2. The U.S. and Great Britain imposed them on South Africa.

_____ 3. He encouraged people to protest apartheid in non-violent ways.

_____ 4. A group of black South Africans that opposed apartheid.

_____ 5. It is located on the plateau of South Africa.

_____ **6.** It means "pulling together" in Swahili.

_____ **7.** Moi changed Kenya's government by allowing this.

_____ **8.** In 1994, he shared the Nobel Peace Prize with Nelson Mandela.

MAIN IDEAS

1. What happened to the Masai and the Zulu in the 1880s and 1890s?

_____

_____

2. How have the lives of Rwandan women recently changed?

_____

_____

3. Why is pastoralism a way of life in Eastern Africa?

_____

_____

4. How did apartheid affect the lives of black South Africans? How did it affect the lives of the Afrikaners?

_____

_____

5. Who is Nelson Mandela, and how did he influence the history of South Africa?

_____

_____

THINKING CRITICALLY

Answer the following questions on a separate sheet of paper.

1. Do you think that Kenya has a good educational system? Explain your thinking.

2. Why do you think that both Nelson Mandela and Willem de Klerk received the Nobel Peace Prize?

Physical Geography

BEFORE YOU READ

In the last chapter, you read about Eastern and Southern Africa.

In this section, you will read about the physical geography of Southern Asia.

AS YOU READ

Copy this web to take notes about the geography of Southern Asia.

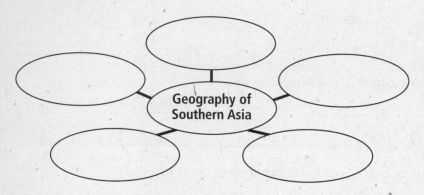

Geography of Southern Asia

TERMS & NAMES

subcontinent a large landmass that is part of a continent but that has its own geographic identity

Himalayas a mountain range that stretches about 1,500 miles across South Asia

Northern Plains plains that lie between the Himalaya Mountains and southern India

delta a triangular deposit of soil at the mouth of a river

sediment small fragments of rock that are moved around by wind, water, or ice

Deccan Plateau a plateau that makes up most of southern India

archipelago a group of islands

monsoon a seasonal wind that brings great amounts of rain

The Variety of Southern Asia
(pages 583–584)

What two regions make up Southern Asia?

The geography of Southern Asia has great variety, including mountain ranges and rain forests. Some places are dry, and others get plenty of water. Some get too much water.

Southern Asia is divided into two regions, South Asia and Southeast Asia. South Asia includes Afghanistan, Bangladesh, Bhutan, India, the Maldives, Nepal, Pakistan, and Sri Lanka. The South Asian subcontinent includes India, Pakistan, Bangladesh, Nepal, and Bhutan. A **subcontinent** is a large landmass that is part of a continent, but is geographically separate from it. India is the largest country on the subcontinent and in Southern Asia.

1. What countries are part of South Asia?

_____

_____

_____

Geographic Regions of South Asia (pages 584–586)

What are the geographic regions of the subcontinent?

The South Asian subcontinent has three main geographic regions—the Northern Mountain Rim, the Northern Plains, and the Deccan Plateau. Off the coast are two island countries, Sri Lanka and the Maldives.

The Northern Mountain Rim is made up of the Hindu Kush Mountains, the **Himalayas,** and the Karakoram Mountains. These mountains separate the subcontinent from the rest of Asia. However, some passes have allowed Asian peoples to get through them since ancient times. One of these, the *Khyber Pass,* connects Pakistan and Afghanistan.

The Himalayas stretch for 1,500 miles across northern India and Nepal. Many of its peaks are four and a half miles high. Few people live in this region.

The **Northern Plains** lie between the Himalayas and southern India. The region includes the Ganges and Indus rivers that form large deltas where they empty into the sea. A **delta** is a triangular deposit of soil at the mouth of a river. The Ganges River carries sediment from the Himalayas to the plains. **Sediment** includes minerals and debris that settle at the bottom of a river. During the rainy season, the Northern Plains flood, and sediment from the Ganges River is deposited there. This makes the plains fertile for farming.

The **Deccan Plateau** makes up most of southern India. The plateau has mineral deposits, as well as forests. The Ghats are mountains that border the plateau. In the interior part of the plateau, the soil is poorer, water supplies are unreliable, and it is hot year round. Fewer people live here than in the Northern Plains.

Sri Lanka and the Maldives lie south and southwest of India. Parts of mountainous Sri Lanka receive a lot of rain. The Maldives is a country with more than 1,200 coral islands called *atolls*. People live on about 300 of these islands.

2. How does sediment get to the Northern Plains?

_____

_____

Regions and Nations of Southeast Asia (pages 587–588)
What is the geography of Southeast Asia like?

Southeast Asia contains both a mainland region and many islands. The countries in Southeast Asia include Brunei, Cambodia, Indonesia, Laos, Malaysia, Myanmar (Burma), the Philippines, Singapore, Thailand, and Vietnam.

The mainland lies on the Indochinese and the Malay peninsulas. Mainland Southeast Asia includes Cambodia, Laos, Myanmar, Thailand, Vietnam, and part of Malaysia. The Mekong River flows through Laos, Cambodia, and Vietnam. This rice-producing region is densely populated.

The islands of Southeast Asia include Borneo, the island of Singapore, and the archipelagoes of Indonesia and the Philippines. An **archipelago** is a group of islands.

Indonesia is the largest nation in Southeast Asia. It is about three times the size of Texas, with the fourth largest population in the world. Indonesia is made up of 17,000 islands.

The 7,100 islands of the Philippines cover an area about the size of the state of Arizona. Only 800 of these islands are inhabited.

3. How would you describe Indonesia?

_____

_____

Climate and Monsoons (pages 588–599)
What is the climate like in South Asia?

Most of South Asia has three seasons—cool, hot, and rainy. The higher elevations are usually cooler. However, most of southern India is hot all year round. Southeast Asia's climate has less variety. It is hot and rainy.

The period from June through September is, generally, monsoon season. A **monsoon** is a seasonal wind that blows over the northern part of the Indian Ocean. In South Asia, heavy monsoon rains fall from June through October. November through February is mostly cool and dry. Because March through late May is hot and humid, the monsoon rains in June bring great relief. In India, school starts in June, and is closed during the spring when it is very hot.

In Southeast Asia, summer lasts from April to September when heavy monsoon rains fall. The winter is cool and dry, and lasts from October to March.

If the monsoons come too early, farmers don't have time to plant seeds. If the rains never arrive or are late, the crops fail. Sometimes the monsoons bring severe flooding.

4. Why do students in India start school in June?

_____

_____

Ancient India

BEFORE YOU READ

In the last section, you read about the geography of Southern Asia.

In this section, you will read about ancient India.

AS YOU READ

Copy this web to take notes about the civilizations, dynasties, and religions of ancient India.

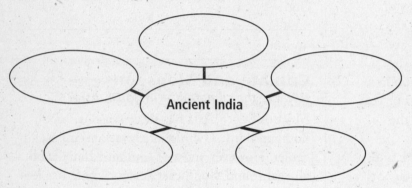

Ancient India

TERMS & NAMES

Mohenjo–Daro a large ancient city in the Indus River valley

Aryans an ethnic group who migrated from southern Russia through central Asia and settled in India

Sanskrit a language of India

Hinduism a religion developed in ancient India

Vedas the Books of Knowledge of the ancient Aryans, which were the basis of Hinduism

caste an inherited social class that separates people from other classes by birth, occupation, or wealth

Ashoka the emperor of ancient India from 269 to 232 B.C.

The Indus River Valley Civilization (pages 591–592)

What civilizations existed in ancient India?

Around 2500 B.C., the Harappan civilization developed in the Indus River valley. This civilization stretched west to what is now Kabul, Afghanistan, and east to what is now Delhi, India. Its center was the rich farmland along the Indus River and its *tributaries*.

The Harappan civilization ended around 1700 B.C. No one knows why. Some think the cause was a climate change. Others think the cities were conquered and destroyed.

Hundreds of towns filled the Indus River valley. Two major cities were Harappa and **Mohenjo-Daro.** Mohenjo–Daro had many well-built homes and public buildings. Canals brought water to farms outside the city.

1. Where was the Indus River valley civilization located?

_____

_____

The Aryan Influence on South Asia (pages 592–593)

Who were the Aryans?

Around 1700 B.C., the **Aryans** migrated to South Asia from southern Russia. The time of the Aryan arrival suggests that they influenced the fall of the Harappan civilization. Over time, the Aryan people and the people of the Indus River valley produced a new culture.

The Aryans were different from the people of the Indus River valley. They spoke a language called **Sanskrit** and were nomads and herders. Their food and clothing came from the animals they raised.

The Aryans brought new technology, animals, and ideas with them to South Asia. Sometime after 1000 B.C., they discovered iron ore in the Ganges River valley. The Aryans settled in towns as they learned to grow rice and use iron plows. Improved iron weapons, and the introduction of the horse, enabled the Aryans to rule northern India.

2. How did the Aryans differ from the Harappans?

_____

_____

Hinduism—A Way of Life
(pages 593–594)
What are the main beliefs and characteristics of Hinduism?

People of ancient India developed **Hinduism,** a religion based on certain Aryan practices. Aryan priests chanted hymns in praise of their gods. For a long time, these hymns were passed down through oral tradition. Later, they and other Aryan religious beliefs were written down and became part of the **Vedas,** or Books of Knowledge. The Vedas contain writings on prayers, hymns, rituals, and philosophy.

The ideas of karma and reincarnation are central to Hinduism. *Karma* is the idea that a person's actions determine future events. *Reincarnation* is the idea that souls are reborn in different bodies after death. Hindus believe that the cycle of birth, death, and rebirth occurs many times. A virtuous person may be reborn wealthy or wise. An immoral person may be reborn poor or sick.

One of the main characteristics of Hinduism is the caste system. A **caste** is an inherited social class. Each person is born to a particular caste for his or her lifetime. Caste determines a person's job, marriage partner, and friends.

The Hindu caste system is based on four major classes—priests, warriors and princes, merchants and farmers, and laborers. Another group, once known as untouchables, was considered inferior. Untouchables did undesirable work and were shunned by society. Today, the caste system has thousands of castes and subcastes, but the four major castes are still the most important. The government is trying to reduce the caste system's influence on society.

3. How has the caste system influenced people's lives in India?

_____

_____

The Maurya and Gupta Dynasties (pages 595–596)
What did the Maurya and Gupta dynasties contribute to India?

Two dynasties—the Maurya and the Gupta—made important contributions to India that still affect our lives today.

The first Indian empire, founded by descendants of the Aryans, was called the Maurya (324–185 B.C.). One of its emperors, **Ashoka,** created a unified government. Artists were known for their sandstone carvings and sculpture.

The Gupta Dynasty (A.D. 320–500) ruled during India's golden age in science, art, and literature. Most Gupta rulers were Hindus. However, both Hinduism and Buddhism were practiced. Hindu and Buddhist beliefs inspired artists. They created sculptures and paintings of Hindu gods, as well as temples with images from Hindu mythology. Architects hollowed out mountain cliffs to create Buddhist temples.

Sanskrit literature blossomed during the Gupta Dynasty. Kalidasa, living during the 5th century A.D., was a great poet and playwright. His mysterious, creative plays taught morals.

Gupta mathematicians made important discoveries. They developed the concept of zero and the numerals that we use today. Centuries after the Gupta Empire fell, Europeans learned these numerals and the concept of zero from the Islamic civilizations of Southwest Asia. Europeans called this number system "Arabic," a name still used today.

4. How did ancient discoveries in mathematics influence the way American students learn today?

_____

_____

Ancient Crossroads

BEFORE YOU READ

In the last section, you read about ancient India.

In this section, you will read about ancient Southeast Asia.

AS YOU READ

Copy this chart to take notes about the ways in which ancient Southeast Asia was influenced by other countries.

	Influences of Other Countries on Southeast Asia
Trade Influences	
Buddhism in Southeast Asia	
Cultural Influences from India	

TERMS & NAMES

Buddhism a religion based on achieving happiness and peace by living life free of desires and pain

Siddhartha Gautama a wealthy Indian prince who founded Buddhism in 500 B.C.

Four Noble Truths the basic teachings of Buddhism

Eightfold Path in Buddhism, a set of guidelines for how to escape suffering

Khmer an ancient ethnic group in Cambodia

Angkor Wat a Hindu temple in India built by the Khmer people

Crossroads of Culture (pages 598–600)

Why was Southeast Asia a major center for trade?

Southeast Asia was one of the crossroads of the ancient world. A crossroads is a place where people, goods, and ideas from many areas come together. In ancient times, travelers from India, China, and other countries came to Southeast Asian shores and made a lasting impression.

Many important skills were developed in ancient Southeast Asia, including making tools from bronze, growing yams and rice, and sailing. In the past, historians thought that people from China or India brought these skills to the region.

Bronze Age items found in Thailand have been dated to 3000 B.C. That is before bronze work was done in China. Eight to nine thousand years ago, rice was grown in Thailand. Yams and other roots were grown in Indonesia between 15,000 and 10,000 B.C. These are some of the earliest examples of agriculture ever found.

The central position of Southeast Asia made it a likely crossroads of trade. Southeast Asian goods reached both India and China. From there, they traveled on to East Africa and Southwest Asia.

Southeast Asian trade goods included rice, tea, timber, and spices such as cloves, nutmeg, ginger, and pepper. Many ideas were shared as well. Religious ideas and knowledge spread. Skills such as farming and metalworking, as well as art forms, crossed to and from Southeast Asia.

Southeast Asia had a thriving culture of its own. However, around A.D. 100, traders, Hindu priests, and Buddhist monks began to bring Indian culture to Southeast Asia, including art, architecture, and religion. These ideas were gradually adopted in the region.

1. What did Hindu priests and Buddhist monks bring to Southeast Asia?

_____

_____

Buddhism in Southeast Asia
(pages 600–601)
What are the origins of Buddhism?

Buddhism is one of the major religions of the world. It came from the same religious roots as Hinduism and began in India around 500 B.C., Hinduism and Islam eventually became more important Indian religions. Buddhism spread to East and Southeast Asia, where it is still strong today.

The founder of Buddhism was **Siddhartha Gautama.** He grew up as a wealthy prince and a member of the warrior class. Gautama lived in a palace with his wife and son. He believed that life involved a lot of pain, and that he needed to leave his family and seek the causes of human suffering.

For six years, Gautama was a wandering monk. He practiced self-denial and ate very little. However, he did not discover the cause of human suffering. One day, he sat under a tree and began to *meditate.* Through meditation, Gautama gained *enlightenment,* or religious awakening. He then felt that he knew the reasons for human suffering and how to escape it. News of his experience spread. People began to call him the Buddha, or the Enlightened One.

The Buddha was influenced by the Hindu beliefs of karma and reincarnation that taught that life is a cycle of death and rebirth. However, he did not like the Vedas, the ancient Aryan texts. He rejected the caste system and the role of priests.

The Buddha taught that the goal of life is to be free from desires and pain. Then one can progress to *nirvana,* a state of happiness and peace. The basic teachings of Buddhism are the **Four Noble Truths.** The first truth is that life is full of pain. The second truth is that suffering comes from the desire for possessions. The third truth explains that people won't suffer if they stop desiring possessions. The fourth truth says that people can escape suffering by following the **Eightfold Path.** These eight guidelines are to strive for the right understanding, purpose, speech, conduct, means of livelihood, effort, awareness, and meditation.

After the Buddha's death, his followers spread the faith throughout southern India, Sri Lanka, and Southeast Asia. Buddhism also spread to Tibet, central Asia, China, Korea, and Japan.

2. According to Buddhism, what is nirvana and how can a person achieve it?

_____

_____

Indian Influence in Southeast Asia (pages 602–603)
How did religion contribute to the rise and fall of empires in Southeast Asia?

As the influence of India spread, new images and religious art became part of Southeast Asian culture. Empires were founded on the beliefs of Hinduism, Buddhism, and, later, Islam. The success of empires often depended on the ongoing popularity of these beliefs.

In the 6th century A.D., the **Khmer** people established a Hindu kingdom in present-day Cambodia. The Khmer built great Hindu temples, including the huge complex, **Angkor Wat.** The Khmer kingdom spread through much of Southeast Asia. Then, as Buddhism grew, Hinduism declined. The Khmer lost power and retreated to Phnom Penh.

Indian influence in the form of Buddhism was also felt in the island nations of Southeast Asia. In Indonesia, a huge Buddhist temple called Borobudur was built in the 6th century.

Indian culture also spread to Myanmar. There, Buddhism was in place by the 5th and 6th centuries. In the 11th century, the powerful king Anawrahta established a strong Buddhist kingdom with the capital city of Pagan. There were soon thousands of Buddhist temples and buildings in the kingdom. The most famous is the Ananda temple.

3. Why did the Khmer leave Cambodia?

_____

_____

Glossary/After You Read

atoll a low, flat, coral island

enlightenment receiving knowledge and inspiration

karma the idea that someone's actions determine his or her fate

Khyber Pass a mountain pass linking Pakistan and Afghanistan

meditate to think quietly and reflectively

nirvana a completely happy, blissful condition

reincarnation the idea that a person's soul is reborn after death

tributary a river or stream that flows into a larger river or stream

TERMS & NAMES

A. If the statement is true, write "true" on the line. If it is false, change the underlined word or words to make it true.

_____ **1.** The <u>Himalayas</u> are located in the <u>Northern Mountain Rim</u> of South Asia.

_____ **2.** The <u>Northern Plains</u> lie north of the <u>Deccan Plateau</u>.

_____ **3.** <u>Buddhism</u> is a religion based on the teachings of one man.

_____ **4.** A <u>subcontinent</u> is a large landmass that is part of a continent.

_____ **5.** <u>Sediment</u> includes minerals that settle in <u>delta</u> regions.

_____ **6.** The hot, dry season in India is called a <u>monsoon</u>.

_____ **7.** <u>Sanskrit</u> is a language spoken in India.

_____ **8.** An <u>archipelago</u> is a deposit of soil at the mouth of a river.

_____ **9.** <u>Mohenjo-Daro</u> is a large ancient city in the Indus River valley.

_____ **10.** <u>Vedas</u> was the emperor of India from 269 to 232 B.C.

_____ **11.** The <u>Aryans</u> are an ethnic group that migrated to South Asia.

_____ **12.** The <u>caste</u> system is based on some beliefs of <u>Hinduism</u>.

B. Write the term next to the description that matches it.

| Angkor Wat | Khmer | Eightfold Path |
| Four Noble Truths | Siddhartha Gautama | Ashoka |

_____ **1.** a Hindu temple built by the Khmer people

_____ **2.** the basic teachings of Buddhism

_____ **3.** guidelines for how to escape suffering

_____   **4.** an ancient ethnic group that built a kingdom in
present-day Cambodia

_____   **5.** the founder of Buddhism

_____   **6.** the emperor of ancient India from 269 to 232 B.C.

MAIN IDEAS

1. Briefly describe the two geographic regions of Southern Asia.

_____

_____

2. How did Aryan culture influence the development of ancient India?

_____

_____

3. Briefly describe the central ideas in Hinduism and Buddhism.

_____

_____

4. Why was the Gupta Dynasty considered a "golden age"?

_____

_____

5. How did Hinduism and Buddhism influence Southeast Asian culture?

_____

_____

THINKING CRITICALLY

Answer the following questions on a separate sheet of paper.

1. Why do you think something like the Hindu caste system is not used
in the U.S.?

2. Why do you think that Buddhism appeals to so many people?

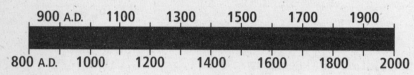
History

BEFORE YOU READ

In the last chapter you read about Southern Asia.

In this section, you will read about the history of India and its neighboring countries.

AS YOU READ

Copy this time line to take notes about important events in the history of India and its neighbors.

History of India and its Neighbors

900 A.D.   1100   1300   1500   1700   1900

800 A.D.   1000   1200   1400   1600   1800   2000

TERMS & NAMES

Mughal Empire an empire lasting from 1526 to 1761 covered most of the subcontinent of India

Indian National Congress in India, a congress formed in 1885 to provide a forum where Indians could discuss their problems

Muslim League a group formed by Muslims in India in 1906 to protect their rights

Mohandas Gandhi an Indian who encouraged his fellow citizens to protest the British using nonviolent methods

Islam Comes to India (pages 609–610)

Why did Islam become widespread in northwest India?

The coast of India has been a site of trade for centuries. Arabs were trading along the coast of India a thousand years before the British arrived. Early in the 8th century A.D., Muslims conquered northwest India. They converted many people to their religion. Even today, the people of this region (now Afghanistan and Pakistan) are Muslim.

Beginning in the 11th century A.D., Turkish Muslims from what is now Afghanistan attacked northwest India, replacing the Arabs. By 1206, the Turkish kingdom stretched south to the Deccan Plateau. The region was ruled from the city of Delhi by a *sultan*. During this time, Mongols from Central Asia began spreading west and south. Because of the mountains in the northeastern part of South Asia, the Mongols never invaded the region. Many people who were threatened by the Mongols fled across the mountains into South Asia. These artists, teachers, officials, and religious leaders brought with them their culture and learning.

1. Why did the Mongols never invade the region?

_____

_____

The Mughal Empire (page 610)

When did the Mughal Empire rule the region?

In the year 1526, Babur, a Mughal ruler and a Muslim, invaded southwards with his army. Eventually, his kingdom included northern India and land west into Afghanistan. Babur involved local leaders in his government and built trade routes, strengthening his rule. Babur's reign was the beginning of the great **Mughal Empire.**

The third Mughal emperor, Akbar, was a strong and intelligent leader. He included Hindus and Muslims in his government, and established policies that made India a place where they could live in peace. He taxed people according to the size and value of their land. Akbar was a strong supporter of the arts. He provided studios for painters and gave awards to the best. He also created a position for a Hindu poet of the nation.

During the Mughal Empire, many new trade routes over land and water were established, making travel between regions easier. The trade routes also connected the empire with other parts of the world. In this way, new ideas and inventions made their way into South Asia. Then, in the year 1707, the last Mughal emperor died, and the empire eventually collapsed.

2. What are a few highlights of the Mughal Empire?

Arrival of the British (pages 611–612)
How did the British gain control of India?

In 1600, Queen Elizabeth I of England gave trade rights to the East India Company, an organization of English merchants, to trade in India and East and Southeast Asia. The Mughals agreed to let the British set up factories and trading centers. The East India Company shipped spices, tea, cotton, silk, indigo (used for dyeing), sugar, and saltpeter (used for gunpowder) to England. Gradually, the British increased their power. By 1818, after the Rajputs and other groups agreed to be ruled by the British, Great Britain's strength in the region was undeniable.

In 1796, Great Britain took possession of the island nation of Sri Lanka, then called Ceylon, and the island nation of the Maldives. The nations of Nepal, Bhutan, and Afghanistan never became colonies of Great Britain, though the British tried to colonize Afghanistan. Nepal and Bhutan depended on their mountainous frontiers to keep out foreigners.

The British army and navy, merchants, and missionaries came to India, bringing new technology for railroads, the telegraph, steamships, and new methods of irrigation. They introduced the British legal system, with new laws regarding land ownership, and made English the official language.

Indians responded to the British in different ways. Some chose to live as they had before the British arrived. Others chose to interact economically with the British by working for

and with them while maintaining their traditions. Others studied British traditions and adopted what seemed useful while keeping their own traditions. Among the higher castes, parents sent their children to British schools so that they could learn English and become successful.

3. How did the lives of Indians change after the British took control of their country?

Independence (pages 612–613)
What did Gandhi encourage people to do?

In 1885, the **Indian National Congress** was formed to provide a forum where Indians could discuss their problems. Muslims formed the **Muslim League** in 1906. After World War I, Indians began to think of independence. They had a great leader in **Mohandas Gandhi.**

Gandhi encouraged people to protest in nonviolent ways to show the British the need for independence. He wanted all Indians to be treated equally, and for women and men to have the same freedoms. He encouraged Hindus and Muslims to find peaceful ways to solve their problems. For example, to protest the British monopoly of salt, Gandhi led a 240-mile walk to the coast to gather sea salt.

Eventually, Great Britain realized that it would have to leave India, but the Indian National Congress and the Muslim League disagreed about how the new government would be formed. Muslims were afraid of losing power, since Hindus were the majority in India. The solution was to divide India into two separate countries, India for the Hindus and Pakistan for the Muslims. The two countries were formed and granted independence in 1947. Sri Lanka became independent in 1948, and the Maldives in 1965.

4. When Great Britain left India, how was the land divided up between the Hindus and the Muslims?

Governments

BEFORE YOU READ

In the last section, you read about the history of India and its neighboring countries.

In this section, you will read about South Asia's governments.

AS YOU READ

Copy this web to take notes about South Asia's governments.

TERMS & NAMES

Taliban a group of fundamentalist Muslims who took control of Afghanistan's government in 1996

martial law temporary military rule that occurs during a time of war or when the normal government has broken down

Dalits a group of people in India, formerly known as the "untouchables," who were previously outside the caste system and considered lower than the lowest caste and who gained some rights under India's new constitution

Indira Gandhi in 1966, she became India's first woman prime minister

panchayat a village council in India

South Asia's Governments
(pages 615–617)

What types of governments did the countries in South Asia choose after they achieved independence?

Since gaining independence, the nations of South Asia have chosen different forms of government. Some are *republics.* In a republic, the people elect leaders to represent them. Some countries, such as India, chose a parliamentary government. Others chose to be constitutional monarchies.

In 1964, a new constitution established a constitutional monarchy for Afghanistan. The monarchy collapsed in 1973 as the result of a coup. In 1979, the Soviet Union invaded Afghanistan and established a Communist government. A UN agreement forced Soviet troops to withdraw from Afghanistan in 1989, leaving behind an Afghani Communist government. This government was overturned and an Islamic republic was declared.

A group of fundamentalist Muslims, the **Taliban,** took control of the government. Under the Taliban, people followed strict rules. Women could not go to school or hold jobs. Going out without a male relative was forbidden. There were harsh punishments for breaking rules.

The Taliban fought opposing Muslim groups for many years. They received help from a few other nations, but most of the world spoke out against them. In 2001, the Taliban was accused of harboring terrorists responsible for attacking the United States on September 11th.

Bangladesh gained independence from Pakistan in 1971. Its constitution, which gives Bangladesh a parliamentary government, was formed in 1972. Since 1975, the military has taken over the government a few times.

For three centuries, Bhutan was ruled jointly by two types of leaders—one spiritual and the other political. In 1907, the spiritual ruler withdrew from public life, and since then Bhutan has had a king only. In 1953, an assembly was formed, which meets twice a year to pass laws. In 1968, a Council of Ministers was created to advise the king.

In 1965, the Maldives gained independence from Great Britain. It became a republic three years later. The Citizens' Council has 48 members, 40 elected by the people and 8 appointed by the president. The president also appoints judges, who follow Islamic law.

For centuries, Nepal was ruled by kings. Prime ministers eventually replaced kings. In 1962, Nepal again became a monarchy and political parties were banned. In the 1990s, the king allowed political parties. The Nepalese wrote a new constitution and set up a parliamentary system.

Pakistan gained independence from Great Britain in 1947 and established a parliamentary government. However, in 1958, **martial law** was declared. The military controlled the government until 1988. Today, Pakistan is a republic, with a prime minister and a president, both of whom must be Muslim.

People in Pakistan have differing views about the role of Islam in the government. Some think Islam holds people together. Others feel that Islam does not meet everyone's needs.

Sri Lanka gained independence from Great Britain in 1948. Today, it is a democracy with a president. As in the United States, political parties struggle for power in the government.

1. How did women live under Taliban rule?

_____

_____

The World's Largest Democracy
(pages 617–618)
How is India a democracy?

India is the world's largest democracy. Approximately 370 million Indians voted in the 1999 elections. The country's official head of state is the president. However, India's prime minister actually runs the government.

India's constitution went into effect in 1950, protecting Indians from being treated unfairly, and assuring all citizens the same basic rights. These include freedom of speech and religion. These rights are protected in the courts.

India's new constitution stated that even the lowest and poorest classes could vote and be represented in the government. Special programs reserve jobs for people of the lower castes and secure places for them in schools. The **Dalits** (formerly called "untouchables") have gained political power. They were outside the caste system and considered lower than the lowest caste. Today, the Dalits vote, though changes are still needed to ensure they have equal rights.

After independence from Britain, Indian women gained many new rights, including the right to vote. It is now against the law in India to discriminate on the basis of gender.

Indian women now work in many fields, such as medicine and education. They also hold public office. **Indira Gandhi** became India's first woman prime minister in 1966.

2. How did the new constitution help the Dalits?

_____

_____

Village Life and Grass-roots Democracy (pages 618–619)
How are the small rural Indian villages governed?

Since ancient times, small rural Indian villages have governed themselves. Today they are governed by the *panchayat* system. A *panchayat* is a village council. India's constitution allows these councils to govern themselves. The *panchayat* collects taxes for maintaining schools and hospitals. It builds roads and digs wells for drinking water. The councils take care of primary school education in India.

Today there are over three million *panchayat* representatives in India. By law, one-third of them must be women. The constitution also makes room for the Dalits and other minorities to participate in the *panchayat* system.

3. What is the panchayat system of government?

_____

_____

CHAPTER
21

Section 3 (pages 622–625)

Economies

BEFORE YOU READ

In the last section, you read about the government systems of South Asia.

In this section, you will read about the economies of South Asian countries.

AS YOU READ

Copy this chart to take notes about the economies of countries in South Asia.

	Economies
Afghanistan	
Bangladesh	
Bhutan and Nepal	
The Maldives	
Pakistan	
Sri Lanka	
India	

TERMS & NAMES

jute a fibrous plant used to make twine, bags, sacks, and burlap

information technology technology that includes computers, software, and the Internet

Green Revolution the introduction of genetically improved grains to farmers of developing nations, beginning in the late 1960s

Developing Economies (pages 622–624)

What economic challenges do countries in South Asia face?

Most people in South Asia live in rural areas that have developing economies. They have low incomes and literacy levels and depend on traditional farming methods to survive. They are farmers, shepherds, and herders. Organizations such as AID (the Association for India's Development) are helping the developing nations of South Asia to move from traditional economies to market economies.

In the 1960s and 1970s, Afghanistan worked to strengthen its economy. It built roads, dams, power plants, and factories. It provided education to more people and began irrigation projects. Then Afghanistan was invaded by the Soviet Union. The invasion was followed by civil war. Afghanistan has not returned to the

improvement program of four decades ago. Today, Afghanistan is one of the poorest countries in the world. Most people work on farms, raising livestock. Only 12 percent of the land in Afghanistan is *arable*, and only half of that is cultivated. Wheat is the chief crop, though cotton, fruits, and nuts are also grown.

Agriculture is a major part of the economy in Bangladesh. About three-fifths of the workers are farmers. The most important cash crops are rice, jute, and tea. Bangladesh supplies one-fifth of the world's **jute,** a fibrous plant used to make twine, bags, sacks, and burlap. Irrigation projects have reached many farms, but the monsoon rains bring floods and disaster to many farmers.

Bangladesh has almost no mineral resources, so its few industries are based on agricultural products, such as bamboo, which is made into paper at mills.

The economies of Bhutan and Nepal are similar. Until the 1950s and 1960s, both countries were largely isolated from the outside world. There were no highways or automobiles. Bhutan did not have a currency. People *bartered* for goods rather than using money. Since that time, with financial help from other countries and organizations, both countries have been working to modernize their economies. For example, they have built major roads allowing the transport of goods and people—especially tourists.

The Maldives is one of the world's poorest nations. The majority of its workers fish or build or repair boats. Tourism has become an important industry as well. Nearly all the food people eat is imported, including rice, which is one of the main foods in people's diets.

Pakistan is the richest country in South Asia. Half its work force is employed in agriculture, forestry, and fishing. Pakistan is the third-largest exporter of rice in the world. Its important industries are fabric and clothing, sugar, paper, tobacco, and leather.

Sri Lanka depends on agriculture and tourism. Its most important agricultural product is rice, followed by tea, rubber, and coconuts. Sri Lanka has not yet been able to benefit much economically from its many mineral resources.

Although some regions of India have many valuable resources, millions of India's people are among the world's poorest. Most people work in agriculture. More than half the farms are smaller than three acres. Farmers practice what is known as *subsistence farming*, which means they grow only enough food to live on. Rice and wheat are India's most important crops. Because many people do not eat meat, chickpeas and lentils are important sources of protein in the diet.

There is a growing information technology industry in India. **Information technology** includes computers, software, and the Internet. Since 1991, India's software exports have been doubling every year.

1. **Which country in South Asia has the healthiest economy, and how do people there make a living?**

_____

_____

The Green Revolution (page 625)
What was the Green Revolution?

In the 1960s, the **Green Revolution** introduced farmers to varieties of grain that were more productive, the widespread use of pesticides, and different methods for farming. In India, farmers grew more rice and wheat than they needed. Much of this surplus was set aside in case of a poor growing season. Some was exported. The Green Revolution had some negative results too. The use of chemicals damaged the land and polluted rivers.

The cost of new methods is too high for some small farmers. As a result, many farmers in South Asia still use old farming techniques despite governments' efforts to introduce reform.

2. **What are a few examples of positive and negative effects of the Green Revolution?**

_____

_____

The Culture of India

BEFORE YOU READ
In the last section, you read about the economies of South Asia.

In this section, you will read about the culture of India.

AS YOU READ
Copy this web to take notes about India's culture.

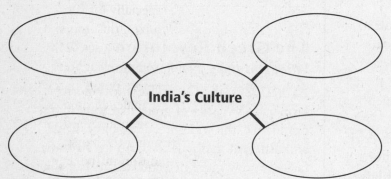

India's Culture

TERMS & NAMES
Taj Mahal the most famous building in India, which was built by the Mughal emperor Shah Jahan in the A.D. 1640s

Mahabharata an epic poem about the growth of Hinduism that is one of two great works of world literature from India

dialect a regional variety of a language

Indo-Aryan related to the family of languages that includes all European and many Indian languages

Dravidian an Indian language

dowry money or property given by a bride to her new husband and his family

The Taj Mahal/India and the Arts (pages 626–627)
What role do the arts play in Indian life?
The Mughal emperor Shah Jahan built the **Taj Mahal** for his beloved wife, Mumtaz Mahal. This white marble building with its onion-shaped domes and thin towers is one of the finest examples of Islamic architecture in the world. Today, it is India's most famous building and a symbol of India's rich artistic heritage.

Two great works of world literature come from India. One, the *Mahabharata,* is an *epic poem*, which means that it tells the story of one or more heroes. The *Ramayana* is another famous epic poem. Both the *Mahabharata* and the *Ramayana* have influenced painters, dancers, and other writers in India. Both are important because they tell about the growth of Hinduism.

India has several styles of music, and each style is unique to a region of India. Music is played and sung in concerts, at parties, or in religious settings. Indians also love to see movies. India makes more films every year than any other country, including the United States.

In rural areas, movie vans travel to villages to show films outdoors.

1. What is the Taj Mahal?

_____

_____

The Languages of India
(pages 627–628)
What languages do Indians speak?
The constitution of India now recognizes 18 official languages. However, Indians speak hundreds of other languages and dialects. A **dialect** is a regional variety of a language. Most languages in India come from one of two families: Indo-Aryan or Dravidian.

Indo-Aryan languages are related to the Indo-European language family, which comes from the ancient Aryan language *Sanskrit* and includes almost all European languages. Today, about three-fourths of the people in northern and central India speak Indo-Aryan languages.

Copyright © McDougal Littell Inc.

About one-fourth of all Indians speak Dravidian languages. **Dravidian** was the language spoken centuries ago in India. As invaders moved into the north, the speakers of Dravidian moved south.

English, which came to India with British colonialism, is spoken by less than 5 percent of the population. However, because it is the language of business, government, and science, knowledge of English is valuable in India.

2. What families do most Indian languages come from?

_____

_____

Religion in Daily Life (page 628)
What religion do most Indians practice?

Most people in India are Hindus. There are no rules dictating how Hinduism is practiced, nor is there one Hindu church. Many Hindus are vegetarians. Some Hindus perform daily rituals on behalf of their gods. The caste system, which is still in place in India, is less rigid than it once was.

Many Muslims who had been living in India moved to Pakistan and East Pakistan, now Bangladesh. Today, 14 percent of Indians are Muslim.

3. How is Hinduism practiced in India?

_____

_____

The Family in India (page 629)
What are some family customs in India?

Family is important to Indians. Often, several related families live together. Parents choose a bride or groom for their children from a family of the same caste. They may consider a potential mate's education, financial status, or even horoscope to help them make a decision. Also, when a woman marries, her parents must provide a **dowry,** money or property given by a bride to her new husband and his family. This can be expensive, especially for rural families. As India modernizes, this, too, is beginning to change.

Parents prefer having sons to daughters, partly because men have more power in this society. Women who have male children have greater influence in their extended families. These attitudes are beginning to change.

Family meals are a tradition in India. A typical meal varies from region to region. In the south and east, a meal usually includes rice. In the north and northwest, people eat a flat bread called a chapati. Along with rice or chapatis, a meal may include beans or lentils, some vegetables, and maybe yogurt. Chili peppers and other spices like cardamom, cinnamon, and cumin give the food extra flavor. Meat is rarely eaten, either because it is forbidden by religion or because it is expensive.

4. What do parents consider when selecting spouses for their children in India?

_____

_____

Pakistan

BEFORE YOU READ
In the last chapter you read about Southern Asia.
In this section, you will read about Pakistan.

AS YOU READ
Copy this chart to take notes about Pakistan.

	Pakistan
History	
Geography	
Language and Religion	
Conflict	

TERMS & NAMES

Mangla Dam a dam built on the Jhelum River in northeast Pakistan in order to control flood waters and provide hydroelectricity

Tarbela Dam a dam built on the Indus River for flood control and irrigation

Punjabi a language spoken in Pakistan

Sindhi a language spoken in Pakistan

Urdu the official language of Pakistan

History of Pakistan (pages 631–633)

What led to the creation of a separate Muslim nation?

Great Britain granted independence to Pakistan and India on the same day. Both South Asian countries have a long and sometimes common history. The Indus River flows through eastern Pakistan, from the mountains in the north to the Arabian Sea. This river valley was the site of one of the world's oldest civilizations. Over time, invaders and immigrants crossed the Himalayas and the Hindu Kush Mountains to reach this fertile area.

In A.D. 712, Arab Muslims brought Islam to the Indus valley region. Then, around the year 1000, Muslims from Central Asia built their kingdom in the Indus River valley. Lahore, today one of the biggest cities in Pakistan, was the capital of their kingdom and a major center of Muslim culture.

In the 1600s, the British East India Company set up trading posts in India, which then included the region that is now Pakistan. When the Mughal Empire, which had been ruling India, grew weak in the 1700s, the company took control.

With British rule, the Muslims lost power in the government. Over time, the Hindus gained power. Because the Indian National Congress was controlled by Hindus, Muslims formed the Muslim League in 1906 as a way of keeping political power. As India moved closer to independence from Great Britain, the Muslim League, led by Mohammed Ali Jinnah, called for an independent Muslim state.

Differences between Hindus and Muslims led to violence. Neither the British nor the Indian National Congress could find a way to settle the differences between the two groups. So on August 14, 1947, at the same time that India gained independence, Pakistan was declared a separate Muslim nation. Millions of Muslims living in India moved to Pakistan, and Hindus in Pakistan moved to India.

When Pakistan became a nation, it included East Pakistan and West Pakistan—separated by 1,000 miles. This distance made Pakistan a difficult country to rule. Although most people of East and West Pakistan were Muslim, they had many differences. Many East Pakistanis were angry that West Pakistan was in charge of the government. War broke out between East and West Pakistan. Over a million people lost their lives. In 1971, East Pakistan became the country of Bangladesh.

1. Why was the country of Bangladesh founded?

_____

_____

The Land of Pakistan (pages 633–634)
What is the physical geography of Pakistan like?

Pakistan (once West Pakistan) is divided into four provinces: Baluchistan, North-West Frontier, Punjab, and Sindh. Most Pakistanis live in the northeast province of Punjab, where the capital, Islamabad, is located.

Western and northern Pakistan are dry and mountainous. The provinces of Sindh and Punjab are less mountainous. They get little rain, but the Indus River flows through them. About two-thirds of Pakistanis are farmers and herders who irrigate their land with water from the Indus river.

In 1967, Pakistan finished building the **Mangla Dam** on the Jhelum River in northeast Pakistan. The dam was built to control flood waters and to provide hydroelectricity. In 1976, Pakistan opened the **Tarbela Dam.** Located on the Indus River, it is used for flood control and irrigation. In 1994, the Tarbela Dam began to produce hydroelectricity, as well.

2. Why were the Mangla and Tarbela dams built?

_____

_____

Language and Religion (pages 634–635)
What languages are spoken in Pakistan?

Language divides the people of Pakistan, but the religion of Islam unites them. Each of Pakistan's four provinces has a unique culture with its own customs and languages.

More than 20 languages are spoken in Pakistan. **Punjabi** and **Sindhi** are the most common. Punjabi is spoken mostly in rural areas. **Urdu,** Pakistan's official language, is taught in schools. Students also learn their regional language. Different languages are spoken in each region.

Pakistani films are usually in Punjabi or Urdu. The most popular newspapers are in Urdu, Sindhi, or English. This variety of languages has caused conflict among Pakistanis.

The country's official name is the Islamic Republic of Pakistan. More than 97 percent of Pakistanis are Muslim. Schools base their teaching on Islam, and most women follow the rules of *purdah.*

3. What do most Pakistanis have in common?

_____

_____

Modern Conflict in Pakistan (page 635)
Why is there conflict between India and Pakistan?

In 1947, when India and Pakistan became independent, each nation claimed the region of Kashmir. This region is important because of its water resources. Pakistan and India have failed to reach an agreement. Within South Asia, Hindus and Muslims have fought over whether Kashmir should join India or Pakistan or become independent.

Relations between Pakistan and India grew increasingly tense in 1998 when both nations tested nuclear weapons and then refused to sign a nuclear test-ban treaty. Since then, both nations have continued to test nuclear weapons, and relations have not improved. However, efforts to forge a better relationship between the two countries continue to be made, with help from other nations.

4. Why do both India and Pakistan want Kashmir?

_____

_____

Glossary/After You Read

arable ready to be cultivated for farming
barter to exchange goods or services without using money
epic poem tells of the deeds of a great person or persons
purdah the practice of keeping women secluded

republic a government in which officials are elected by the people and represent them
Sanskrit the ancient, classical language of India
subsistence farming growing crops for survival
sultan the ruler, or emperor of a Muslim country

TERMS & NAMES

A. Write the term next to the description that matches it.

Mohandas Gandhi	Dalits	martial law
Indian National Congress	jute	*panchayat*
Mughal Empire	Muslim League	Indira Gandhi
Taliban	information technology	Green Revolution

_____ **1.** a fibrous plant used to make twine and burlap

_____ **2.** formerly known as the "untouchables"

_____ **3.** a group formed in 1906 to protect Muslim rights

_____ **4.** He encouraged non-violent protest.

_____ **5.** formed so Indians could discuss their problems together

_____ **6.** fundamentalist Muslims who once ruled Afghanistan

_____ **7.** temporary military control of a government

_____ **8.** India's first woman prime minister

_____ **9.** the Internet, computers and software

_____ **10.** a village council in India

_____ **11.** It lasted from 1526 to 1761.

_____ **12.** It helped farmers learn new methods for growing crops.

B. Fill in the blanks with the name or term that best completes the sentence.

Mangla	*Mahabharata*	Indo-Aryan
Urdu	Punjabi	Sindhi
dowry	Tarbela	Taj Mahal
dialect	Dravidian	

1. In India a _____ is given by a bride's family to her new husband and family.

2. The emperor Shah Jahan built the _____ for his wife.

3. The _____ is an epic poem that tells about the growth of Hinduism.

4. Two important dams built in Pakistan are the _____ and the _____.

5. _____ and _____ are the most commonly spoken languages in Pakistan.

6. A _____ is a regional variety of a language.

7. Most languages in India come from the _____ and _____ families.

8. _____ is Pakistan's official language and is taught in schools.

MAIN IDEAS

1. How did Mohandas Gandhi help India achieve independence from the British?

_____

_____

2. Why and how was the Taliban government overturned in 2001?

_____

_____

3. How has India's 1950 constitution affected the lives of Indians?

_____

_____

4. How do most people in South Asia earn a living?

_____

_____

5. Why was Pakistan founded?

_____

_____

THINKING CRITICALLY

Answer the following questions on a separate sheet of paper.

1. Why do you think Gandhi's teachings and example have had such a lasting impression on the world?

2. Is it important for Pakistan and India to quickly reach a compromise about Kashmir? Explain.

Name _____ Date _____

CHAPTER 22 Section 1 (pages 643–647)

Reading Study Guide

History and Governments

BEFORE YOU READ

In the last chapter you read about Southern Asia.

In this section, you will read about the history and governments of Southeast Asia.

AS YOU READ

Copy this chart to take notes about the history and governments of Southeast Asia.

Cultural Influences	
Colonialism	
Governments after Independence	

TERMS & NAMES

mandala in Southeast Asia, a political system in which a central ruler works to gain support from others and uses trade and business to influence others and maintain power

military dictatorship a government ruled by a person whose power comes from the army

East Timor an island nation in Southeast Asia

New Cultures in Southeast Asia
(pages 643–645)

How did Chinese and Indian cultures influence South Asia?

Around the year A.D. 500, Southeast Asia was under the influence of two strong, advanced cultures: China and India. China made Vietnam part of its empire. Vietnam was not able to gain independence until A.D. 939. India never ruled any part of Southeast Asia, but its culture had a lasting influence on the region.

New religions—Hinduism, Buddhism, and Confucianism—came to Southeast Asia from China and India. So did writing systems, literature, and ideas about government and social class.

Instead of states or nations, Southeast Asia was made up of mandalas. A **mandala** had a ruler who worked to gain support from others. The ruler used trade and business to influence others and maintain power. Some mandalas were larger than others, some depended on agriculture, and some had more advanced technology. The mandala system stayed in place in many parts of Southeast Asia until the 19th century.

One ancient mandala, called Oc Eo, was located in southern Vietnam. Ships from its port carried goods to and from places as far away as Rome. Over time, the mandalas developed into states, and the people considered themselves citizens. Because of trade and communication, new ideas were exchanged and each state developed into a unique nation.

Trade with other parts of the world also brought Christianity and Islam to Southeast Asia. In the 9th or 10th century, Muslim traders brought Islam to the islands of Sumatra and Java, part of what is now Indonesia. Islam spread gradually throughout the other islands of Indonesia and Malaya.

In the early 1500s, Christian missionaries came to Southeast Asia from Portugal, France, and Spain. The Spanish missionaries met with success in the Philippines, where there was no organized religion to combat, although each group of Filipinos had its own set of beliefs. Today, about 90 percent of Filipinos are Christians. However, in the rest of Southeast Asia, the missionaries were not so successful. Buddhist monks kept missionaries from converting people.

Copyright © McDougal Littell Inc.

1. How were mandalas organized?

_____

_____

European Colonialism (pages 645–646)

When did European nations begin to colonize Southeast Asia?

Europeans came to Southeast Asia as traders and as missionaries. The Portuguese arrived in 1509. The Spanish, the Dutch, the British, and the French followed. These European traders came for spices, gems, and gold, not power. The Europeans mostly controlled port cities and nothing more for the first three centuries.

In the 19th and early 20th centuries, these nations began to *colonize* the nations of Southeast Asia. The Philippines was under Spanish rule until 1898, when it came under the rule of the United States. Cambodia, Laos, and Vietnam were all ruled by France. The British ruled Burma, most of Malaysia, and Singapore, and the Dutch ruled Indonesia. Only Thailand never became a colony.

During World War II, the Japanese pushed out most Europeans from the region. When the war ended in 1945, Cambodia, Vietnam, Laos, Malaysia, and Indonesia fought for independence. The Philippines won independence peacefully.

2. When did European nations leave Southeast Asia, and why did they leave?

_____

_____

After Independence (pages 646–647)

What kinds of governments do the nations of Southeast Asia have?

After gaining independence, many nations in Southeast Asia found themselves in turmoil. Political parties fought one another to gain power. In Vietnam, Myanmar, and Indonesia, the military eventually took control of the government. Over the next twenty years, the nations of Southeast Asia worked out their own unique government systems.

Brunei, Malaysia, Cambodia, and Thailand are all *constitutional monarchies*. Indonesia, the Philippines, and Singapore are republics. Myanmar was also a republic, but in 1988, the military overthrew the government. Since then, it has been a **military dictatorship,** ruled by one man whose power comes from the army. Laos and Vietnam are both Communist states.

The island nation of **East Timor** declared its independence from Portugal in 1975. A month later, the neighboring country of Indonesia invaded and took over. The United Nations said the people of East Timor could decide their government for themselves. In 1999, they voted for independence.

However, Indonesia did not accept the people's ruling. The United Nations has accused the Indonesian army of killing and deporting people because of the vote. UN peacekeeping forces were stationed in East Timor. In August of 2001 East Timor held its first democratic elections.

3. What is the difference between a constitutional monarchy and a military dictatorship?

_____

_____

Section 2 (pages 650–653)

Economies and Culture

BEFORE YOU READ

In the last section you read about the history and government of Southeast Asia today.

In this section, you will read about the economies and culture of Southeast Asia.

AS YOU READ

Copy this chart to take notes about the economies and culture of Southeast Asia.

Economies	
Culture	

TERMS & NAMES

developing nation newly industrialized nation

Bahasa Indonesian the national language of Indonesia

pagoda Buddhist tower built in many levels, with sculptures or carvings of Buddha on each level

thatch woven palm fronds used to build roofs

batik a method of dying fabric in which any parts of the fabric not intended to be dyed are covered in wax that is later removed

An Agricultural Economy
(pages 650–651)

How do people earn a living in Southeast Asia?

Three-fourths of the people in Southeast Asia live in *rural* areas. Many of them live on small farms where they grow rice to feed their families, not to sell for profit. Many nations of Southeast Asia are **developing nations.** They are working to improve their economies and to help people live safe, healthy, successful lives.

The *Green Revolution* and irrigation have helped some farmers grow more food. But many others have small plots of land and cannot afford to buy fertilizers, chemicals, and modern equipment. They must rely on good weather and hard work for successful harvests.

In the last 50 years, industry has become more important in Southeast Asia. Small factories that process crops, make clothing and fabric, and produce small electronic parts are the most common. Many people have moved into the larger cities looking for work.

The small country of Singapore is an exception in Southeast Asia. Virtually everyone lives in the city, also called Singapore. Though small in size, Singapore is one of the richest nations

in the world, and has one of the busiest ports. The production of electronic goods is its most important industry, and more than half are exported.

1. Why is Southeast Asia considered a developing region?

_____

_____

The Cultures of Southeast Asia
(pages 651–653)

How would you describe the various cultures of Southeast Asia?

The people of Southeast Asia live in widely differing geographical regions. In rural communities, people's lives have not changed much in the last century. In the big cities, however, history and tradition stand side by side with modern architecture, automobiles, and fast-food restaurants.

In Indonesia, the Philippines, and Myanmar, where people are separated by water, dense forests, or mountains, people speak many languages. However, most people from Indonesia also speak **Bahasa Indonesian,** the national language. In places where there is a large Chinese population, dialects are spoken. Indians who live in parts of Southeast Asia speak Hindi or Tamil.

A form of Buddhism is the most common religion in mainland Southeast Asia. Islam, brought by Muslims who came to Southeast Asia several centuries ago, is practiced in Malaysia, the Philippines, Thailand, and Indonesia. Spanish and Portuguese missionaries spread the Catholic faith, which is most important today in southern Vietnam and the Philippines. Protestantism and Hinduism are also practiced in the region.

Statues of the Buddha can be seen in temples all over Southeast Asia. Often the temples consist of one or more **pagodas,** or towers, built in many levels, with sculptures or carvings of Buddha on each level. Houses, built of wood or bamboo, have roofs made of **thatch,** or woven palm fronds. In areas where there is flooding from monsoons, houses are built on stilts.

Dancing is a popular art form in much of Southeast Asia. The dances might tell a story from history or the *Ramayana,* one of India's great epic poems. Dancers must train for years. They wear elaborate and beautiful costumes. The motions of their hands often tell the story.

Weavers in Southeast Asia use available resources. In the Philippines, fabrics are sometimes made of pineapple fiber. In Indonesia, weavers make cotton **batik,** using wax and dye to make intricate patterns on fabric. In Laos, they weave cotton and silk from fibers that are grown there.

2. How do some countries in Southeast Asia honor the Buddha?

_____

_____

Vietnam Today

BEFORE YOU READ

In the last section you read about the history and government of Southeast Asia today.

In this section, you will read about Vietnam.

AS YOU READ

Copy this web to take notes about Vietnam.

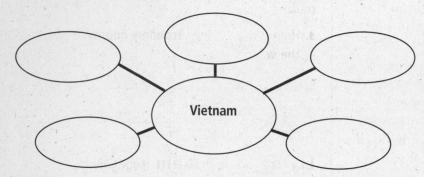

TERMS & NAMES

Ho Chi Minh president of North Vietnam from 1954 to 1969 who studied communism in the Soviet Union and China, and was a leader in Vietnam's independence movement

Politburo the group that heads a Communist party

doi moi the name of a Vietnamese policy, meaning "change for the new"

supply and demand an economic law that says the price of a good rises or falls depending on how many people want it (demand) and on how much of that good is available (supply)

Tet the Vietnamese New Year

History of Struggle (pages 655–656)

What countries ruled over Vietnam during its early history?

The Vietnamese have endured unrest for centuries. China ruled Vietnam for more than a millennium, until A.D. 939. They built roads and waterways and introduced metal plows, farm animals, and better irrigation methods. Still, the Vietnamese kept their culture and traditions.

China invaded Vietnam again in 1407, but was soon forced out. For a time, Vietnam was peaceful and prosperous. But during the 1500s and the 1600s, Vietnam was disrupted by civil wars and has continued to face much unrest since.

In 1858, Napoleon III, the ruler of France, invaded Vietnam. He wanted to increase his empire and have access to more trade in Southeast Asia. Over 25 years, France took control of Vietnam, Cambodia, and Laos.

The French took natural resources such as rice, coal, gems, and rubber out of Vietnam. They exported French goods to Vietnam, making the Vietnamese buy them at high prices.

1. How did the French treat the Vietnamese?

_____

_____

War (pages 656–657)

Who fought for control of Vietnam?

Over time, the Vietnamese organized against the French. Some Northern Vietnamese looked to China for help. **Ho Chi Minh,** who studied *communism* in China and the Soviet Union, became a leader in the independence movement.

France tried to maintain its rule over Vietnam, but Ho Chi Minh and his government began fighting the French. He received support from China's Communist government. The United States government, worried that communism would spread to Vietnam and elsewhere, helped the French.

In 1954, Vietnam was divided into two parts: Communist North Vietnam and U.S.-supported South Vietnam. In South Vietnam, no government was successful. Soon the *Vietminh* were looking for ways to overthrow South Vietnam and unite Vietnam as a Communist nation.

Not wanting South Vietnam to fall to communism, the United States provided military support and then began bombing North Vietnam in 1965. By 1973, opposition to the war by United States citizens led to the withdrawal of troops. North Vietnam overwhelmed South Vietnam, and the war ended in 1975. Three million Vietnamese died during the war, and four million were wounded. Much of Vietnam was destroyed leaving more than half the people homeless. The country reunited in 1976 as the Socialist Republic of Vietnam. Many South Vietnamese fled to the U.S. and other nations.

2. What was the outcome of the Vietnam War?

_____

_____

Vietnam Today (page 658)

What kind of government does Vietnam have?

Vietnam is now a Communist nation. People elect representatives to the National Assembly, which then chooses the prime minister. A group called the **Politburo** heads the only political party, the Communist Party.

A Communist nation owns and runs industries and services. After the Vietnam War, many people lived in poverty. Many educated people left the country. In an effort to improve the economy, the government restricted trade with other nations. This made the economic situation worse.

In 1986, the government began a policy called *doi moi,* or "change for the new." Under *doi moi,* individuals gain more control of some industries. The state still owns the land, but farmers decide how to work it. Businesses control prices, which rise and fall according to **supply and demand.** The price of a good goes up or down depending on how many people want it and how much of it is available.

Most of Vietnam's farmland is in the deltas of the Red and Mekong rivers and is planted with rice, the main staple of the Vietnamese diet.

Plantations grow rubber, bananas, coffee, and tea. Woven silk is exported worldwide. The most profitable industry is food processing. Seafood is exported to nations such as Japan and the U.S.

When Vietnam opened up trade with the rest of the world, foreigners started businesses and invested in Vietnam, bringing money and modern technology with them.

In 1994, the United States and Vietnam reopened diplomatic relations and began trading again.

3. How has Vietnam's economy improved since the war?

_____

_____

Living in Vietnam (page 659)

What are living conditions like in Vietnam today?

In the large cities of Vietnam, many people live in crowded apartment buildings. In the country, families live in stone houses in the north and in bamboo and wood houses in the south. Many have no electricity or running water.

Along the Mekong River many people live in houseboats or in houses built on stilts to be safe from floods. In the mountains, people live in *longhouses*—long, narrow buildings that hold up to 30 or 40 people.

Tet is the Vietnamese New Year. This three-day festival includes parades, fireworks, feasts, dances, and family gatherings, and marks the beginning of spring. Families feast on fruit, vegetables, candy, and rice cakes. People also wear new clothes, pay debts, and settle old arguments. Children receive money wrapped in red rice paper as gifts.

4. What is Tet?

_____

_____

Glossary/After You Read

colonize to control a territory or country

communism an economic and political system in which property is owned collectively and labor is organized in a way that will benefit all people

constitutional monarchy a government ruled by a king or queen whose power is determined by the nation's constitution and laws

Green Revolution the introduction of genetically improved grains to farmers of developing nations, beginning in the late 1960s

longhouses long narrow buildings that hold up to 30 or 40 people

Ramayana one of India's great epic poems

rural of or having to do with the country

Viet Minh the government of Communist North Vietnam

TERMS & NAMES

A. If the statement is true, write "true" on the line. If it is false, change the underlined word or words to make it true.

_____ **1.** <u>East Timor</u> is an island nation in Southeast Asia.

_____ **2.** *Doi moi* means "change for the new."

_____ **3.** <u>Ho Chi Minh</u> is the Vietnamese New Year.

_____ **4.** A <u>politburo</u> is a group that heads a Communist party.

_____ **5.** A <u>pagoda</u> is a newly industrialized nation.

_____ **6.** <u>Bahasa Indonesian</u> is a Buddhist tower built in many levels.

_____ **7.** Rising prices for goods that many people want is an example of <u>supply and demand</u>.

_____ **8.** The national language of Indonesia is <u>Tet</u>.

B. Write the term next to the description that matches it.

Ho Chi Minh   thatch

mandala   batik

developing nation   military dictatorship

_____ **1.** a method of dying fabric

_____ **2.** a Southeast Asian political system

_____ **3.** president of North Vietnam from 1954 to 1969

_____ **4.** woven palm fronds used to make roofs

_____ **5.** a government ruled by a person whose power comes from the army

_____ **6.** a country working to improve its economy and help its people

MAIN IDEAS

1. What countries make up Southeast Asia?

_____

_____

_____

2. How do people in Southeast Asia earn a living?

_____

_____

_____

3. What religions are most commonly practiced in Southeast Asia today?

_____

_____

_____

4. What caused the Vietnam war?

_____

_____

_____

5. What kind of government does Vietnam have today, and how is it working to improve the economy?

_____

_____

_____

THINKING CRITICALLY

Answer the following questions on a separate sheet of paper.

1. Why do you think that there are more languages spoken in Singapore than there are in any country in Southeast Asia?

2. Do you think that the United States made a good decision when it intervened in the Vietnam War? Explain.

Physical Geography

BEFORE YOU READ

In the last chapter, you read about Southeast Asia today.

In this section, you will read about the physical geography of East Asia, Australia, and the islands of Oceania.

AS YOU READ

Copy this chart to take notes about the geography of the region.

	Geography of East Asia, Australia, and the Islands of Oceania
China	
Japan	
The Koreas	
Australia	
New Zealand	
Islands of Oceania	

TERMS & NAMES

Mount Everest on the border of China and Nepal, the highest mountain peak in the Himalayas and in the world

Mount Fuji the tallest mountain in Japan

Ring of Fire an area of volcanic activity along the borders of the Pacific Ocean

typhoon a hurricane that occurs in the western Pacific Ocean

outback the vast, flat plain that extends across most of central Australia

Great Barrier Reef a coral reef off Australia's northeastern coast, which is the world's largest coral reef system

The Lands of the Region (page 675)

What countries are located in the region?

East Asia, Australia, and the islands of Oceania include many countries. East Asia includes China, Japan, North Korea, South Korea, Mongolia, and Taiwan. Australia is an island, a nation, and a continent. New Zealand is a neighbor. The thousands of islands of Oceania are grouped into three subregions—Melanesia, Micronesia, and Polynesia.

1. How is Australia geographically unique?

_____

_____

China (pages 676–677)

What are some features of China's geography?

Mountains cover much of China. Rivers and plains are found in the eastern part of the coun-

try. To the southwest, there are high plateaus, and to the northwest, there are long deserts.

China's highest mountains are in the west. The Himalayas run along China's southwestern border. The highest peak is **Mount Everest**, at 29,035 feet. The Plateau of Tibet spreads across one-fourth of China's land and is nicknamed the "roof of the world."

China's major rivers are the Huang He, the Chang Jiang, and the Xi Jiang. The Chang Jiang is the longest—over 3,400 miles long.

The Taklimakan desert covers northwestern China and is one of the world's largest deserts. East of the Taklimakan is the Gobi. Temperatures there rise to 113°F and fall to ‾40°F.

2. What are China's major rivers and deserts?

_____

_____

Japan (pages 677–678)

What are some characteristics of Japan's geography?

Japan is a country of islands. The four main islands are Hokkaido, Honshu, Shikoku, and Kyushu. Honshu is the largest and is home to Japan's capital, Tokyo.

Mountains cover much of Japan. Instead of forming ranges, these mountains are blocks separated by lowlands. This formation results from *faults,* or cracks in the rock.

Japan's tallest mountain, **Mount Fuji,** is an active volcano. Japan is part of the **Ring of Fire,** an area of volcanic activity along the borders of the Pacific Ocean. Japan records up to 1,500 minor earthquakes annually.

Japan's climate is largely controlled by monsoons. In the winter, the monsoons bring cold rain and snow to Japan's western coast. In the summer, they bring warm rains to the south and east. Storms and **typhoons** occur in the Pacific during the summer and early fall. A typhoon is a hurricane.

3. Why are there frequent earthquakes in Japan?

_____

_____

The Koreas (pages 678–679)

What is the geography of North and South Korea like?

North and South Korea lie on the Korean Peninsula. North Korea is filled with mountains and valleys. Its major rivers, the Yalu and Tumen, mark the border with China. North Korea has cold, dry winters and hot, humid summers. Most rain falls in the summer, brought by Pacific monsoons. South Korea is a mix of mountain, coastal plains, and valleys. Its main rivers are the Han, the Kum, and the Naktong.

4. What rivers mark the border between North Korea and China?

_____

_____

Australia (pages 679–680)

How is Australia different from other countries?

Australia is one of Earth's largest countries, though it is the smallest continent. Its landscape is unique in that it has not changed dramatically for more than 250 million years.

The mountains of the Great Dividing Range run along Australia's eastern coast. To their west, a vast, flat plain, called the **outback,** extends across most of Australia.

Australia is the flattest and driest continent. Deserts cover one-third of the country. Most people live along the northern and eastern coasts, where most fresh water is found.

Off Australia's northeastern coast stretches the **Great Barrier Reef.** Made of more than 2,500 individual reefs and islands, it extends 1,250 miles. Over 400 species of coral and other ocean life call the reef home.

5. What is the Great Barrier Reef?

_____

_____

New Zealand and Other Pacific Islands (page 680)

How many islands are located north and east of Australia?

Thousands of islands are located north and east of Australia. New Zealand is one of the largest. Most of the others are tiny.

The roughly 20,000 islands of Oceania are of three types: continental, high oceanic, and low oceanic. Continental islands, such as New Guinea and New Zealand, are parts of Earth's crust that sit above the surface of the water. They often have active volcanoes. High oceanic islands, such as Tahiti, are mountainous islands formed by volcanic activity. Most islands of Oceania are low and formed from coral reefs.

6. What kinds of islands are found in Oceania?

_____

_____

Ancient China

BEFORE YOU READ

In the last section, you read about the physical geography of East Asia, Australia, and the Pacific Islands.

In this section, you will read about Ancient China.

AS YOU READ

Copy this web to take notes about ancient China.

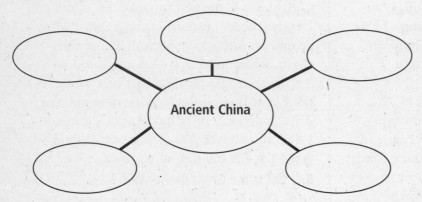

Ancient China

TERMS & NAMES

dynasty family of rulers

Genghis Khan Mongol leader who invaded China in A.D. 1200s

Kublai Khan leader of China who founded the Yuan Dynasty in 1279

Confucius Chinese philosopher who taught the importance of moral character and individual responsibility

bureaucracy the administration of a government through departments called bureaus

Taoism a Chinese philosophy based on the importance of finding harmony with nature

Lao Tzu a Chinese philosopher who founded Taoism in the 500s B.C.

Foundations of Chinese Civilization (pages 681–683)

When was China's early culture established?

Over the course of thousands of years, the Chinese have built the longest-lasting culture in the world. As early as 5000 B.C., Chinese people lived in the fertile river valley of the Huang He. Sometime in the 1700s B.C., their lives changed drastically when invaders, called the Shang, entered their valley. These invaders established China's first permanent, organized civilization.

For most of China's history since the Shang take-over, the country was ruled by **dynasties,** or families of rulers. Some lasted only 15 years, others continued for hundreds of years.

In 1211, the Mongols invaded China, led by **Genghis Khan** and later by his grandson **Kublai Khan.** In 1279, Kublai Khan conquered China's Song Dynasty and founded the Yuan Dynasty. He established its capital at Ta-tu.

Warfare eventually broke out among the Mongols, weakening the Yuan Dynasty. The Ming dynasty took over. Ming founder, Zhu Yuanzhang, was called the Hongwu emperor—meaning "vast military achievement." He won the Yunnan province and unified the region that is China today.

When the Hongwu emperor died, one of his grandsons took power, naming himself the Yongle emperor—meaning "eternal contentment." He rebuilt the Yuan capital, which he named Beijing. He ordered a huge palace to be built in the capital. This was called the Forbidden City because only the emperor, his family, and some officials could enter it.

The Ming Dynasty came to an end in 1644 at the hands of invaders from northeastern China, called the Manchus. These attackers established China's last dynasty, the Qing, which ruled China until 1911.

1. What is a dynasty and when did China's last dynasty end?

_____

_____

_____

Copyright © McDougal Littell Inc.

Religion and Philosophy
(pages 683–684)

Which religions and philosophies came about during the reign of the Chinese dynasties?

China's dynasties are known for their military, technological, artistic, and spiritual achievements. Some of the world's most influential philosophies and religions arose in China.

Towards the end of the Zhou Dynasty, a man named Kongfuzi—later called **Confucius** by Europeans—developed a new philosophy. Confucius taught the importance of moral character and of individual responsibility. He also taught that a ruler should treat his people with care and kindness. After he died, his students succeeded in spreading his philosophy.

In 121 B.C., the Han emperor Wudi established Confucianism as the official philosophy guiding the Chinese bureaucracy. **Bureaucracy** is the administration of a government through departments, called bureaus. The officials that staff the bureaus are called bureaucrats. The Han called their bureaucracy the civil service and staffed it with scholars of Confucianism.

The Zhou period also gave rise to **Taoism,** a philosophy developed in the 500s B.C. by **Lao Tzu.** He wrote the main Taoist book—the *Tao-te Ching.* Lao Tzu described the force that guides the universe as the Tao, which means "way of nature." The greatest achievement for any person, in Taoist belief, is to find harmony with the Tao and with nature.

During the A.D. 200s, Buddhism made its way to China through traders from India and other areas in Asia. During the Tang Dynasty, Buddhist teachings of how to escape suffering appealed to many Chinese. However, Buddhism did not replace Confucianism or Taoism. The Chinese belief system today includes elements of all three philosophies.

2. What are some major ideas of Confucianism?

_____

_____

_____

Achievements of the Dynasties
(pages 684–685)

What were some achievements of the Chinese dynasties?

China has also given the world some important inventions. Around 2700 B.C., the Chinese invented silk cloth and a new system of writing. In the first two centuries A.D., the Chinese invented paper and a type of pottery called porcelain. In the A.D. 1200s, Chinese navigators began using the compass. These inventions helped shape Asia and Europe.

The ancient Chinese kept the secret of how to manufacture silk for centuries, and earned all the profits of the silk trade. Caravans carried the precious fabric to Europe and Southwest Asia, along a trade route named the *Silk Road.*

The first records of travel and trade along the 4,000 mile route date to the Han Dynasty, around 114 B.C. Along it, the Chinese carried silk, porcelain, tea, incense, and spices. Travelers on the Silk Road faced danger from robbers, harsh weather, sickness, and lack of water. Nevertheless, it stayed in use until sea routes to Asia proved safer and until the Ming Dynasty decided to limit foreign trade.

During the Shang Dynasty, the Chinese developed a written language. As in *cuneiform,* the Chinese system used pictograms to represent objects or ideas. Later, pictographs were simplified into symbols, called characters, that do not look exactly like what they represent. About 50,000 characters exist in the Chinese written language. Most words are made up of two or more characters. Both the Japanese and Koreans use Chinese characters in their writing systems.

The ancient Chinese had large construction projects like the Great Wall. The Grand Canal, built in the 600s B.C., is more than 1,000 miles long and connects Beijing with Hangzhou.

3. What was the Silk Road used for?

_____

_____

_____

CHAPTER
23

Ancient Japan

BEFORE YOU READ

In the last section, you read about Ancient China.
In this section, you will read about Ancient Japan.

AS YOU READ

Copy this web to take notes about Ancient Japan.

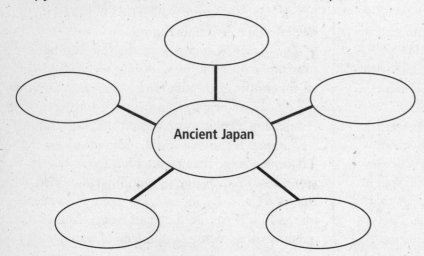

Ancient Japan

Copyright © McDougal Littell Inc.

TERMS & NAMES

Shinto a Japanese religion that developed around 300 B.C.

clan a group of families who trace their descent from a common ancestor

Heian Age the golden age of Japanese culture, from 794 to 1185

The Tale of Genji the first novel ever written, it describes life at Heian-kyo's imperial court

Zen a branch of Buddhism practiced in Japan, which emphasizes that people can achieve enlightenment suddenly

samurai Japanese warriors who each pledged to serve a particular lord and protect his estate

shogun in feudal Japan, the emperor's chief general, who held most of the country's power

Early Japan (pages 690–691)

What was life like in early Japan?

From 10,000 to 300 B.C., hunters, gatherers, and skilled fishermen lived along Japan's eastern coast. Towards the end of this period, the Japanese began practicing a religion called **Shinto.** Shinto teaches that supernatural beings live in all objects and forces of nature.

The early Japanese lived in kingdoms organized around clans. A **clan** is a group of families who trace their descent from a common ancestor. Clans in Japan were each led by a chief who inherited the position. Around A.D. 250, the Yamato clan emerged as the most powerful and established a government that ruled Japan for hundreds of years.

1. What is Shinto, and when did the Japanese begin practicing it?

_____

_____

Outside Influences (pages 691–692)

How was Japan influenced by Korea and China?

Around the time that the Yamato clan took power, Japan began using new ideas and practices from its neighbors, Korea and China. From Korea, the Japanese gained knowledge of how to use bronze and iron to make tools and weapons, as well as how to grow rice. Japanese religious life also changed when the Koreans introduced Buddhism into Japan. This was one of many ideas and customs that Koreans brought to Japan from China. In the A.D. 500s, China began to influence Japan's culture directly.

At that time, Japanese rulers believed an understanding of Chinese civilization would help them gain political power in East Asia. Prince Shotoku Taishi became a Buddhist and a student of Chinese literature and culture. He established relations with China and sent priests and students there to study. Through this exchange, the Japanese adopted China's writing system, calendar, and system of government.

In A.D. 794, the emperor Kammu built a new capital called Heian-kyo. The period from that year to 1185 is called the **Heian Age** and is considered Japan's golden age. Japanese culture flourished. A population of 100,000 aristocrats, servants, and artisans lived in Heian-kyo.

Members of the royal court lived in luxury. Many aristocratic women wrote about life in the court. Lady Murasaki Shikibu wrote the world's first novel, called *The Tale of Genji.*

After first being established at the Heian-kyo court, Buddhism became a national religion. One branch of Buddhism, called **Zen,** was the most influential in Japan. Zen emphasizes that people can achieve enlightenment suddenly, rather than through years of painful study. Zen teaches that to reach enlightenment, a person must focus to understand certain concepts.

2. What did Japan learn from Korea and China?

_____

_____

Feudal Japan (pages 692–693)

How did Japan change in the 1100s?

By the 1100s, the Heian-kyo aristocracy lost control of the country to powerful lords. The strongest lords enlisted warriors to fight rival lords. Japan began to develop a feudal system similar to that of medieval Europe, with the country divided into huge estates.

While the aristocracy at the Heian-kyo court lived lavishly, violence spread throughout the country. Lords needed protection against outlaws and bandits. They relied on warriors called **samurai** to protect their estates. The samurai pledged to serve a particular lord and provide military and bureaucratic services. They became a distinct social class.

During the 1100s, Japan was torn by a war between two clans. After 30 years of fighting, the Minamoto clan claimed victory. In 1192 in Kamakura, the clan's leader, Yoritomo, established a new kind of warrior government called a *shogunate.* He took on the role of **shogun**—or the emperor's chief general—and held most of the country's power.

In 1274 and again in 1281, the shoguns faced their greatest challenge—Kublai Khan attempted to invade and conquer Japan. The war drained the treasury, and the shogun was unable to pay the samurai. They turned to individual lords for support, and many years of fighting among lords followed.

3. What is a shogunate?

_____

_____

Tokugawa Shogunate (pages 693–694)

What was the Tokugawa Shogunate's biggest challenge?

Finally, in the 1560s, the fighting began to settle down. The lord Tokugawa Ieyasu defeated his rivals and became shogun in 1603. In that year, he moved the capital to Edo.

In 1543, just before the Tokugawa Shogunate began, the first Europeans arrived in Japan. They brought firearms and other goods to trade for gold and silver. In 1549, Catholic missionaries arrived in Japan. By 1614, 300,000 Japanese had converted, including peasants.

By the 1630s, Tokugawa Ieyasu was worried about foreigners in Japan. He heard that the Spanish had established a settlement in the Philippines. He ordered all Christians to leave the country and declared that any Japanese who left the country and then returned would be killed. He banned most European trade and freed Japan of European influences. This situation continued for 200 years, during which Japan isolated itself from most outside contact.

4. What actions did Ieyasu take in the 1630s?

_____

_____

Glossary/After You Read

cuneiform ancient writing that uses characters
fault A break in the Earth's crust causing rock layers to shift

shogunate a warrior government in which the emperor and his court only had ceremonial duties
Silk Road a 4,000-mile trading route used by the Chinese to carry silk, porcelain, and other items

TERMS & NAMES

A. Write the term next to the description that matches it.

Genghis Khan   typhoon   Kublai Khan

Taoism   Heian Age   samurai

Mount Everest   Lao Tzu   Mount Fuji

The Tale of Genji

_____ **1.** the tallest mountain in Japan

_____ **2.** the first novel ever written

_____ **3.** Mongol leader of China who founded the Yuan dynasty

_____ **4.** Japanese warriors

_____ **5.** the highest mountain in the world

_____ **6.** Chinese philosophy based on finding harmony with nature

_____ **7.** Mongol leader who invaded China in A.D. 1200s

_____ **8.** the golden age of Japanese culture

_____ **9.** Chinese philosopher who founded Taoism

_____ **10.** a hurricane that occurs in the western Pacific Ocean

B. If the statement is true, write "true" on the line. If it is false, change the underlined word or words to make it true.

_____ **1.** <u>Zen</u> taught the importance of moral character and individual responsibility.

_____ **2.** <u>The Great Barrier Reef</u> is a belt of volcanic islands in the Pacific Ocean.

Copyright © McDougal Littell Inc.

         3. Each Japanese <u>clan</u> was led by a <u>dynasty</u> who inherited the post.

         4. A <u>bureaucracy</u> is run through departments called bureaus.

         5. In 1192, <u>Confucius</u> became the first <u>shogun</u> in Japan.

         6. <u>Taoism</u> is a religion that means "the way of nature."

         7. The <u>outback</u> is the vast plain that extends through the <u>Ring of Fire</u>.

MAIN IDEAS

1. Why is Australia geographically unique?

2. What are the differences among the three types of islands in Oceania?

3. Describe some of the inventions, religions, and philosophies that came about during the Chinese dynasties.

4. How did China and Korea influence ancient Japan?

5. Why did the Japanese shogun Tokugawa Ieyasu isolate Japan from outside contact for 200 years?

THINKING CRITICALLY

Answer the following questions on a separate sheet of paper.

1. Why do you think that the Han emperor staffed his bureaucracy with scholars of Confucianism?

2. How would you feel if the U.S. government decided that you could not have any contact with the world outside the United States? How would your life be different?

Establishing Modern China

BEFORE YOU READ

In the last chapter, you read about East Asia, Australia, and the Pacific Islands.

In this section, you will read about the establishment of modern China.

AS YOU READ

Copy this web to take notes about the establishment of modern China.

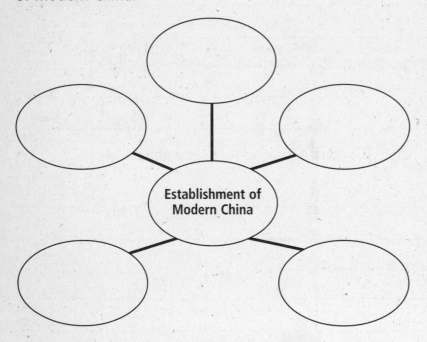

Establishment of Modern China

TERMS & NAMES

Opium War a war over the trade of the drug opium, which was fought between the Chinese and the British from 1839 to 1842

Taiping Rebellion the greatest of the peasant revolts in China that occurred in response to the signing of the Treaty of Nanking

Boxer Rebellion a rebellion led by a group called the Boxers in China in 1900

Sun Yat-sen founded the Chinese Nationalist Party, which overthrew the Qing Dynasty in 1911

Chiang Kai-shek Nationalist Party leader who ruled over China from 1927 to 1949

Mao Zedong Communist leader of the People's Republic of China from 1949 to 1976

Great Leap Forward a program that Mao Zedong began in China in 1958 to speed up economic development

Cultural Revolution a movement that Mao Zedong began in China in 1966 in an attempt to remove opposition to the Communist Party

China's Last Dynasty (pages 701–703)

Why did the Qing dynasty end?

In 1644, the Manchus established the Qing Dynasty—China's last empire. The Qing drew Taiwan and part of Tibet into China. By the mid-1800s, China's population had more than tripled, straining its ability to produce food. Shortages, famines, and wars helped end the Qing empire.

The Qing rulers faced turmoil early on because of a drug called opium. They tried unsuccessfully to prohibit the sale of opium in China. In the late 1700s, the British began smuggling opium from India into China. They used opium to buy Chinese goods, which hurt China's economy.

In 1839, China seized all of Britain's opium, and the first **Opium War** began. The British overpowered the Chinese. The war ended in 1842 with the *Treaty of Nanking*. This treaty forced China to pay Great Britain money, turn Hong Kong over to British control, and allow British traders into more Chinese ports.

Angered by the treaty, peasants rebelled. The greatest revolt, the **Taiping Rebellion,** raged for 14 years and took 20 million lives. The Chinese military crushed the revolt in 1868.

In 1900, a rebel group called the Boxers rose up in the **Boxer Rebellion.** The Boxers hoped to defeat the Qing Dynasty and force all foreigners out of China. British, French, Russian, Japanese, and American troops defeated the Boxers, leaving China in turmoil.

Many Chinese wanted a new government. One leader, **Sun Yat-sen,** hoped China would become a democracy. He founded the Chinese Nationalist Party, which toppled the Qing Dynasty in 1911. China became a republic, and Sun Yat-sen became the first provisional president. For political reasons, he gave up the first presidency to Yuan Shigai.

Over the next 16 years, China was in turmoil. Yuan struggled with rebels for power, and before and during World War I, China fought against Japan. At this time, the Nationalist Party gained more members. The Chinese Communist Party also formed.

In 1927, the two parties joined forces and **Chiang Kai-shek** became China's leader. Soon, Chiang turned against the Communists, and the two parties began a long fight for power. In 1934, the Communists retreated on the *Long March.* About 100,000 Communists marched 6,000 miles to escape from the Nationalists.

Chiang Kai-shek controlled China until 1949. During this time, transportation, education, and industry improved. However, the lives of peasants and workers did not improve. Many of these people turned to the Communist Party.

1. What was Sun Yat-sen's role in Chinese history?

_____

_____

Communist Revolution (page 703)
Who was Mao Zedong?

By the end of the Long March, a leader emerged in the Communist Party—**Mao Zedong.** When World War II began and Japan invaded China, Chiang Kai-shek turned to Mao and the Communist Red Army for help. At the end of the war in 1945, China's two parties again turned on each other. In 1949, the Communists defeated the Nationalists, forcing Chiang Kai-shek to flee to Taiwan. Mao declared China a Communist state called the People's Republic of China.

2. What government has China had since 1949?

_____

_____

Reform and Revolution (pages 704–705)
What changes occurred when the Communists took control?

Mao Zedong became head of China's Communist Party and government. The party set policy and the government carried it out, giving Mao nearly absolute power.

The Communists seized land from the wealthy and gave it to the peasants. They controlled China's industry. As in the Soviet Union, peasants worked on collective farms.

In 1958, Mao Zedong launched a program called the **Great Leap Forward** to speed up economic development. Collective farms grew crops, ran small industries, and provided education and health care for members. By 1959, the program had failed. Poor agricultural production, droughts, and floods caused a terrible famine. In one year, this program shattered China's economy.

Many people began calling for reform. In 1966, Mao launched the **Cultural Revolution.** Mao's new supporters, the Red Guards, punished people who spoke against Mao or who had contact with Western people or ideas. During this time the economy weakened and the government could not carry out its duties. More Chinese called for reform.

3. How successful was the Cultural Revolution?

_____

_____

The Governments of East Asia

BEFORE YOU READ

In the last section, you read about establishing modern China.

In this section, you will read about the governments of East Asia.

AS YOU READ

Copy this chart to take notes about East Asia's systems of government.

Governments of East Asia	
China	
Japan	
North Korea	
South Korea	
Mongolia	
Taiwan	

TERMS & NAMES

Deng Xiaoping Communist leader of China beginning in 1977, who tried to restore order and economic growth after the Cultural Revolution

human rights rights to which every person is entitled

Tiananmen Square a square in Beijing, China, where thousands of protesters gathered in demonstration and were injured or killed by the military in 1989

Diet Japan's parliament

Working Toward Change/China's Government Today (pages 708–709)

What do North Korea and China have in common?

North Korea and China are Communist nations, and both have seen war and conflict in the past 50 years. Through efforts from within and from organizations and nations around the world, both nations are working to improve the lives of their people. They are also gradually becoming a part of the world market.

When Mao Zedong died in 1976, the Cultural Revolution ended. Moderates who wanted to restore order and economic growth took power in 1977. Their leader was **Deng Xiaoping.**

Under Deng, the Chinese government established diplomatic relations with the United States and increased trade with other countries.

It also made reforms, such as allowing farmers to own land. It released many political prisoners and reduced the police force's power. However, the government was not willing to give up any of its basic control.

Officially, China's highest government authority is the National People's Congress. In practice, the Chinese Communist Party holds the real power. It controls what happens locally. The government allows only churches and temples that are closely linked to this party to operate.

1. How did Deng Xiaping change the Chinese government in 1977?

_____

_____

The Fight for Human Rights
(page 709)

What are human rights?

China's Communist government has a history of repressing criticism of its policies. Such actions often lead to the violation of **human rights**— rights to which every person is entitled. They include the freedom to say or write what you think, to worship as you believe, to be safe from physical harm and political persecution, and to have enough to eat.

In 1989, the Chinese military denied citizens a basic human right—freedom of speech—when it attacked protesters calling for democracy in **Tiananmen Square.** For weeks, protesters occupied this 100-acre square in Beijing. Demonstrations soon occurred in other Chinese cities. The military killed hundreds and wounded thousands in their attempts to end the protests. As the events of 1989 unfolded, people around the world spoke out against the Chinese government. Since then, efforts have been made to help the people of China in their struggle for human rights.

2. What happened in Tiananmen Square in 1989?

_____

_____

China's Neighbors (pages 710–711)

Who are China's neighbors?

The United States occupied Japan after it was defeated in World War II. General Douglas MacArthur helped set up a constitutional monarchy with a parliamentary government and a separate judiciary. The parliament is called the **Diet.** The Diet chooses the country's prime minister, who is then officially appointed by the emperor.

The constitution states that the emperor's position is symbolic. In practice, the emperor has had limited power, though many people regard the emperor as partly divine. The constitution also gives the Japanese people

rights and responsibilities similar to those of Americans.

Korea used to be one country, but it was divided after World War II. The Soviet Union helped set up a Communist dictatorship in the north, and the United States helped set up a democratic republic in the south. Each government thought it should govern the whole of the Korean Peninsula. In 1950, North Korea invaded South Korea. For three years, during the Korean War, the borders did not change. In June of 2000, the two nations started talking about reuniting.

North Korea, or the Democratic People's Republic of Korea, is still a Communist state. Although there is a president and a cabinet, the Korean Workers' Party holds power. The people have little freedom, and the legislature—the Supreme People's Assembly—has little power.

South Korea, or the Republic of Korea, is a republic with a government similar to that of the United States. Power is divided among legislative, executive, and judiciary branches. People vote for the president as well as the legislature—the National Assembly. The government guarantees its citizens freedom of the press and of religion.

One of the world's oldest countries, Mongolia was under either Chinese or Russian domination for years. It has been an independent republic since 1991 and has a constitution that guarantees its citizens certain basic rights. However, there is still a strong element of Communist party control in Mongolia's government.

Also a republic, Taiwan has a multiparty democratic system. For years it was a Chinese colony, but since 1949, the Chinese Nationalist government has been based there. The question of whether Taiwan and China will unify under one government has long caused conflict.

3. How are the government systems of North and South Korea different?

_____

_____

The Economies of East Asia

BEFORE YOU READ

In the last section, you read about the governments of East Asia.

In this section, you will read about the economies of East Asia.

AS YOU READ

Copy this web to take notes about the economies of East Asia.

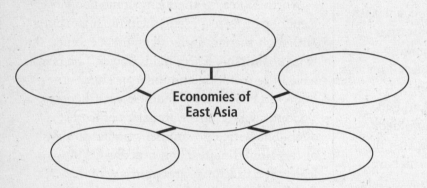

Economies of East Asia

TERMS & NAMES
tungsten a type of metal
antimony a type of metal
textile a cloth manufactured by weaving or knitting
cooperative a large farm on which up to 300 families work

Economies of the Region (page 712)

How have the economies of East Asia grown since WW II?

Since World War II, East Asia's countries have grown more active in the world market. Today, Japan has one of the strongest economies in the world. Consumers in the United States regularly purchase goods made in China, Taiwan, Japan, and South Korea. However, wars, droughts, and internal conflicts have made economic growth difficult for some countries, such as North Korea.

1. What challenges do some countries in East Asia face in achieving economic growth?

_____

_____

_____

China's Economy (page 713)

What are some characteristics of China's economy?

Although this has begun to change, China's government controls most of its economy. It owns all financial institutions, such as banks, and the larger industrial firms. The government also sets the prices on goods and plans the quantity of goods each worker should produce.

China has put a strong emphasis on improving its industry. It has become one of the world's largest producers of cotton cloth and of two metals—**tungsten** and **antimony.** The industries that have seen the most growth are machine building, metal production, and the making of chemical fertilizers and clothing.

Many people in China live in the countryside and make a living by farming. They use traditional methods, such as plowing with oxen, rather than using farm machinery. Much of the land in China—in the deserts and mountainous regions—cannot be farmed. Nevertheless, China is the world's largest producer of rice. It is also a major source of wheat, corn, soybeans, peanuts, tobacco, and cotton.

2. How do many Chinese people earn a living?

_____

_____

Other East Asian Economies
(pages 714–715)

How have the economies of East Asia changed over time?

Taiwan has a growing market economy that relies heavily on manufacturing and foreign trade. Since 1988, Taiwanese businesses have invested billions of dollars in mainland China, significantly contributing to China's fast-growing economy.

North Korea's government controls the economy, and, like China, has emphasized the growth of industry. Iron, steel, machinery, chemical, and textile production are the main industries in North Korea. A **textile** is a cloth manufactured by weaving or knitting.

Many people in North Korea are farmers. They work on large **cooperatives,** where some 300 families share the farming work. These farms have become more productive as improvements in irrigation, fertilizers, and equipment have been made.

For most of the 20th century, North Korea traded with other Communist nations. Since the fall of the Soviet Union, North Korea has opened its borders to investment and trade with other countries.

The economy of South Korea has changed dramatically since the early 1960s. At that time, it was a poor nation of subsistence farmers. Since then, however, the government has supported the expansion of the textile industry and the building of factories that make small appliances, electronics, and equipment. The government also helped develop iron, steel, and chemical industries. Today, South Korea has one of the world's strongest economies. It is a major producer of automobiles and electronics and trades with many countries.

The government of Japan does not control its economy in the way the governments of China and North Korea control theirs. However, it does oversee and advise all aspects of the economy including trade, investment, banking, and production.

Like South Korea, Japan has an economy that has grown significantly since the mid-20th century. Japan is a small nation with few natural resources and little farmland. Industry and a skilled, educated work force are vitally important to Japan's economy.

Japan imports the raw materials it needs and transforms them into goods for export. Ships, automobiles, steel, plastics, machinery, cameras, and electronics are Japan's major exports. The United States is Japan's biggest customer, although Japan also exports goods around the world. It is currently one of the world's largest economic powers.

3. What are some of Japan's major exports?

_____

_____

The Cultures of East Asia

BEFORE YOU READ

In the last section, you read about the economies of East Asia.

In this section, you will read about the cultures of East Asia.

AS YOU READ

Copy this web to take notes about the cultures of East Asia.

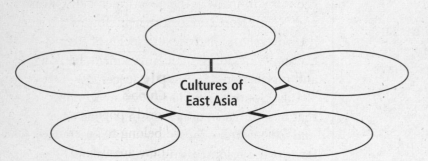

TERMS & NAMES

zither a type of stringed instrument

haiku a Japanese form of poetry that uses only 17 syllables

Han the main ethnic group in China

Cultural Exchange/Exchange Within East Asia (pages 716–717)

What is cultural exchange?

Cultural exchange has occurred for centuries in East Asia. Recently, these countries have also been influenced by Western culture, and aspects of East Asian cultures have spread outside the region. Events like the Olympics are sure to generate more awareness of the region around the world.

East Asian cultures have much in common because of cultural exchange. Many of the shared aspects of culture originated in China. For example, the Japanese and Koreans adapted China's writing system to their own languages. The Japanese also adopted Chinese ideas about urban planning, government, and painting. Similarly, the Koreans picked up Chinese printing techniques and methods of governing.

The religions of East Asia are strong indicators of cultural exchange within the region. Buddhism, for example, originated in India. The Chinese learned about the religion

around 1,700 years ago. They then passed on their understanding of it to the Koreans, who later transmitted their knowledge to the Japanese. Some elements of Buddhism were incorporated into Japan's native Shinto religion. The Koreans and Japanese also developed interest in Confucianism. It, too, spread from China to their countries.

Throughout East Asia, many people still practice Buddhism and Confucianism. They also practice other religions, such as Christianity and Taoism. The Communist government of North Korea discourages religious freedom. South Koreans, however, practice Buddhism and Christianity. Mongolians practice Tibetan Buddhism. Taiwan's dominant religion is based on Buddhism, Confucianism, and Taoism. Japan's two major religions are Zen Buddhism and Shinto.

1. How has Buddhism moved through East Asia?

_____

_____

_____

_____

Arts Past and Present (page 718–719)
What art forms have been exchanged in East Asia?

Art forms also reflect cultural exchange in East Asia. For example, similar methods of painting and making pottery are used. However, each country has its unique traditions.

Chinese art forms date back thousands of years. The art of bronze casting was developed around 1100 B.C. Music and dance are also ancient art forms in China. Bells, flutes, drums, and a stringed instrument called a **zither** are played.

Porcelain dishes and vases are among China's greatest treasures. The paintings, designs, and words that decorate them have helped historians understand life in ancient China.

Today, theater is a popular art form in China. It has at least 300 forms of traditional opera. At the Beijing Opera, actors wear elaborate costumes to perform dramas based on Chinese stories, folklore, and history.

Buddhist ideas have influenced the arts in Japan. Artists consider simplicity, delicacy, and tradition to be important in their artwork. Painting, printing, dance, music, and theater all reflect these ideals. In literature, the **haiku** is a world-famous form of Japanese poetry. The goal of haiku is to suggest, in a short description, much more than is stated.

Some artists in Japan work to preserve traditional crafts. Potters and weavers, in particular, receive money from the Japanese government to continue their work and teach others. These artists are considered living treasures.

2. What art forms are practiced in Japan?

_____

_____

Culture and Communism (page 720)
How has communism affected East Asian cultures?

Communism has significantly affected some of East Asia's cultures. In North Korea and China,

Communists repressed artistic freedom. During the Cultural Revolution in China, artwork was frequently damaged or destroyed. Writers were forced to create propaganda instead of expressing their own ideas. Artists who created work about Communist ideals were allowed to continue their work. Artists who criticized the government through art were punished.

In North Korea today, the government still controls the work of artists. The Chinese government has shown greater willingness to allow artists to pursue their own ideas.

3. Why are Communists concerned about art?

_____

_____

The Chinese People (pages 720–721)
How do families live in China?

About one-fifth of the world's population lives in China. Most Chinese belong to an ethnic group called the **Han.** There are also about 55 minority groups. Each minority group has its own language. Students speak their native language in school. Mandarin Chinese is taught as the official language.

The Chinese have traditionally lived in large, *extended families.* To slow down population growth, the government decreed in the 1980s that each married couple in a city may have only one child. Rural families may have a second child, and families in ethnic minorities may have more than one child. Most Chinese households today are made up of small family units that may include the grandparents.

Family members in China depend on one another and follow traditions. Elders are respected. Children are given lots of attention. In the past, marriages were arranged by the parents, but that is no longer common. In China today, most parents work, so grandparents often care for the children.

4. What are some features of Chinese family life?

_____

_____

Name _____ Date _____

Establishing Modern Japan

BEFORE YOU READ

In the last section, you read about the cultures of East Asia.

In this section, you will read about the establishment of modern Japan.

AS YOU READ

Copy this web to take notes about modern Japan.

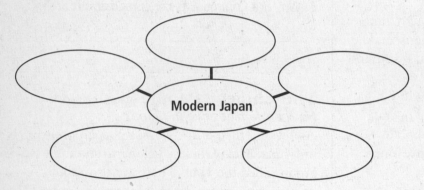

TERMS & NAMES

Meiji Restoration the period from 1868 to 1911 during which Japan again was ruled by an emperor

Hiroshima a Japanese city on which the United States dropped an atomic bomb in 1945

Nagasaki a Japanese city on which the United States dropped an atomic bomb in 1945

homogeneous largely the same

Ainu the descendents of Japan's early settlers from Europe

History (pages 722–724)

How has Japan changed over time?

In the past century, Japan has seen changes in its government, economy, and relations with the world. From the mid-1600s to the 1800s, Japan was a fairly isolated nation. It traded with China but was unaffected by most of the world.

Japan's location made it a convenient place for ships from the United States to stop and replenish supplies. In 1853, American naval vessels commanded by Commodore Matthew C. Perry landed in Japan. Perry opened Japan to the West, ending nearly 200 years of Japanese isolation.

In 1867, a group of samurai overthrew the Tokugawa Shogunate and restored the emperor as head of government. The period that followed, from 1868 through 1911, became known as the **Meiji Restoration,** because the new emperor was called Meiji. During this time, Japan became wealthy and powerful. It built modern industries and developed the economy.

Following a series of wars, Japan assumed control of Taiwan, Korea, and Manchuria.

Japan, allied with the United States, Britain, and France, defeated Germany in World War I and thus was able to expand its holdings of ex-German colonies in the Pacific. The Great Kanto Earthquake in 1923 hurt Japan's economy, and so did the Great Depression. During the 1930s, the military took control of Japan's government. In 1937, Japan invaded China. Also at this time, Japan developed closer relations with Nazi Germany and Fascist Italy. As a result, the United States stopped selling oil to Japan. In 1941, Japan bombed the U.S. naval base at Pearl Harbor in Hawaii, bringing the United States into World War II.

By 1942, the Japanese military had won many victories in East Asia and the South Pacific. But by 1943, Japan had lost several battles, which turned the tide of the war. In 1945, the United States dropped atomic bombs on two Japanese cities—**Hiroshima** and **Nagasaki.** Emperor Hirohito then surrendered, ending the war.

1. How did World War II end?

_____

_____

_____

Economy and Government
(pages 724–725)
How did Japan recover after World War II?

After World War II, Japan's economy and government were in shambles. Its cities had been bombed. Many Japanese were homeless and without jobs. The Japanese values of hard work and saving money helped to rebuild the economy. The United States also gave Japan help through loans and advice. By the mid-1950s, Japanese industrial production matched its prewar levels.

Today, Japan has one of the most powerful economies in the world. It encourages *free enterprise,* which can motivate people to develop new ideas and expand their businesses with little government interference.

Women's participation in the work force has grown since World War II. However, discrimination exists, and ideas about women's roles are changing slowly. About two-fifths of Japanese women hold jobs, but many are temporary or part-time. Few women hold management positions.

After World War II, the United States occupied Japan until 1952. It helped set up a new government. Under the new constitution, the rights and responsibilities of the Japanese are similar to those of Americans.

Today, Japan has a constitutional monarchy with a parliamentary government. The Diet is the highest law-making body in the country. Before 1945, Japan's emperor headed the government. He is now a symbolic head of state.

2. How are the U.S. and Japan similar today?

_____

_____

_____

Culture (pages 725–726)
How would you describe Japanese life?

Japan's population is **homogeneous,** or largely the same. Most of the Japanese are descended from the Mongolian people who settled Japan thousands of years ago. The exception is the approximately 15,000 **Ainu** people. Scholars believe that the Ainu came to Japan from Europe well before the majority of settlers arrived.

In Japan, as in most of Asia, people think of themselves first as part of a group, not as individuals. Social behavior in Japan is governed by an idea called *on* (ohn). This value is based on Confucian principles about relationships. The Japanese take the relationship between children and their elders seriously. People are respectful toward their parents and elders. They also put their elders' needs before their own. Japanese people also seriously consider an elder's judgment when making decisions.

More than 90 percent of Japanese families live in urban areas. Many live in apartment buildings, because houses are expensive and there is little space for them.

Many people commute to work or to school. Most cities have subway systems. During rush hour, high-speed trains are packed with people and connect many of the big cities. Railway tunnels also connect the islands. The world's first undersea railway tunnel was built to connect the islands of Kyushu and Honshu.

Some aspects of Japanese culture have gained popularity in the United States, including the Japanese tea ceremony, sushi, and Japanese flower arranging. Japanese gardens have been built in many parts of the world. Baseball and soccer are also popular in Japan and draw huge crowds.

3. What are some ways in which Japanese culture is different from American culture?

_____

_____

_____

Glossary/After You Read

Treaty of Nanking after the Opium War, a treaty that forced China to pay Great Britain money, turn Hong Kong over to the British, and allow more British traders in Chinese ports

Long March held in 1934, when 100,000 Communists marched more than 6,000 miles to escape from the Nationalists

extended family a group of families who live together

free enterprise an economic system based on private ownership and operation of business with little or no governmental control

TERMS & NAMES

A. Write the term or names next to the description that best matches it.

Tiananmen Square	Sun Yat-sen	human rights
Ainu	Opium War	cooperative
Han	Diet	Taiping Rebellion
zither	Deng Xiaoping	Boxer Rebellion

_____ **1.** Demonstrators protested there in 1989.

_____ **2.** It occurred in response to the Treaty of Nanking.

_____ **3.** Every person is entitled to them.

_____ **4.** It was fought between the Chinese and the British between 1839 and 1842.

_____ **5.** the main ethnic group in China

_____ **6.** a large farm on which many families work

_____ **7.** the descendents of Japan's early settlers from Europe

_____ **8.** He founded the Chinese Nationalist Party.

_____ **9.** a type of stringed instrument

_____ **10.** Communist leader after the Cultural Revolution

_____ **11.** Japan's parliament

_____ **12.** fought by a rebel group that hoped to defeat the Qing dynasty

B. Fill in the blank with the term or name that best completes the sentence.

Mao Zedong	textile	Chiang Kai-shek
tungsten	antimony	Cultural Revolution
homogeneous	Nagasaki	Hiroshima
haiku	Great Leap Forward	Meiji Restoration

1. A _____ is a Japanese form of poetry, and a _____ is cloth.

2. During the _____, supporters of Western ideas were punished.

3. _____ and _____ were bombed by the Americans at the end of World War II.

4. The _____ in China was meant to speed up economic development.

5. _____ ruled China from 1927 to 1949, and _____ ruled from 1949 to 1976.

6. China is a leader in producing _____ and _____.

7. Japan has a mostly _____ population.

8. During the _____, Japan became wealthy and powerful.

MAIN IDEAS

1. How did life change in China under Chairman Mao?

   _____

   _____

2. What led to the protest in Tiananmen Square in 1989? What was the result?

   _____

   _____

3. How do the economies of China and North Korea compare to South Korea's and Japan's?

   _____

   _____

4. How has cultural exchange affected the countries in the region?

   _____

   _____

5. How did Japan recover after World War II?

   _____

THINKING CRITICALLY

Answer the following questions on a separate sheet of paper.

1. Do you think that Mao Zedong was a popular leader? Explain.

2. Do you think that the violence at Tiananmen Square could have been avoided? Explain.

CHAPTER 25

History and Governments

Copyright © McDougal Littell Inc.

BEFORE YOU READ

In the last chapter, you read about China and its neighbors.

In this section, you will read about the history and governments of Australia, New Zealand, and the islands of Oceania.

AS YOU READ

Copy this chart to take notes about the history and governments of Australia, New Zealand, and the islands of Oceania.

	History	Governments
Australia		
New Zealand		
Islands of Oceania		

TERMS & NAMES

Maori the first settlers of New Zealand

Aborigines the descendents of Australia's first inhabitants

Melanesia one of the three regional groups of islands in Oceania

Micronesia one of the three regional groups of islands in Oceania

Polynesia one of the three regional groups of islands in Oceania

Commonwealth of Nations a group of countries, including Australia and New Zealand, that were once British colonies and that share a heritage of British law and government

History of the Region (page 733)

What is the history of the region?

Long before the British arrived in New Zealand, the country's first settlers—the **Maori**—lived there. In fact, people inhabited many of the islands in the Pacific and Indian oceans for thousands of years before any Europeans arrived. Today, we know this region as Australia, New Zealand, and the islands of Oceania.

1. Who were the Maori?

_____

_____

People of the Region (pages 734–736)

Who were the people who migrated to the region?

Australia's first inhabitants migrated there from Southeast Asia at least 40,000 years ago. Their descendants are called **Aborigines.** Settlers from Southeast Asia arrived in the islands of Oceania about 33,000 years ago. The three regional groups of Oceania are **Melanesia, Micronesia, and Polynesia.** Southeast Asians migrated first to Melanesia, then spread into Micronesia and finally Polynesia. About 1,000 years ago, Polynesians settled New Zealand. These settlers were the Maori.

Geography influenced which islands people settled. If an island had fresh water, wildlife, and vegetation, people settled there. If an island was too dry, too small, or lacked sources of food, it remained unpopulated.

Most of the early islanders fished or farmed. They also traded with nearby islanders. Because of the vast expanses of ocean, however, distinct languages and cultures developed over time.

In the 1500s, Europeans explored the Pacific for spices. In the 1600s and 1700s, missionaries and other settlers arrived. Some of them carried diseases, such as smallpox. Many of the native islanders died from these diseases. Some settlers also brought hardship upon the islanders by enslaving them.

Britain, France, Germany, Spain, the United States, and later Japan all established colonies in the Pacific. Since 1962, many islands have gained independence. Others are still colonies. For example, France governs New Caledonia, and the United States controls Guam.

In the 1700s, Great Britain sent many people to Australia. Some were convicts who labored on farms and others were free colonists. By 1859, six British colonies made up Australia. In 1901, these colonies became states of the Commonwealth of Australia.

In the 1790s, New Zealand was settled by whale hunters and traders from Great Britain, the United States, and France, as well as European missionaries and colonists. In 1840, the Maori and the British signed the Treaty of Waitangi, which gave control of New Zealand to Britain. New Zealand did not become a self-governing country until 1907.

When Europeans first came to Australia, as many as 750,000 Aborigines populated the continent. As more settlers arrived, Aborigines were forced into the country's interior. Today, only 1 percent of Australia's population is of Aborigine descent. Similarly, in New Zealand, only about 14 percent of the population today is of Maori descent.

2. What happened to the Aborigines when Europeans came to Australia?

_____

_____

Governments (page 736)

What kinds of governments do Australia, New Zealand, and the island nations of Oceania have?

The governments of Australia, New Zealand, and the island nations of Oceania are quite varied. Some are democracies, some are monarchies, and some are ruled by other nations. Many countries have governments that resemble that of the nation that colonized them.

Australia and New Zealand belong to the **Commonwealth of Nations.** This is a group of countries that were once British colonies and share a heritage of British law and government. Great Britain's monarch is their head of state but has no real power.

A few islands of Oceania still have official ties to various countries. For example, the United States still defends the Federated States of Micronesia, while the French Polynesians vote in French elections. Other islands rule themselves, such as Tonga, which is a constitutional monarchy.

3. In what way do Australia and New Zealand both share a heritage of British law and government?

_____

_____

Economies and Cultures

BEFORE YOU READ

In the last section, you read about the history and governments of Australia, New Zealand, and the islands of Oceania.

In this section, you will read about the economics and cultures of the region.

AS YOU READ

Copy this chart to take notes about the economics and cultures of Australia, New Zealand, and islands of Oceania.

	Economies	Cultures
Australia		
New Zealand		
Islands of Oceania		

TERMS & NAMES

copra dried coconut meat

matrilineal societies societies in which ancestry is traced through the mother's side of the family

patrilineal societies societies in which ancestry is traced through the father's side of the family

Resources and Economies
(pages 737–739)

What industries do people in the region rely on to earn a living?

The economies of Australia, New Zealand, and the islands of Oceania have various foundations. On the one hand, tourists travel to the region to enjoy its beaches, mountains, *fjords*, and unusual plant and animal life. Thousands also came to Australia for the 2000 Summer Olympic Games. On the other hand, agriculture is the traditional base of the region's economies. Australia and New Zealand still depend more on farming than do most other developed countries.

Most people in Oceania fish, grow their own food, and build their own homes. However, some commercial agriculture does exist on the islands. **Copra**—dried coconut meat—and coconut oil are important agricultural exports. Tourism also contributes significantly to the economies of some islands in Oceania, such as Tahiti.

Australia has a strong market economy and relatively free trade with other nations, especially Japan. Service industries—including health care, tourism, news media, and transportation—provide nearly three-fourths of the country's jobs.

Australia's strong economy also depends on mining and farming. Australia is the world's leading producer of bauxite, lead, and zinc. It has also developed vast fields of natural gas. Wheat is Australia's most important cash crop, and about 80 percent of the harvest is exported. Sugar cane is also an important cash crop.

During colonial times, Australia and New Zealand mostly traded with Great Britain. Today, Australia's main trading partners are Japan and the United States, while New Zealand's main trading partner is Australia. Asian countries are now also playing a bigger role in New Zealand's economy. In 1983, Australia and New Zealand signed a *free-trade agreement* to boost the trade between them.

1. What are the main industries in Australia?

_____

_____

Cultures and Change (pages 739–740)
How has modernization affected life in the region?

Despite their remote locations, the islands of the region have attracted immigrants from around the world. *Modernization* and tradition both play strong roles in the region.

Modernization has affected life in some of the islands of Oceania. For example, modernization has clearly changed modes of transportation. For short trips, villagers take canoes just as they always have. However, for longer trips, they outfit canoes with modern outboard motors or travel by ship or airplane.

Tradition continues to be strong, especially in art forms and family structures. For example, matrilineal societies are less common than patrilineal societies, but they are still found in parts of the islands of Oceania, such as Papua New Guinea. In **matrilineal societies,** ancestry is traced through the mother's side of the family. In **patrilineal societies,** ancestry is traced through the father's side.

Australia has a diverse population. People worship in mosques, churches, synagogues, and Buddhist temples. In the past 50 years, immigrants have come from many parts of the world, such as Cambodia, Laos, and Vietnam. Some came escaping war or other danger.

In New Zealand, over half a million people are Maori. Most others are descendants of Scottish, English, Irish, and Welsh settlers. Many Asians also live in the cities, such as the capital, Wellington, and the largest city, Auckland.

2. What are some traditional family structures that are still common in the region?

_____

_____

Antarctica

BEFORE YOU READ

In the last section, you read about the economies and cultures of Australia, New Zealand, and Oceania.

In this section, you will read about the land, the climate, the history of exploration, and the resources of Antarctica.

AS YOU READ

Copy this web to take notes about Antarctica.

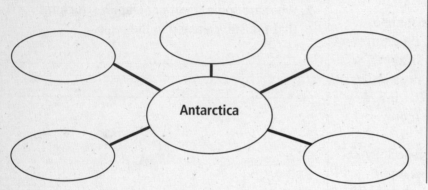

TERMS & NAMES

ice shelf a sheet of ice that floats on water but connects to land on one side

The Continent of Antarctica (page 742)

What continent is the coldest and windiest?

Antarctica was the last continent to be explored. It is the coldest and iciest continent on Earth. It is also the windiest and driest continent. No one lives in Antarctica all the time.

Antarctica is farther south than any region on Earth. It is the fifth largest continent. It covers more than five million square miles in area.

1. How much area does Antarctica cover?

_____

_____

Land and Climate (page 743)

What covers 98 percent of Antarctica?

An ice cap is a thick layer of ice and snow. An ice cap covers 98 percent of Antarctica. It holds about 70 percent of the world's fresh water. Under it lie mountains, plateaus, and valleys.

The Transantarctic Mountains divide the continent into two regions. They are East Antarctica and West Antarctica. A high plateau covers the central part of East Antarctica. The South Pole is on this plateau. The South Pole is Earth's southernmost point.

Much of West Antarctica is below sea level. The icecap covers this region. Under the ice are mountainous islands and a large peninsula. It is called the Antarctic Peninsula.

Antarctica is so cold and dry, it is called a polar desert. Inland areas are colder and drier than the coast. Winter lasts from May through August. Winter temperatures can drop to more than 100°F below zero. Inland areas receive no rain and just a few inches of snow each year.

The Atlantic, Indian, and Pacific oceans meet around Antarctica to form the Southern Ocean. Almost 60 percent of the Antarctic coastline is made of glaciers and ice shelves. An **ice shelf** is a sheet of ice that floats on water but connects to land on one side.

2. In Antarctica, how long does winter last?

_____

_____

History of Exploration (page 743)
When did the exploration of Antarctic begin?

Since ancient times, people thought there might be a continent in the far south. For hundreds of years sea captains searched for it. Whalers had landed on Antarctica by the 1890s.

People began to explore Antarctica in the early 1900s. Two British explorers were Robert Falcon Scott and Ernest Shackleton. They each led teams of men and braved harsh conditions. Robert Scott lost his life in Antarctica.

Richard Byrd was a U.S. naval officer. In 1929, he flew over the South Pole. He was the first person to do this. People in planes took photographs of Antarctica. Later satellites also took photographs. These pictures gave more information about Antarctica's geography.

As time passed, scientists set up stations to do research in Antarctica. By the 1950s, 12 nations had more than 50 research stations.

3. What kind of photographs gave more information about Antarctica's geography?

_____

_____

Resources (page 744)
What are some of the animals that live along the coast of Antarctica?

Few plants and animals can live in Antarctica's cold, dry climate. Lichens, mosses, and insects are found in the interior. The Southern Ocean has a lot of wildlife, such as whales. The whales eat small, shrimplike animals called krill. Large numbers of birds, penguins, and seals live along the coast. They find food in the ocean.

Antarctica has minerals. These include coal and iron. They would be costly to mine.

Some nations claim to own parts of Antarctica. Other nations reject those claims. In 1959, 12 nations signed the Antarctic Treaty. In the treaty, the nations agreed to use the continent only for scientific research. They also agreed to share their results. Since 1959, more than 30 other countries have signed the treaty.

4. In the Antarctic Treaty, how did 12 nations agree to use Antarctica?

_____

_____

The Scientific Community (page 744)
What is global warming?

Scientists from more than 25 countries do research in Antarctica. In the summer, about 20,000 people come to the continent. They include scientists, support staff, and tourists. Only about 1,000 stay through the winter. The scientists study wildlife, glaciers, and stars.

The scientists also study climate change. One way they do this is by studying ice samples. Over the past 50 years, temperatures in the Antarctic Peninsula have gone up. They have risen 4.5°F. Some scientists believe this change supports the *theory* of global warming. Global warming is the theory that world temperatures are rising because of human activity. One such activity is the burning of fossil fuels. Not all scientists believe in global warming.

Warmer temperatures caused an ice shelf to break apart in 2002. It was on the Antarctic Peninsula. It was larger than Rhode Island.

5. Over the past 50 years, how much have temperatures in the Antarctic Peninsula risen?

_____

_____

Glossary/After You Read

fjord a long, narrow inlet of the sea between high cliffs or banks

free-trade agreement an agreement between nations that allows trade without restrictive charges on imported or exported goods

modernization changing or bringing up to current ways or standards

theory an explanation that has not been proven to be fact

TERMS & NAMES

A. Write the term next to the description that best matches it.

copra   ice shelf

Maori   Aborigines

matrilineal society   patrilineal society

_____ **1.** descendents of Australia's first inhabitants

_____ **2.** dried coconut meat

_____ **3.** a sheet of ice that floats on water but connects to land on one side

_____ **4.** the first settlers of New Zealand

_____ **5.** a society that traces its ancestry through the mother's side of the family

B. If the statement is true, write "true" on the line. If it is false, change the underlined word or words to make it true.

_____ **1.** <u>Patrilineal societies</u> are more common than matrilineal societies in Oceania.

_____ **2.** People from <u>Melanesia</u> settled New Zealand 1,000 years ago.

_____ **3.** Australia and New Zealand both belong to the <u>Commonwealth of Nations</u>.

_____ **4.** Southeast Asians first migrated to <u>Polynesia</u>, and then to other islands.

MAIN IDEAS

1. Who lived in New Zealand and Oceania before the Europeans arrived? How did these people survive?

_____

_____

2. Why were European countries interested in the region?

_____

_____

3. How has modernization affected life in Oceania?

_____

_____

4. Describe Australia's economy.

_____

_____

5. How do people who live in Oceania earn a living?

_____

_____

THINKING CRITICALLY

Answer the following questions on a separate sheet of paper.

1. Why do you think that the Aborigine population in Australia is so small today?

2. Do you think that the European colonists had the right to establish colonies in Australia, New Zealand, and Oceania? Explain.